Environmental History of Modern Migrations

In the age of climate change, the possibility that dramatic environmental transformations might cause the dislocation of millions of people has become not only a matter for scientific speculations or science-fiction narratives, but the object of strategic planning and military analysis.

Environmental History of Modern Migrations offers a worldwide perspective on the history of migrations throughout the nineteenth and twentieth centuries and provides an opportunity to reflect on the global ecological transformations and developments which have occurred throughout the last few centuries. With a primary focus on the environment/migration nexus, this book advocates that global environmental changes are not distinct from global social transformations. Instead, it offers a progressive method of combining environmental and social history, which manages to both encompass and transcend current approaches to environmental justice issues.

This edited collection will be of great interest to students and practitioners of environmental history and migration studies, as well as those with an interest in history and sociology.

Marco Armiero is Director of the Environmental Humanities Laboratory at the KTH Royal Institute of Technology in Stockholm, Sweden, where he is also Associate Professor of Environmental History. He is the author of *A Rugged Nation. Mountains and the Making of Modern Italy* (2011) and co-editor of *A History of Environmentalism. Local Struggles, Global Histories* (2014), and *Nature and History in Modern Italy* (2010). Armiero is a senior editor of *Capitalism Nature Socialism* and associate editor of *Environmental Humanities.*

Richard Tucker is Adjunct Professor in the School of Natural Resources, University of Michigan, USA. His earlier publications addressed the history of environmental change in the colonial and tropical world, including *Insatiable Appetite: The United States and the Ecological Degradation of the Tropical World* (2000) and *A Forest History of India* (2010). His recent work addresses the environmental history of warfare. He is the author of numerous essays and co-editor of several multi-author books on the subject, including *Natural Enemy, Natural Ally: Toward an Environmental History of War* (2004).

At last, a careful look at the linkages between migration and environmental change in modern history! With an admirably international set of authors, this collection ranges far and wide, both geographically and conceptually. It should be a landmark in both global environmental history and the history of migration.

J.R. McNeill, Georgetown University, USA

All too often, studies that claim to be ground-breaking fail to live up to the brag. This stimulating and very timely collection of essays exploring the multiple and complex connections between human migration and biophysical environments represents a refreshing exception. In a study that is politically committed to the cause of socio-environmental justice as well as intellectually innovative, the authors engage with key notions such as corporeal ecology, environmental nativism, nativist environmentalism and the environmental refugee/migrant. Editors Marco Armiero and Richard Tucker, who remind us that 'migrants are themselves nature on the move', are to be congratulated for launching a new research area within environmental history of urgent contemporary importance internationally.

Peter Coates, University of Bristol, UK

This innovative and timely volume will surely change the way we think about the history of immigration. As these essays show, modern migrations are not only a social and political processes; they also have important environmental dimensions. Covering a wide geographic range—from Polynesia to Siberia, from Brazil to China, the authors lay the groundwork for a new research agenda.

Linda Nash, University of Washington, USA

The editors have assembled an innovative group of contributors who challenge scholars of migration and environmental studies to develop a new analytical lens—one that posits mobile humans as part of nature and nature as constitutive of mobile cultures and societies. A must-read.

Donna Gabaccia, University of Toronto, Canada

Routledge Environmental Humanities

Series editors: Iain McCalman and Libby Robin

The *Routledge Environmental Humanities* series is an original and inspiring venture recognising that today's world agricultural and water crises, ocean pollution and resource depletion, global warming from greenhouse gases, urban sprawl, overpopulation, food insecurity and environmental justice are all *crises of culture*.

The reality of understanding and finding adaptive solutions to our present and future environmental challenges has shifted the epicenter of environmental studies away from an exclusively scientific and technological framework to one that depends on the human-focused disciplines and ideas of the humanities and allied social sciences.

We thus welcome book proposals from all humanities and social sciences disciplines for an inclusive and interdisciplinary series. We favour manuscripts aimed at an international readership and written in a lively and accessible style. The readership comprises scholars and students from the humanities and social sciences and thoughtful readers concerned about the human dimensions of environmental change.

Environmental History of Modern Migrations

Edited by
Marco Armiero and Richard Tucker

Routledge
Taylor & Francis Group
LONDON AND NEW YORK

from Routledge

First published 2017
by Routledge

2 Park Square, Milton Park, Abingdon, Oxfordshire OX14 4RN
52 Vanderbilt Avenue, New York, NY 10017

Routledge is an imprint of the Taylor & Francis Group, an informa business

First issued in paperback 2018

British Library Cataloguing-in-Publication Data
A catalogue record for this book is available from the British Library

Library of Congress Cataloging-in-Publication Data
A catalog record for this book has been requested

ISBN: 978-1-138-84317-2 (hbk)
ISBN: 978-0-367-17262-6 (pbk)

Typeset in Bembo
by Swales & Willis, Exeter, Devon, UK

Contents

PART II
Racializing natures   109

PART III
Naturalizing causes   157

Figures

Tables

Contributors

Editors

Marco Armiero is Director of the Environmental Humanities Laboratory at the KTH Royal Institute of Technology in Stockholm, Sweden, where he is also Associate Professor of Environmental History. He is the author of *A Rugged Nation. Mountains and the Making of Modern Italy* (2011) and co-editor of *A History of Environmentalism. Local Struggles, Global Histories* (2014), and *Nature and History in Modern Italy* (2010). He is also a senior editor of *Capitalism Nature Socialism* and *Environmental Humanities*.

Richard Tucker is Adjunct Professor in the School of Natural Resources, University of Michigan, US. His earlier publications addressed the history of environmental change in the colonial and tropical world, including *Insatiable Appetite: The United States and the Ecological Degradation of the Tropical World* (2000) and *A Forest History of India* (2010). His recent work addresses the environmental history of warfare. He is the author of numerous essays and co-editor of several multi-author books on the subject, including *Natural Enemy, Natural Ally: Toward an Environmental History of War* (2004).

Contributing authors

Giovanni Bettini is a lecturer at Lancaster University, UK. He is a co-editor of *Life Adrift: Climate Change, Migration, Critique* (2017) and has published a number of articles on the connections between climate change, security and resilience, and human mobility.

Miguel Mundstock Xavier de Carvalho is a Professor at the University of Southern Frontier, Brazil, Campus Laranjeiras do Sul – Paraná. He was a post-doctoral fellow at the University of Guelph, Canada, from 2015 to 2016. His research focuses on the history of Araucaria Forest and the colonization of south Brazil.

Linda L. Ivey (PhD, Georgetown University) is Associate Professor of History at California State University, East Bay, US. She specializes in environmental history, looking at the intersections of this field with cultural, ethnic and labor history. She completed her doctoral work on the ecological and social consequences of capitalist agriculture on the Central Coast of California, and is currently researching cultural environmental expectations and the Japanese in the US. She has published several essays in journals and edited volumes. She is also the co-author of *Citizen Internees: A Second Look at Race and Citizenship in Japanese American Internment Camps* (2017).

Carol MacLennan (PhD in anthropology at the University of California at Berkeley) is an anthropologist who writes about the industrialization of mining and sugar plantation communities and their environmental consequences for landscape and people. She is the author of *Sovereign Sugar: Industry and Environment in Hawai'i* (2014). She is currently writing a book on how mining communities engage with their toxic histories, *Laid to Waste: Lessons from One Hundred Years of Mining*, based upon ethnographic and historical inquiries into two copper mining communities.

Eunice Sueli Nodari is Full Professor at the Federal University of Santa Catarina (UFSC) in Florianópolis, Brazil, where she is also the coordinator of the Laboratório de Imigração, Migração e História Ambiental (LABIMHA). From 2015 to 2016 she was visiting scholar at Center for Spatial and Textual Analysis (CESTA) at Stanford University, US. For more than 15 years Professor Nodari has been doing research on the environmental history of Brazil, and in particular on the transformations of the landscape in southern Brazil, the devastation of Araucaria Forests, environmental disasters, and migrations and agriculture.

Lisa Sun-Hee Park is Chair and Professor of the Department of Asian American Studies at the University of California, Santa Barbara, US. She is also the author of several books, including *The Slums of Aspen: Immigrants vs. the Environment in America's Eden* (2011), which she co-wrote with David Naguib Pellow.

David Naguib Pellow is the Dehlsen Chair and Professor of Environmental Studies and Director of the Global Environmental Justice Project at the University of California, Santa Barbara, US. He is a co-editor of *Keywords for Environmental Studies* (2016) and co-wrote *The Slums of Aspen: Immigrants vs. the Environment in America's Eden* (2011) with Lisa Sun-Hee Park.

Fei Sheng is an environmental historian and associate professor at the Department of History, Sun Yat-Sen University in Guangzhou, China. He has a PhD in world history from Peking University. His first book, *The Struggling Chinese El Dorado: Cantonese Immigrants in the Australia and New Zealand Colonies* (2017, forthcoming), is an environmental history of early Chinese migration to Australia and New Zealand.

Mark Sokolsky is a Visiting Instructor in History at Colby College, Maine, US. His doctoral dissertation, *Taming Tiger Country: Colonization and Environment in the Russian Far East, 1860–1930* (Ohio State University, 2017) examines settlement, ecological change, and conservation in Russia's Maritime Province (Primor'e) during the late-tsarist and Soviet eras.

Daniele Valisena is a PhD Candidate at the Royal Institute of Technology, Stockholm, Sweden, within the Environmental Humanities Laboratory at the Division of History of Science, Technology and Environment. His project on the environmental history of Italian immigrants in Belgium is funded by the Innovative Training Network Marie Curie Environmental Humanities for a Concerned Europe (ENHANCE).

Angus Wright is Professor Emeritus of Environmental Studies at California State University, Sacramento, US. He is the author of *The Death of Ramon Gonzalez: The Modern Agricultural Dilemma* (University of Texas Press, 1990, 2nd ed. 2005) and co-author of *To Inherit the Earth: The Landless Movement and the Struggle for a New Brazil* (2003) and *Nature's Matrix: Linking Conservation, Agriculture and Food Sovereignty* (2012).

Ying Xing is a sociologist. His main area of research is political sociology and historical sociology. He is the author of *Dahe yimin shangfang de gushi* (History of the Petitions of the Migrants of the Great River) (2001) about the Three Gorges Project, and *A Study of the Stability of Contemporary Rural Chinese Society* (2011). He is a professor in the School of Sociology, China University of Political Science and Law.

Figure I.1 Brazil, Rio Grande do Sul, early twentieth century. Men, women and children at work in a furnace.

Source: Fondazione Paolo Cresci per la storia dell'emigrazione italiana

Introduction

Migrants in environmental history

Marco Armiero and Richard Tucker

Histories in the present tense

It seems redundant to explain why there is a need for a book like this. We are writing these lines in the midst of a massive migration crisis as Europe is transforming itself into an impenetrable fortress. The times when walls were falling and barbed wires removed seem so far away. Everywhere rich nations are trying to isolate themselves from the waves of desperate people fleeing from wars, poverty, persecutions, and disruptive environmental changes. "A wall will save us"; this is the easy mantra repeated by the professionals of fear, the gardeners of the new and pernicious hate plantations. Xenophobia, racism, and nationalism are gaining terrain, breeding on a toxic narrative which redirects class conflicts towards the "outside." According to this narrative, if in the Global North the working class is becoming poorer, this is because of immigrants and not the unequal distribution of wealth, the attack against workers' rights, and the neoliberal erosion of the welfare state. When hard times come, having an "other" to blame has always been a handy resource in order to preserve the privilege of the few. The rise of terrorism has even aggravated this situation with a continuous overlapping in the public discourse of migrants and terrorists. An exotic name does all the work here; the fact that often the terrorists were born and raised in the West is easily buried under the inflammatory rhetoric of the new right-wing nationalists.

Lampedusa, Idomeni and Ventimiglia are the centers of a new geography of Europe, places which embody the fact that migration, borders, and bodies intertwine, creating a political ecology of humans' movement and state's control. Routes of hopes and desperation crisscross the Mediterranean; acts of violence and disobedience dot the fortified borders of Europe. The situation is not different in the United States and in Australia, where similar fears are agitated in the public discourse, deeply affecting the political agenda of those countries. A simple textual analysis of the 2016 American presidential campaign could prove beyond any reasonable doubt that migration is a keyword in the public discussion.

In the face of all this, do we really need to explain why an environmental history of migrations (hereafter EHM) is needed? Environmental history—at least as a self-conscious disciplinary field—was born with a strong connection to the ecological movement rising especially in the US society in the 1970s. As the New Social History, Environmental History also looked at what was occurring outside the university's walls, conceptualizing its function as the study of the past in order to address the challenges of the present. In this sense, dealing with migration is going back to the very roots of environmental history as an intellectual project; we might say that it implies the reinforcement of the political conatus of a field which, in gaining academic prestige, sometimes seems to have lost its militant soul (Armiero 2016).

The connections between migration and the environment may not be self-evident; nonetheless, there is a growing body of literature as well as a wider narrative in the public discourse which is enhancing the reflection on this theme. The most fertile terrain where migration and environment have met is that of climate change induced migration. Scholars, policy-makers, journalists, the military, writers and artists, NGOs, and the general public have engaged with the issue of the so-called climate refugees. From the Intergovernmental Panel on Climate Change (IPCC) reports to the biblical migrations of catastrophe blockbuster films such as *The Day After Tomorrow*, and from the 2008 National Intelligence Council's assessment to European Union-funded research programs, the idea that climate change will cause massive and ominous movement of people has increasingly gained authority. Although everyone would agree that significant climate changes will imply the migration of more vulnerable people, it is more controversial to establish a direct and unequivocal cause–effect connection between the two. In other words, defining climate change migrants might be a difficult task, especially since this is not only a matter of academic disquisitions and it might have a legal implication connected to the ongoing debate on the status of people seeking asylum in the Global North. The ghost of the climate refugee is haunting fortress Europe, and for that matter fortress Australia as well; it continuously reappears in the pages of scholarly works and policy briefings. The temptation to reduce everything to some ecological truth might be strong among those who believe that nature matters in humans' affairs. Wars and poverty, two crucial causes of migration, can also be explained as consequences of environmental—more specifically climate—changes. Is this the task for environmental historians? Are we supposed to concur in demonstrating that migration is caused by environmental—better-off climate—changes? With this volume we propose a wider and less deterministic research agenda. Rather than isolating the environmental, searching for the supposed clear ecological causes—or effects—of migration, the challenge is to think ecologically of the processes which have led to—or spring from—migration. Connecting rather than isolating should be our research mantra. A good example might help to explain our vision of an EHM.

In his influential book, *Dust Bowl*, Donald Worster (1979) studied a clear case of migration connected to a major environmental event. The Okies—as the Dust Bowl's refugees were called—left the Great Plains covered by sand

and hit by tornadoes, trying to reach the dreamed-of valleys of California. For an environmental historian the Okies and the Dust Bowl could work as the perfect tale; the environmental is extremely visible and powerful in that story, and no one could question its relevance in the Okies' migration. Nonetheless, Worster avoids a simplistic narrative based on a narrow understanding of the "environmental," adopting instead what we have called above ecological thinking, that is, an approach which looks for the connections rather than for ultimate causes. Drought, tornadoes, sand, and a fissured soil pushed people away from the Great Plains, but Worster rightly connects those "natural" facts to less "natural" processes as the imposition of capitalistic agriculture and farmers' outstanding debts with banks. In this sense, the Okies were climate refugees at least as much as capitalism refugees. In his analysis Worster overcomes the binary division of ecological vs. social. Paraphrasing the critical geographer David Harvey we can state that capitalistic agriculture was an ecology of soil and communities disruption which dispersed both dust and people. Worster's *Dust Bowl* offers a model for an environmental history of migrations which is not obsessed with proving the "environmental" ultimate causes of the movement of people, but rather unpacks the dichotomy nature/society, showing the intertwining of economies, cultures, and ecologies.

Looking at the current refugees' crisis through the lens adopted by Worster, it would seem irrelevant to trace impenetrable borders among environmental, economic, and political migrants as if those were parallel universes and not the intertwined socionatures of which our world is made. If we wished to be provocative, we would argue that we need an environmental history of migration which should not be obsessed with the "environmental." The point is not to depart from the relevance of "nature," which is the very foundation of the field, but to subvert the commonsense assumption that in order to see nature we need to separate it from the "rest," be it culture, economy, or society. After all, by and large the ways in which the environment has been framed in the discipline has not allowed us to see migrants; evidently we need to change what we mean and understand for the environment, and maybe to change where we place environmental history in respect to the broader historical field. If we wish to stay safe and sound in our "green ghetto," satisfied with the space of maneuver that is granted to us as environmental historians, we should not dare to trespass. But if instead we believe that environmental history can enter into every space of the past and change our way of looking at it, then migration is indeed a theme for our discipline.

Beyond conquistadores and Her Majesty's subjects

Indeed, if there is something that "general" history might learn from environmental history, it is the ecological approach to the study of human migration. Alfred Crosby's, Jared Diamond's, Thomas Dunlap's, and Richard Grove's studies, even with a significantly diverse range of determinism and mono-causality, have shown that ecology, culture, and economy mix when environments and people meet (Crosby 1972, 1986; Diamond 1997; Dunlap 1999; Grove 1995).

Some stories are more significant than others; the impact of the Europeans on Australia and the Americas and on their environments has been particularly dramatic, even if the ecological implications of the "discovery" have been less obvious than we imagined, considering that only with Crosby's books have historians started to consider those aspects. The movements of people around the world have affected not only economy, societies, and cultures, but even nature itself, both in the places of departure and of arrival. Scholars such as Crosby and Diamond prefer to speak about the complex biota that each ethnic group has brought with it: animals, plants, and germs. Thus, the intensity, and therefore the interest, of these physical changes depended to a great degree on how much the new environment was different from the old one, or, in other words, how distant the two worlds were before they met. Crosby's and Diamond's approach to people's movements has been intensively used in the study of the great geographical explorations that connected people and environments long separated from each other. According to those narratives, the moment of discovery is particularly dramatic; the major ecological transformations have generally occurred in the first phase of the meeting between discoverers/conquerors and discovered/conquered. Today, it would be impossible to address the making of the modern world without any reference to the Columbian Exchange. Potatoes, horses, and smallpox are more or less part of the mainstream narrative about the conquest of the Americas. The popularity of Diamond's *Guns, Germs, and Steel* (1997) is the proof of the success of that kind of explanation.

But what about the age of modern and contemporary migrations? Is it possible that after this phase the movement of people around the world has not had ecological implications again? Indubitably that movement did, if we think about the age of imperialism in the nineteenth to twentieth century. The environmental historians of Africa have led the field in showing how much the natural environment of that continent both affected (for instance, in terms of the resistance of white people to particular diseases) and was affected by European colonialism (Beinart 2000; McCann 1999; Sunseri 2002). Probably, in this case, it was more a matter of policies than of biological expansion. Today Africa is not a Neo-Europe—using Crosby's expression—in terms of human, animal or plant populations, but this recognition does not mean that the colonial policies had had little impact on African environments. Thinking "ecologically" about imperialism means considering the biological power of different groups, looking at the consequences of the invasion on the environment, and vice versa, that is, the effects of nature on the colonial expansion. Big game hunting and animal reserves, forestry agencies and policies, have been connected to colonial environments; even some powerful ideas about nature, such as wilderness, are considered to be the result of the encounter between people from elsewhere and the nature they have found (Davis 2007; MacKenzie 1988; Neumann 2002; Sivaramakrishnan 1999).

While these authors have emphasized the ecological effects of discovery and imperialism, what about the age of mass migrations? Can we look ecologically at this phenomenon? As Alfred Crosby once put it, with the advent of mass migration the earth was involved in the largest and quickest movement of biomass across the ocean (Crosby 1995, 178). Speaking of migrants in terms of biomass did not help to interest historians in the subject because generally historians pay attention to topics other than biomass. Therefore, as we have argued above, we are challenged to overcome a dichotomist approach which divides nature and human experiences. The passage of that special biomass, the mass migration, implied the movement of both nature and culture. Human migrants crossed the oceans carrying with them cultures and hopes, bodies and works, techniques and crops. Generally, in the nineteenth and twentieth century migrants did not bring with them an entire biota, with its plants, animals, and germs, never before seen in the places of arrival—perhaps with a few exceptions. Although they did not bring with them an entire ecosystem, they moved around the world with their ideas about nature, with their knowledge about ways of using natural resources; sometimes they transplanted some of their home crops, adapting old practices to new environments. Again, they brought with them their bodies, their resistance or weakness to the pathogenic agents encountered in the New Worlds (Kraut 1994). Too often, environmental historians have forgotten that nature is not external to human beings. Working in the mines or on the malarial plantations of the south, building railroads, and living in overcrowded urban ghettos were not without consequences for the migrants. The experience of migration often left indelible traces in the bodies of those who were exposed to unfamiliar threats and hazards.

Thus, to approach mass migrations from an environmental perspective, we need to adjust our ideas about nature and its historical relationship with humans. First of all, we need to enlarge our concept of nature. Migrants did appreciate nature but often following different paths and in general without leaving clear evidences of this relationship. But if planting grapes, harvesting the sea, mining coal, or simply surviving in the tenements of the metropolis had a "natural" substance, then migrants do indeed have their environmental stories waiting to be told. Moreover, an environmental history of migrations shows that the environment has not changed only through the *longue durée*, but that the transformations can occur even in shorter periods of time. Sometimes the time of nature and that of humans meet; the age of mass migration was one of those moments.

EHM: a toolkit

Environmental historians have not been significantly active in studying the history of mass migrations, nor have the historians of migration ever been interested in the environment. Of course, there are exceptions (Chiang 2009; Fisher 2015; Kraut 1994; Mitchell 1996; Nash 2006; Rome 2008; Valencius 2002), but by and large migration has not attracted environmental historians with the same intensity as other topics. This lack of attention is particularly remarkable in US environmental history, comparing it to the role of immigration in the history of that country. It is hard to find in-depth references about migrants in several general textbooks on American environmental history (Fiege 2012; Opie 1998; Steinberg 2002), as well as in the few books dedicated to the environmental history of Europe and European countries (Delort and Walter 2001; Rackham and Grove 2001; Simmons 2001). There are significant exceptions, such as, for instance, John McNeill's remarkable fresco of the Mediterranean mountains in which he rightly considers the issue of migrations crucial to his research (McNeill 1992). In his extensive review of the field, John McNeill has corroborated this impression, writing that "[t]he environmental effects of human migration also deserve more scrutiny" (McNeill 2003, 41–42).

This volume contributes to filling the gap, but before illustrating our research contribution, we will reflect on the challenges and possibilities of doing EHM. First of all, it is worth asking the reasons for such a gap: why did environmental historians not embrace migrations/migrants as a recurrent theme for their research? Above we have argued that a strong disciplinary approach did not help in expanding the field in that direction. A narrow understanding of what the environment is—or should be—excludes humans' migration from the picture. An environmental history too concerned with building its own territory, patrolling borders and checking its rate of "environmental," cannot be interested in migration. As migrants, environmental historians too must trespass borders, traveling between disciplinary territories blending a crumb of adaptation and some doses of experimentation. This attitude also implies a welcoming practice towards any fellow traveler who wishes to join us, even only for a short piece of the journey.

However, a narrow disciplinary approach cannot be the only explanation for environmental historians' lack of interest in migration. An important part of the problem is the undeniable difficulty in finding relevant sources on the subject. In other words, where can we find sources to write the environmental stories of migrants? Even when migrants had left a few written sources, they were concerned with job opportunities, accommodation, or travel suggestions, but hardly with landscape and other "natural subjects." At least not in these terms. As Patricia Nelson Limerick wrote:

> A landowning-literati class is indeed the source of much of the Anglo-American literature of discovery of landscape [....] Without a margin of assured subsistence, without the opportunity for contemplation and introspection, without a way to enter one's memories into a permanent, written source, a group's response to a new geography can be close to impossible for posterity to hear.
>
> (Limerick 2000: 195)

The point is well made, but rather than being a capitulation to the limits of the sources, it is a call to arms, a request to mobilize creativity in order to overcome those bounds. Indeed, in the pages which followed those lines, Patricia Nelson Limerick described the Chinese agency in shaping the Californian landscape, stressing their ingenuity in transforming useless things into resources. To cite just a few examples: the mustard plants, seen by the Americans as a nuisance, became raw materials for valued Chinese spice; and the willows, which were perceived by the "whites" as useless, for the Chinese were evidence of fresh water and therefore fertile land (Limerick 2000, 196). Nonetheless, there is no doubt that it is quite improbable to find the diary of a Chinese farmer who describes his idea of the California soil or the reminiscences of an Italian scavenger reflecting about nature in the city. As always when historians wish to uncover the lives of the subalterns, there is a need to look for new sources as well as to interrogate the usual one with new questions. The chapters gathered in this volume will show the strategies which can be employed in order to escape the limits of the sources.

In an attempt to systematize approaches and strategies for EHM, we propose three possible paths, or styles: the assertive style, the constructivist style, and the embodied style. Those are ideal-types which, rather than being mutually exclusive, are often blended in the empirical work of researchers. As in Worster's foundational essay on "Doing Environmental History" (1988), here also the organization of the research along three paths does not imply that researchers must opt for one of them; instead, we argue that the best experiments will be produced by a blend of the three.

The assertive style, or strange pioneers on the frontier

EHM may aim to uncover the contribution of migrants in the making of the landscapes where they settled. The connection to studies on the empires and colonial expansion of Europe is evident. Since the beginning of the discipline, environmental historians have researched the ecological transformations imposed by the imperial arrangements of the world. Looking at migrations, especially at the age of mass migrations, means to enlarge those kinds of studies beyond the limits of the colonial settings. Those limits are not only chronological— mass migrations arrived later than the age of the first colonial expansion—but they are also inherent to the nature of Empire. The military support of the Fatherland, the expropriation of natives' lands, and the construction of a legal and institutional system at the service of the colonizers' interests were the basis of the imperial movement of people. The late nineteenth and early twentieth century migrants did not have that kind of cargo and by and large did not have such a close encounter with natives, rather with other ethnic groups or the descendants of the colonizers. In the classical Turnerian plot, those migrants do not fit; according to this historiographical myth, they were not pioneers and the Frontier was far from their experience. About thirty years ago the emergence of the New Western History radically undermined the Turnerian plot, reclaiming the agency of indigenous people, minorities, and women as well as uncovering the varieties of the ecologies of the frontier vs. the uniformity of the mythical West. EHM proceeds in the path traced by the New Western History, challenging the male, Anglo-Saxon, white, and Protestant pioneer ideal-type.

But precisely following the New Western History model, EHM should also challenge the classic idea of Frontier. The frontier was not only somewhere west of the Mississippi in America or wherever "wild nature met civilization." There was also an urban frontier where immigrants were pushed to live. There was an industrial and agricultural frontier in which immigrant workers were exposed to hazards precisely because they were immigrants. In other words, EHM not only expands the pioneers' tale to encompass other actors, but also questions the triumphalist tone of pioneers taming the frontier. Migrants were not the epitomes of free settlers shaping nature for the best. Many times, theirs are stories of exploitation, of competition with other ethnic groups over access and control of natural resources, of failure in adapting to new socioecologies. The risk of celebration is rather strong in the assertive style; EHM can easily embrace a research agenda aiming to prove that immigrants were also pioneers, contributing to the taming of "nature" (a very informative example is Rolle 1968). Nonetheless, we argue that as with the New Western History and the Turnerian paradigm, EHM can also open up a possibility for going beyond celebration and still exploring how immigrants have shaped the environments where they settled.

The constructivist style, or seeing the environment through others' eyes

Migrants not only shaped the environment where they settled; they also saw it in different ways, applying categories and visions which belonged to their own cultures or which emerged in the blending of the migratory experience. In many cases they were able to shape the environment because they saw it differently, recognizing in it things that others could not see. Following Worster's organization of environmental history, one could say that this is the cultural part of the EHM; through it researchers should be able to uncover migrants' perceptions and understandings of nature. Although rather appropriate, we find this explanation of what we call the constructivist style limited and problematic. It seems to reproduce a binary opposition between cultural and material, or even cultural and natural which we believe should be overcome. Seeing nature and giving it meanings was not the cultural side of migrants' relationships to the environment. In the very process of making sense of the environment, migrants transformed it, or at least affected it, and as we will see later, themselves. In a seminal essay on EHM, Adam Rome (2008) has illustrated the clash between Anglo-Saxon conservationist cultures and immigrants' understandings of nature, which left very little room for contemplation of wilderness. Peter Coates has uncovered the intertwined human and more-than human histories of migration in the United States, stressing the concept of "alien" and its load of nativism and natural belonging (Coates 2006). Louis Warren (1997) has uncovered the struggles between US conservationists and immigrants' hunting practices. Something occurred almost in the same way in Brazil, as explained by Elenita Malta Pereira and Regina Weber (2012). A xenophobic line of reasoning might be detected even today in some "environmentalist" discourses about the need to stop migration in the rich countries in order to avoid the ecological problems brought by immigrants (Armiero 2012; Hartman 2004).

As the assertive style should not be concerned with some pioneers' celebration, we do not envision the constructivist style as the reinvention of the ecological immigrant—after the ecological Indian, indigenous nations, etc. The point is not to prove that immigrants' ways of seeing nature were by definition "ecologically friendly," but to scrutinize them beyond xenophobic stereotypes. It is worth remembering that bison and passenger pigeons were not made (almost) extinct by hordes of Italians or Mexicans. An EHM constructivist style may be a good way to rethink different ideas and practices of nature. We argue that the conservationist problem with immigrants' vision of nature was not so much its destructive consequences, rather the fact that it proposed a porous nature, one where the spaces of work, living, and leisure were not drastically separated. What were the Italian backyards, full of vegetables, rabbits and chickens, if not a different appreciation of land and natural resources and a porous space blending work, living, and leisure times? The constructivist style can contribute to urban environmental history, rethinking ecologically the ethnic enclaves, exploring how immigrants understood and activated urban commons, including garbage, that is, a space traditionally occupied by immigrant workers.

The embodied style, or the nature of/in the immigrant's body

EHM leads also to cross the frontier between human and natural realms, reinforcing the position of those environmental historians who have argued for including the body as a critical field of exploration (Sellers 1997). Here we need to borrow some sentences from Linda Nash's *Inescapable Ecologies*, one of the few and most inspiring EHM experiments:

> The central [California] valley, like all of North America, is now a complicated mixture of human and nonhuman elements, a hybrid landscape: aquifers and aqueducts, soils and chemicals, native plants and commercial crops. But change did not occur in only one direction. As people have shaped the landscape, the landscape has shaped the bodies of its inhabitants.
> (Nash 2006, 209)

Migrants are themselves nature on the move. This was true not only during the early years of the Columbian or Magellan Exchange. People continued to cross the oceans bringing with them their bodies, their resistance or weakness to pathogenic agents, their ability to cope with different climate and food. EHM needs to break the boundaries between bodies and nature. However, what we are looking for is not just a map drawing the distribution of health hazards in respect to migrants. In the mines, farms, factories, or urban environments, often immigrants—and of course we are speaking here of the large majority of them—were exposed to the worst conditions. However, a map like this runs the risk of being blind to how much power relations and social structures have constructed both hazards and migrants' exposure to them. Was the environment or rather the capitalistic organization of labor, based on race, the cause of illness among the Mexicans working in the plantations in California (Alamillo 2006, 40–41; Mitchell 1996)? Was it just an unfortunate accident that killed 146 workers, mostly immigrants, at the Triangle Shirt Factory in New York, or rather the special combination of a powerful capitalistic discipline of labor and a weak immigrant labor force? Historian Alan Kraut has reminded us that one of the first workers interviewed by Alice Hamilton—the pioneer of occupational health—for her studies was O.V., an Italian immigrant; and the fact that he was an Italian was absolutely central to his experience of factory hazards, doing the worst job and being incapable of understanding what he was doing due to the language barrier (Kraut 1994, 176). Morris Kavitsky, a Polish Jew arriving in New York in 1914, remembering his first impressions of the New World, said:

> Most of the Jews seemed to have lost their health here while working the sweatshops. I had never seen so many people with false teeth and eyeglasses. Was this part of the process of becoming Americanized? How about tuberculosis and appendicitis? I was shocked at the physical condition of my people in this country. It seemed to me that hardly any one of them escaped the surgical knife. The air was damp [...] and people worked harder here.
>
> (Stave 1994, 49)

Thereby, EHM must join forces with those environmental historians who have contributed to renovating the field, calling attention to the connections linking work, ecologies, and health (Barca 2014; Mitman 2005; Montrie 2008; Sellers 1997). This is not only a movement inside the environmental history field, but it also comes strongly from civil society organizations, and especially from the environmental justice movement that has emerged in the environmentalist cultures. In this sense, it is the right time to foster the EHM agenda.

Around the world in eleven chapters

Wide ranging themes in this collection shine light on the environmental complexity of modern migrations. The case studies are organized around three broader themes: Changing natures, Racializing natures, and Naturalizing causes. Although we do see a coherent thread connecting the chapters in each section, we also stress that this organization of the volume should not undermine both the general unity of the book and the diversity of themes touched by the authors. Addressing migration in environmental history should not lead to neat and compartmentalized narratives; rather the challenge is to stick with the messiness of socionatural intertwines blending racism, ecologies, cultures, class and gender, politics and economies.

In almost every instance the migrants—whatever the degree of coercion under which they moved—took their environmental knowledge systems from one ecological home to another, applying them with adaptation. Most of the migrant communities in this book were relatively homogeneous in class and subculture, and took relatively homogeneous packages of environmental knowledge with them, applying it as means of survival in initially unfamiliar new settings. This aspect is especially developed in the Changing natures section. The essays gathered under that label all have a distinctive interest in the understanding of migrants–environments metabolic relationships. The ecological transformations of the immigrants' new home areas are at the core of these papers. Deforestation, soil depletion, and reduction of biodiversity emerge as themes in several of these chapters. Eunice Nodari and Miguel Carvalho trace the work of German and Italian immigrants in clearing the forest frontier of southern Brazil into productive agriculture and vineyards, but at the cost of losing 90% of the original forest biota. Mark Sokolsky describes the ethnic Russian "Great Migration" to eastern Siberia in the late nineteenth century, showing the complexity of transplanting both Russian and Chinese biotas to different ecological settings. Another variation is Carol MacLennan's long time-frame study of Polynesians, then Asians, and then Euro-Americans migrated to Hawaiʻi islands. Each layer of what became modern Hawaiʻi's socioenvironment took its own package of species. The long term result has been the classic case of invasive species overwhelming native species of flora and fauna, severely reducing the islands' biodiversity as the cultural diversity has become more diverse and stratified in its place in the global economy. Marco Armiero's chapter bridges the transformation of the environment with the transformation of the immigrant's very body. While making vineyards out of the desert or soil out of waste, migrants were deeply affected by the environment, or, as Armiero insists, by the power relationships organizing their metabolic relationships with it. The body also becomes a central theme in Valisena's and Armiero's chapter on the Italian miners in Belgium. The sobering story of Italian coal miners in southern Belgium links migrations to industrial ecology, and specifically to capitalist ecologies, more directly than the other cases presented in the volume. Against the violence of the capitalistic organization of labor, which even placed an expiration date on miners' bodies, stand migrants' sabotage of their own bodies and their re-appropriation of the environment through gardening.

In this chapter Valisena and Armiero mention what they define as a xenophobic spatialization, that is, an organization of space meant to exclude migrants from public spaces. This theme easily drives the reader to the following section on Racializing natures. That migrants have been discriminated against is anything but a new finding for scholars. Trying to connect this to environmental discourses and issues is, instead, a rather new path of research (see Coates 2006 and Rome 2008). Fei Sheng explores how environmental arguments were mobilized in building a racist discourse against Chinese immigrants in Australia. While their mining methods were blamed for negatively affecting water, in an escalation of nativism and racism their own bodies became a matter of controversy, a place of moral and biological impurity.

Linda Ivey traces the troubles of Filipino farm workers in the industrialized lettuce fields of central California in 1930. She places this case of environmental nativism against the previous generation of Chinese immigration and the longer history of environmental nativism in California's agriculture. The ecology of lettuce, the capitalistic organization of labor, sex and race all intertwine into Ivey's story, providing a compelling case of an environmental history of nativism and migrants' struggles.

David Pellow and Lisa Park demonstrate that the connections between nativism, racism and environmental discourses are not only a matter of history. In their study of the tourist Mecca of Aspen, Colorado, they describe ethnic injustice in the Anglo-American effort to save "pristine nature" from immigrants from Latin America by severely restricting immigration for the service economy. The hypocrisy of blaming immigrants' impact on the local environment while ignoring the astonishing level of consumption on which that exclusive community is built seems the perfect metaphor for so many mainstream discourses on the Anthropocene. At the heart of the ideological problem Pellow and Park identify the Euro-American elite's environmentalism, based on the defense of a Romantic image of "wilderness." Mixing anti-immigration into local environmental politics is explosive.

Finally, the last section of this volume is dedicated to the environmental causes of migrations. By no means do the three chapters gathered in this section pretend to cover such an enormous field of studies. Rather, they aim to indicate some major lines of inquiry such as the issue of the natural causes of migration, the need to excavate the intellectual history of the environment/ migration debate, and the case of forced migrations due to development projects. Angus Wright reflects on the creation of an environmental explanation of the emigration from the Brazilian northeast to the industrial south and Amazonia. As Wright uncovers, "Drought as an explanation for 'backwardness' and migration had several advantages over the competing explanations. It did not require a confrontation with the entrenched political economy of the plantation complex and those powerful families and politicians who controlled it." He warns against reducing complex causes to "oversimplified explanations to serve exploitive purposes." Giovanni Bettini's essay complements this, adding a survey of the deep ideological roots of the recent controversy in the two-century debate about population and resources. He warns us against falling into the trap of identifying overpopulation in the Global South as the core of the contemporary crisis. Ying Xing shifts our attention to megadevelopment projects as potential cases of forced migrations. His chapter addresses one of the world's largest displacements of people because of the construction of a dam.

The Three Gorges Dam has caused the removal of a million Chinese (both urban and rural) out of the lower Yangtze valley by their own government, in pursuit of its grandiose development project. As with hydro-development projects in many countries, planning and provision for the displaced population has been woefully inadequate, resulting in socioenvironmental degradation on a large scale. Xing's proposal to speak of ecological resettlers rather than project resettlers reinforces the systemic transformations triggered by both the remaking of the environment and the reshuffling of its people.

We are well aware that relevant themes and crucial geographical areas are not included in this volume. Nonetheless, producing an exhaustive work was not our aim. Rather, we wished to ignite a renewed interest in researching the histories of migrants and their contradictory metabolic relationships with the environment. In doing so, this volume also contributes to locating environmental history at the frontline of current global challenges, reclaiming the public or, dare we say, the political relevance of the discipline. On the other hand, this volume also has the ambition of debunking what we perceive as a too narrow disciplinary scope, probably a side-effect of the field finally gaining academic recognition. While arguing for the need to trespass across disciplines and thematic territories, we think that this book has experimented with an open border disciplinary policy, including geographers, sociologists, and political scientists, together with environmental historians. Not building walls but demolishing them will save us. And we are not speaking only of disciplines.

References

Alamillo, J.M. (2006) *Making lemonade out of lemons. Mexican American labor and leisure in a California town 1880–1960*. University of Illinois Press, Chicago.

Armiero, M. (2012) The green-washing of the anti-immigration discourse. An environmental history perspective paper presented at the workshop The Securitisation of Climate-Induced Migration: Critical Perspectives. Hamburg 10–12 June.

Barca, S. (2014) "Laboring the earth: transnational reflections on the environmental history of work," *Environmental History* 19.1: 3–27.

Beinart, W. (2000) "African history and environmental history," *African Affairs* 99.395: 269–302.

Coates, P. (2006) *American perceptions of immigrant and invasive species: strangers on the land*. University of California Press, Berkeley and Los Angeles.

Chiang, C.Y. (2009) *Shaping the shoreline: fisheries and tourism on the Monterey coast*. University of Washington Press, Seattle.

Crosby, A.W. (1995) "The past and present of environmental history," *The American historical review* 100.4: 1177–1189.

Crosby, A.W. (1986) *Ecological imperialism: the biological expansion of Europe, 900–1900*. Cambridge University Press, Cambridge.

Crosby, A.W. (1972) *The Columbian Exchange: biological and cultural consequences of 1492*. Greenwood Press, Westport, Connecticut.

Davis, D.K. (2007) *Resurrecting the granary of Rome: environmental history and French colonial expansion in North Africa*. Ohio University Press, Athens, Ohio.

Delort, R. and Walter F. (2001) *Histoire de l'environnement européen*. Presses universitaires de France, Paris.

Diamond, J. (1997) *Guns, germs, and steel: the fates of human societies*. W.W. Norton, New York.

Dunlap, T.R. (1999) *Nature and the English diaspora: environment and history in the United States, Canada, Australia, and New Zealand*. Cambridge University Press, Cambridge.

Fiege, M. (2012) *The republic of nature: an environmental history of the United States*. Washington University Press, Seattle.

Fisher, C. (2015) *Urban green: nature, recreation, and the working class in industrial Chicago*. University of North Carolina Press, Chapel Hill.

Grove, R.H. (1995) *Green imperialism: colonial expansion, tropical island Edens, and the origins of environmentalism, 1600–1860*. Cambridge University Press, Cambridge.

Hartmann, B. (2004) "Conserving racism: The greening of hate at home and abroad," *Different Takes* 27 [no page numbers].

Kraut, A. (1994) *Silent travelers: germs, genes, and the "immigrant menace."* Basic Books, New York.

Limerick, P.N. (2000) *Something in the soil*. W.W. Norton and Co, New York.

MacKenzie, J. (1988) *The empire of nature: hunting, conservation, and British imperialism*. Manchester University Press, Manchester, New York.

McCann, J.C. (1999) *Green land, brown land, black land: an environmental history of Africa, 1800–1990*. Heinemann, Portsmouth, New Hampshire.

McNeill, J.R. (2003) "Observations on the nature and culture of environmental history," *History and theory* 42.4: 5–43.

McNeill, J.R. (1992) *Mountains of the Mediterranean world: An environmental history*. Cambridge University Press, Cambridge.

Mitchell, D. (1996) *The lie of the land: Migrant workers and the California landscape*. University of Minnesota Press, Minneapolis.

Mitman, G. (2007) *Breathing space: how allergies shape our lives and landscapes*. New Haven: Yale University Press.

Montrie, C. (2008) *Making a living: work and environment in the United States*. University of North Carolina Press, Chapel Hill.

Nash, L. (2006) *Inescapable ecologies: a history of environment, disease, and knowledge*. University of California Press, Berkeley and Los Angeles.

Neumann, R.P. (2002) *Imposing wilderness: struggles over livelihood and nature preservation in Africa*. University of California Press, Berkeley and Los Angeles.

Opie, J. (1998) *Nature's nation: an environmental history of the United States*. Brace, New York.

Pereira, E.M. and Weber R. (2012) "Roessler vs. bird hunters: 'passarinhada' and ethnic conflicts in the south of Brazil," *Miradas En Movimiento* 1 (2012): 98–124.

Rackham, O. and Grove, R. (2001) *The nature of Mediterranean Europe: an ecological history*. Yale University Press, New Haven.

Rolle, A. (1968) *The immigrant upraised. Italian adventurers and colonists in an expanding America*. University of Oklahoma, Oklahoma.

Rome, A. (2008) "Nature wars, culture wars: immigration and environmental reform in the Progressive Era," *Environmental History* 13.3: 432–453.

Sellers, C.C. (1997) *Hazards of the job: from industrial disease to environmental health science*. University of North Carolina Press, Chapel Hill.

Simmons, I.G. (2001) *An environmental history of Great Britain: from 10,000 years ago to the present.* Edinburgh University Press, Edinburgh.

Sivaramakrishnan, K. (1999) *Modern forests: statemaking and environmental change in colonial Eastern India.* Stanford University Press, Stanford.

Stave, B.M. and Sutherland, J.F. with A. Salerno (1994) *From the old country. An oral history of European migration to America.* Twayne Publishers, New York.

Steinberg, T. (2002) Down to earth: nature's role in American history. Oxford University Press, New York.

Sunseri, T.R. (2002) *Vilimani: labor migration and rural change in early colonial Tanzania.* Heinemann, Portsmouth, New Hampshire.

Valencius, C.V. (2002) *The health of the country: how American settlers understood themselves and their land.* Basic Books, New York.

Warren, L.S. (1997) *The hunter's game: poachers and conservationists in twentieth-century America.* Yale University Press, New Haven.

Worster, D. (1988) "Appendix: doing environmental history," in *The ends of the earth: perspectives on modern environmental history*, ed. D. Worster, Cambridge University Press, Cambridge, 289–307.

Worster, D. (1979) *Dust Bowl: the southern plains in the 1930s.* Oxford University Press, New York.

Part I

Changing natures

The authors of the following chapters have dealt with the idea of *Changing natures* from different perspectives. Some of them have stressed the impact of immigrants on external nature (MacLennan; Eunice Nodari; and Miguel Carvalho); others have focused on the changing natures immigrants have found where they settled (Sokolsky). Other authors have analyzed how immigrants per se were changing natures blending their own bodies with the environments where they settled (Armicro, and Valisena and Armicro). Talking of human/ environment relationships can be a tricky business. One can very easily fall into the usual dichotomist trap of placing culture vs. nature. An environmental history of migrations is interested in understanding how immigrants have affected the places where they settled. This kind of approach is rather strong in several of the chapters gathered in this part of the volume. We will learn about the making of the Hawaiian landscape as a stratification of various ethnic groups (MacLennan) and about the deforestation of the Brazilian Atlantic Forest due to Germans' and Italians' economic activities (Eunice Nodari and Miguel Carvalho). Armiero will illustrate how the US landscape was made of the work of various immigrant groups both in the rural as well as in the urban space. It might be said that the chapters collected in this part deal with the ways in which immigrants have shaped the environment around them. Though it has the beauty of a clear argument, limiting the theme of Part I to the immigrants' effects on the environment is misleading. It risks reproducing the dichotomist vision of humans vs. nature. In some of the following chapters the authors argue that immigrants were also nature, their bodies were nature imbricated in a mutual relationship with the matter which makes both themselves and the world—what the ecocritical scholar Stacy Alaimo has called transcorporeality. This is the case of the Italian miners who were part of the metabolism of coal, producing both bodies and landscapes (Valisena and Armiero). Armiero also illuminates the porosity of the immigrant's body in his chapter on the United States. However, not only is the body nature; the chapters in this section also show that nature is never just "natural." The capitalistic organization of plantations and agriculture, the discipline of labor in the factories and in the mines, even the forms of the urban segregation of spaces and people were not "natural" at all.

1 Waves of migration

Settlement and creation of the Hawaiian environment

Carol MacLennan

Abstract

Three major waves of human migrants mark the major alterations in the Hawaiian environment: Polynesians, Europeans and North Americans, and Asians, primarily from China, Japan, and the Philippines. In this chapter I will explore the phases of landscape transformation produced by those immigrants and how the interactions among them shaped the modern environment. In understanding those ecological transformations, it will become clear that they have also implied major changes in human history of production, political development, and social organization.

Setting the scene

Humans settled the Hawaiian archipelago in the Central North Pacific relatively late in human history. Polynesian navigators from the Marquesas and Tahiti began voyages to the islands around AD 1000, followed by two additional sizable migrations of people from Asia and from the temperate climates of North America and Europe. For nearly one thousand years these waves of migrants arrived and settled the islands introducing plants, animals, insects and human cultures that layered one upon the other to create an island society that is urban, agricultural, and militarized. One cannot understand the physical character of Hawai'i today without peeling away the waves of human migrations and settlement among the six major islands—Kaua'i, O'ahu, Maui, Moloka'i, Lana'i, and Hawai'i Island. Known as high volcanic islands in the Pacific, the archipelago of settled and uninhabited islands rise over 13,000 feet (Mauna Kea and Mauna Loa on Hawai'i Island) at the southerly end where Kilauea Volcano is still active. Underwater seamounts mark the northerly end of the Hawaiian–Emperor Seamount Chain, eroded ancient volcanoes that inhabit the ocean floor to the south of the Aleutian Islands in the North Pacific. Slowly colonized over millennia by only one mammal (a bat) and primarily by birds and insects, Hawai'i's environment was characteristic of "remote" islands with limited diversity composed of mostly endemic species. Human habitation in the valleys and along the fertile volcanic coastal soils created a cascade of consequences that altered every niche of the complex wet and dry ecosystems.

Three major waves of human migrants mark the major alterations in island ecology: Polynesians who introduced agriculture, new species, and populated the islands with 250,000 to 800,000 individuals[1] between AD 1000 and 1780 created a highly stratified state society based upon intensive agricultural production. Europeans and North Americans arrived in the North Pacific in the late eighteenth century, initiating a slow but powerful wave of migration of seamen, merchants, missionaries, and their families, that settled and aggressively strove to apply their agricultural and cultural norms to the subtropical environment. Asians, primarily from China, Japan, and the Philippines arrived in Hawai'i primarily to work on sugar and, later, pineapple plantations. Many became permanent settlers, while others returned home or migrated to California.

Peeling back the layered environment produced by migrants over one thousand years, I will examine the phases of landscape transformation produced by Polynesian, Euro-American, and Asian immigrants, and how the interactions among them shaped the modern environment. It becomes clear that multiple migration histories record not only the transformation of landscapes but also major changes in human history of production, political development, and social organization. As we trace one thousand years of migration settlement in Hawai'i we also witness the major transformations in global society as etched on the Hawaiian landscape.

Polynesian arrival and settlement

Around AD 900–1000 Polynesian navigators launched long voyages from the Marquesas and Society Islands in central Polynesia, settling Hawai'i and Rapa Nui (Easter Island) sometime between AD 1000 and 1200.[2] Later, they extended their range to Aotearoa (North Island of New Zealand), thus completing what today we call the Polynesian triangle. An astounding feat, the voyaging expeditions utilized star charts and expert readings of currents and animal migrations. Polynesians sailed the Pacific in double-hulled canoes that carried families, animals, plants, and food thousands of miles on their quest for new settlements. For a period of time, until around 1400, regular voyaging back and forth from Hawai'i to the Marquesas and Society Islands continued, indicating that Hawai'i was discovered and settled not by accident but by design. Hawai'i's isolation is a major factor in its environmental history. Part of what archaeologists call Remote Oceania, the islands have unique evolutionary histories prior to human arrival. As the first wave of migrants, Polynesians introduced environmental changes during the first several hundred years that produced a type of feedback loop between humans and ecosystems and set the stage for human migrations from subsequent eras.

Polynesians traveled with their food staples and animals to their new homes. Hawai'i supplied little in the way of plant food except for ferns, but fish, shellfish, and limu were abundant. Along the coastal regions, and particularly in the wet, wide windward valleys, Hawaiians added their chickens, pigs, dogs, taro, yams, breadfruit, bananas, kava, and sugar cane. The Pacific Rat, as a stowaway on the canoes, also populated the islands with consequences for ground-nesting birds and native coastal trees. The older, western islands of Kaua'i and O'ahu, surrounded by coral reefs, were the likely first homes of the colonizers (Kirch 2012, 83).

The early Polynesians altered the coastal landscapes with their wet and dry agricultural systems. Evidence of fire in lowland forests indicates Polynesian clearing of vegetation to introduce their imported plants (Athens 1997, 267). Gradually settlers occupied the windward valleys on the major islands and slowly expanded their population. Archaeologists have determined that extensive changes to the lowlands occurred within two to three hundred years after canoes landed in O'ahu. Soil erosion was a major factor of landscape change, as cleared lands released soils downslope, filling bays and estuaries (Allen 1997, 241). Birds, such as the flightless *moa nalo* (extinct gooselike duck) disappeared quickly; palm (*Prichardia*) forests more slowly; and the landscape became one of "managed organization" (Kirch 2012, 111).

By AD 1500 there was virtually nothing left of the lowland forests. Besides agricultural clearing and fire, other factors at work depleted the endemic vegetation and birds. Rats introduced by the newcomers had a hand in the extinction of native palms and some ground-nesting bird species.

In the tradition of ancient Polynesia (Hawaiki—the Hawaiians' Polynesian homeland), chiefs ruled society, and individuals held rights to home and land through their ancestors. Genealogy was important for identity and land rights. This began to change in the early fifteenth century about the time that voyaging ceased. First on O'ahu, then on the other islands, one chief rose to power. Land claims were organized in a hierarchical order under an *ahupua'a*, a self-sufficient economic unit made up of smaller districts, which included coastal, valley, and mountain resources all in one slice. According to Kirch (2012, 139–142), this marked the first steps toward the transition from a chiefdom to a kingship. Within three hundred years, on the eve of contact with Europeans, Hawai'i had become a society of island states based upon divine kingship (Kirch 2010).

During this time of political transformation, the population expanded significantly and agricultural production intensified. The islands of Maui and Hawai'i hosted new settlements and agriculture expanded into the dry leeward sides of islands. New districts such as Kohala (Hawai'i) and Kahikinui (Maui) developed into zones of dryland cultivation, characterized by cropping cycles of taro, sweet potatoes, yams, and sugar cane in bounded fields. Fishpond aquaculture emerged in harbors and bays using lava rock for walls and constructed gates for cultivation of *'Ama'ama* (mullet) and *Awa* (milkfish). In the older valleys, new irrigation systems were applied to the earlier wet-agriculture locations, expanding the food supply and populations of these original settlements. Maui and Hawai'i populations expanded exponentially over three to four centuries under the new agroecosystems, particularly with the intensification of the rain-fed dryland cultivation (Kirch 2012, 198–201). Between AD 1400 and 1600 the Hawaiian population grew at a rate of 1.2 percent annually, after which it stabilized until contact with Europeans (Kirch 2007).

As Hawaiians expanded their agrosystems to all islands and new powerful chiefs arose to control land and production, the ecological consequences also mounted. The surpluses produced within the *ahupua'a* for a new class of *ali'i* (ruling chiefs) by *maka'āinana* (farmers) utilized multiple ecological zones and spread the expanding population over all available agricultural land. Dryland cultivation, vulnerable to rains, had been pushed to maximum expansion by the eighteenth century. Famines were not uncommon when rains were late. Evidence from interdisciplinary research of archaeologists and ecologists shows a measurable decline in soil quality over time in the Kohala fields (Kirch 2012, 200). Hawaiian mammals (especially feral pigs) penetrated the forests of upland zones with their routing habits that damaged fragile volcanic soils. Tree and fern species that had not co-evolved with island mammals other than bats proved vulnerable to soil disruption and drying, adding to further deforestation (Cuddihy and Stone 1990). Hawaiian feathered capes that adorned the *ali'i* came from brightly colored endemic birds, of which some were hunted to extinction. By the arrival of Captain James Cook on the third of his famous Pacific voyages, virtually the entire lowland forest (dry and wet) below 1,500 feet on Hawai'i's main islands had disappeared (Athens 1997).

The rise of archaic states in Hawai'i is notable for several reasons. It represents an interesting experiment in social evolution because of Hawai'i's isolation. Unlike continental examples of archaic state formation where cultural developments were subject to continual modification from contact with outsiders, the rise of Hawaiian island states comes from internal cultural changes. European contact at the height of state formation provides us with written records from outside observers, and not dependent upon archaeological investigation, as is the case with other ancient states. In addition, contemporary Hawaiian access to oral traditions provides a genealogy of generations and lineages to trace through the centuries. Unlike earlier state formations in human history, Hawaiians altered island environments, expanded their population, and settled all productive island regions, all without interference from outside populations. As Kirch notes:

> [I]n Hawai'i we have an especially good opportunity to understand the conditions—whether environmental, demographic, economic, social, ideological, or, most likely, some combination of all of these, that led to the emergence of primary states, along with their most salient feature, divine kingship.
>
> (Kirch 2010, 2)

In short order around the beginning of the seventeenth century two chiefs unified Hawai'i and Maui. The building of massive temples (*heaiu*)—a testament to their rule—signified high levels of organization and a ritual basis for organizing agriculture and collecting tribute (Kirch 2012, 216). 'Umi from Hawai'i and Kiha-a-Pi'ilani of Maui represented a new era in Hawai'i. The characteristics of the early Hawaiian state mirrored similar developments in early civilizations. Land ('*āina*) was no longer controlled by lineages. Incest taboos were broken with unions between brothers and sisters, which became a godly practice. Ritual human sacrifice emerged along with separation of society into two classes. Finally, the rise of the *ahupua'a* brought the development of a new, more efficient land use management system.[3]

Polynesian migration to the isolated Hawaiian archipelago transformed the landscape into an agrosystem that evolved a large and dense population, marked by a radical social transformation. Because of the absence of interference from outside peoples and the availability of eyewitness accounts from Europeans at its height, it represents a model in human development. The link between this ancient migration and ecological change also sets the table for the study of subsequent migrations to the islands—Europeans and North Americans in small but ecologically influential numbers and the later Asian mass migrations of Chinese, Japanese, and Filipinos.

Europeans and North Americans—contact and settlement

The arrival of British explorer James Cook in Hawaiian waters in 1778 and again in 1779 where he met his death initiated a period of rapid contact between Hawaiians, Europeans, and North Americans. Within two decades fur traders traveling between the Pacific Northwest and China, European explorers, and by 1811 American sandalwood traders, entered Hawaiian waters. Within fifty years, by mid-century, a cascading ecological and social effect of this exchange set off another epoch in the Hawaiian transformation that endured for a century. The migration of Europeans and especially Americans who settled in the islands introduced Western trade in the Pacific, plantation agriculture, and new forms of political and economic organization to a society that had been in place for two centuries. Contact with European trade goods, ships, and weapons had the initial effect of turning Hawai'i from island-based states into a unified kingdom under one leader. American missionaries and merchants collaborated with Hawaiian chiefs and the king in transformation of the Hawaiian agrosystem into one based upon plantation agriculture for export. As Hawai'i entered into the world of Pacific trade in the nineteenth century, it transformed itself into a modern nation state. The history of the ecological and social changes introduced with those contacts reflects the effects of Euro-American migration into the Pacific at a point in global history in which mercantilism gives way to capitalism. Hawai'i's continued history of immigration reflects this transformation as the next two waves of settlers from the West (North America) and the East (Asia) play a significant role in environmental change.

When Cook landed, Hawai'i was divided into three states—one, O'ahu and Kaua'i; a second, western Maui and Molokai'i; a third composed of Hawai'i and parts of Maui—all ruled by a god-king (*ali'i akua*) (Kirch 2012, 299). The agricultural systems supporting the eastern islands with irrigation systems and fishponds and the younger western islands with rain-fed field systems supported around a half a million people. Kamehameha, a powerful chief on the Island of Hawai'i, was one of the first to meet Cook and actively engage in trade with early Europeans. Within a decade he had created an armory of European firearms in trade for meat, vegetables, water, and firewood. He used his firearms to gain control over Hawai'i Island, Maui, and O'ahu by 1795, and Kaua'i by 1810. As king, Kamehameha began to dominate all trade with foreigners. He took on Westerners for advisors and began construction of Western sailing ships. With the conquest of O'ahu, he resided in and controlled Honolulu, the more favorable port for visiting ships to replenish in their trading voyages between North America and China. Gradually, with more vessels in port, the *ali'i* on O'ahu (under the direction of Kamehameha) traded food, wood, water, and sandalwood for Western goods. They extended the labor of the *maka'āinana* into service for provisioning ships as well as maintaining agricultural production. Coupled with the toll that Western diseases took on the population, this tributary system taxed villagers beyond their capacity. By 1820, the Hawaiian population had declined from over 400,000 in 1779 to 150,000 (Kirch 2012, 286).

After Kamehameha's death in 1819, his queen (Ka'ahumanu) called for abolishment of the *kapu* system and demolishment of the temples, along with the old religious order. She invited American missionaries from Boston to settle and open churches and schools, proclaiming a new religious order. Between 1820 and 1850, twelve companies of missionaries, mostly couples, established missions and schools throughout the islands. The earliest of them were witness to the environmental consequences of European contact and trade. Cattle and goats given to Kamehameha roamed Hawai'i Island unrestrained and reproduced in numbers, which damaged upper elevation forests and trampled Hawaiian fields. Diseases continued to ravage the Hawaiian population such that by 1850 the missionary census recorded a population of 86,000, recording a decline of 150,000 Hawaiians from thirty years earlier. The provisioning of foreign vessels with yams, pigs, wood, and water altered agricultural rhythms and led to depopulation of whole villages. The introduction of ungulates (hoofed animals), especially cattle and goats, into a landscape not adapted to their disturbance of soil structure and vegetation, led to deforestation above the agricultural districts and disrupted Hawaiian dryland agriculture. Missionary reports to Boston from these isolated island stations chronicled these changes.[4]

Missionaries also brought Western political ideas to the kingdom, influencing Kamehameha's descendants. Within thirty years Hawai'i, now a constitutional monarchy, entered the Western world of nations. It engaged in foreign trade, negotiated treaties with European nations, legalized and protected private property, developed a market-based agriculture, established a monetary system, developed a written language, and created a government composed of courts, a legislature, and an executive administration under direction of the king.

Kamehameha's unification of the islands and Ka'ahumanu's abolishment of the *kapu* system prepared the groundwork for Hawai'i's emergence as a modern nation state. Unlike much of the island Pacific, Hawai'i remained a sovereign and independent kingdom. It transformed itself into a political economy that blended Hawaiian cultural forms from the era of the archaic state with those of emergent mercantile and capitalist economies of Western nations enmeshed in an industrial revolution. Immigrants from North America settled and over the course of the century gained control over trade and agriculture, remaking multiple Hawaiian ecosystems into zones of production for export.

Europeans and North Americans migrated to Hawai'i in small numbers during the nineteenth century. Merchants, seamen, ships captains, and missionaries populated the emerging port towns of Lahaina (Maui), Hilo (Hawai'i Island), and Honolulu (O'ahu) with their shops and merchant houses. They provisioned ships in port and supplied the outer districts with Western goods. As their numbers grew, so did the town centers, which became their primary population base (especially Honolulu). Their businesses attracted Hawaiians who entered the skilled trades or established businesses of their own. Hawaiians called them *haoles,* a term originally defined as "foreigner," but today associated with Caucasian. British, German, and American settlers dominated the early Caucasian migration to Hawai'i which began with American missionaries in the 1820s and gradually included British and German merchants, plantation supervisors, and businessmen by the 1870s. Portuguese families added to this population beginning in the 1880s.

Euro-American immigrants also brought plantation agriculture to the islands, establishing small sugar plantations as early as the 1830s and 1840s. Small in scale and poor in comparison to sugar businesses in the Caribbean or Brazil, these plantations failed more often than they succeeded. Maui was one of the more popular islands for sugar cultivation, attracting missionary families, sea captains, and even Hawaiians to plant cane and import small mills (MacLennan 1995). Sugar exports increased considerably after the boom period during the Civil War with the decline of Louisiana sugar production and the rise of the California market. Missionary families, primarily the second generation, were prominent planters. After 1880, production increased rapidly as investors from San Francisco, England, and Germany purchased and leased cane lands and erected modern industrial mills. By the end of the century the sugar industry, now fully industrialized, was the dominant economic force in the islands and the planter class exerted its muscle by deposing the Hawaiian queen, Lili'uokalani, and established an independent Hawaiian republic that sought annexation to the US.

Euro-American plantation agriculture brought significant environmental changes to Hawai'i. Organized as the Hawaiian Sugar Planters' Association (HSPA), the increasingly cohesive resident planter class drastically altered the demographics of the islands. Industrial sugar production required large numbers of field laborers for each plantation that serviced the large, modern mills. The HSPA, in cooperation with the kingdom and later the territorial government, imported thousands of workers from Asia to populate the plantation camps and villages, fueling another migratory wave to the islands. In just fifty years (1850–1900) Hawai'i switched from a majority Polynesian to a nation based upon a plurality of Asians. In 1850 during the early years of the constitutional monarchy, foreign-born numbered only 1,828 in a total population of 73,138 in which the vast majority were Hawaiian. By the turn of the century in 1896, island population totaled 109,000. Native and part-Hawaiians numbered 39,500 (just over a third) and non-Hawaiians accounted for 69,500 (nearly two-thirds). Within fifty years Hawaiians had flipped from a large majority to a minority population. The largest sector of non-Hawaiians was Asian: Chinese (21,600) and Japanese (24,400) accounted for 42 percent of the total population in 1896. Europeans and North Americans (13,200) represented only 12 percent (Schmitt 1968, 74–75). It is worth noting that the majority of Europeans brought to work on sugar plantations at that time were Portuguese workers and their families from both Madeira and the Azores islands. They composed nearly three-quarters of the Europeans at the turn of the century.[5]

By the end of the century, the American missionary sector dominated the economy and political society and thus had a significant hand in alteration of Hawai'i's multiple ecosystems. They and their descendants helped establish land, water, forest, and other policies that shaped the future environment. After decades of service to the American Board of Commissioners for Foreign Missions (ABCFM), their missionary financial support was terminated in 1860. Many missionaries and their adult children opted to remain in the islands and start new lives on small plots of land as business owners, or continue their work through independent churches. They became landowners, something originally prohibited by the ABCFM. They also played important roles as advisors to the king, members of the legislature and courts, and administrators in the growing national bureaucracy.

The eventual success of plantation agriculture in the islands was rooted in missionary influence over Hawaiian kings which began with Ka'ahumanu's conversion to Christianity, and in particular, the education of royal children steeped in curriculum promoting Western notions of private property, free labor, and a market economy. It led to the abandonment of chiefly control over land and the labor of the *maka'āinana* and to the disintegration of the *ahupua'a* system of land management. Land became property, to be bought and sold by individual owners. The *Māhele* (1840), the name for the land privatization legislation initiated by Kamehameha III, divided all lands between the Crown, chiefs, and commoners. The vast majority of land fell into the hands of the Crown, government, and chiefs, who registered their claims, whereas the commoners ended up with only small parcels, called *kuleanas*. American missionary William Richards (who left the mission to advise the king) tutored Kamehameha III in Wayland's *Elements of Political Economy* during 1838–1839, a popular text in the US which promoted the idea that the right of private property and free labor was the natural order and that it was the duty of the law to recognize this right. At the core of missionary schooling of chiefs and royal children was the idea of the natural right of property as well as the belief that manual labor and agricultural development for markets created wealth and social stability (MacLennan 2014, 53–61).

Missionary settlers exerted influence on royal decisions in the 1840s, which created new government forms, laws, and a national bureaucracy. The effect on land tenure, agriculture, and natural resources was profound. During his long reign of nearly fifty-five years, Kamehameha III adapted Western concepts of economy and governance as a means to maintain Hawaiian sovereignty in a rapidly colonized Pacific. The *Māhele* (land ownership agreement) severed the final relationship between *ali'i* (elite) and *maka'āinana* (commoners) and introduced a market economy that was protected and promoted by the state. Probably the most significant environmental impact of the migration and settlement of Euro-Americans on the island environment is their role in influencing the implementation of the *Māhele*.

Free to sell their lands and engage in paid labor, many Hawaiians entered the new economy by moving to towns, shipping onto whaling vessels, or becoming plantation workers. The shifting land tenure gradually depopulated Hawaiian villages and shifted subsistence production to isolated regions, which provisioned towns and plantations with Hawaiian foods such as *poi* (taro), yams, and fish.

In the 1860s foreigners acquired large parcels of land. Even Crown and government lands ended up in their hands. Missionaries were especially well placed in the rural districts to know which lands were available and agriculturally productive. Between 1849 and 1877, sixteen missionaries purchased 37,800 acres of government and Crown lands from the kingdom. Six plantation companies (Kohala, Haiku, Wailuku, Brewer, Hana, and Lihue) were organized using these land purchases (MacLennan 2014, 289–291).

Kamehameha III's bargain to privatize land paid off for the new resident Euro-American planter class and their descendants. By the early 1880s, 28,400 tons of sugar was produced on 89 plantations capitalized at $15.8 million, populated by 12,350 plantation workers in nearly all the rural districts where rainfall was adequate for the thirsty sugar crop.[6] As whaling declined in the North Pacific and other experimental crops tried by Europeans and Americans failed to thrive in the sub-tropical environment, the sugar plantations remained the most salient economic base. King Kalākaua recognized this in 1875 when he signed the Reciprocity Treaty with the US allowing Hawaiian sugars duty-free into American ports in return for duty-free American goods in Hawai'i. Reciprocity ensured the rapid industrialization of sugar production.

The Hawaiian sugar industry grew rapidly as new investors arrived from San Francisco (Claus Spreckels) and Britain (Theo. H. Davies), acquired land, bought large modern mills, built plantation railroads, and financed irrigation projects. The infusion of capital into the islands also aided the smaller missionary plantations, whose agents borrowed from California banks. Spreckels' Hawaiian Commercial Sugar Plantation on Maui became the model of industrial sugar production with its 17,000 acres, irrigated by water delivered in concrete ditches from distant streams in the East Maui Mountains, sugar delivered to the largest mill in the islands by railroad, and over 1,000 field, mill, and transportation workers. H. Hackfeld, a merchant from Bremen, Germany financed large plantations on Kaua'i, Maui, and Hawai'i. Yet only the American missionary planter class settled in the islands. Capitalists Spreckels, Davies, and Hackfeld maintained their primary residences in San Francisco, England, and Germany, and their children did the same, while managing plantation business with surrogate managers. By the early 1900s, the capitalist class was distinctly American with German and British capital in a minority position. By 1920, after World War I, missionary descendants and their companies controlled the assets of the Hackfeld and Davies companies (MacLennan 2014).[7]

While Caucasians accounted for a small sector of the total population—only 15,000 (7.7 percent) of the 191,900 total island populations—their influence over the landscape and natural resources was extraordinarily large (Schmitt 1968, 120).[8] Through their influence with the Hawaiian monarchy they acquired favorable leases of Crown and government land for sugar cultivation, won licences to divert water from distant streams and irrigate new cane fields on dry lands, and helped design natural resource laws that served plantation agriculture. By 1930, the sugar capitalists controlled, either directly or indirectly, most land (agricultural, ranching, forest reserves), harnessing their resources for production of sugar cane, pineapple, and cattle.

Figure 1.1 illustrates the capture of land on O'ahu, showing plantation (sugar and pineapple) and ranch lands in 1930. Forestland, controlled by the government, was managed for watershed protection and delivery of irrigation water to the 'Ewa plains area adjacent to Pearl Harbor, for sugarcane cultivation. The other main islands, Maui, Kaua'i, and Hawai'i, replicated this pattern. Small producers of coffee, taro, and vegetable crops made up a minor sector of the economy and land utilization.

What were the environmental effects of this small, but powerful, settler community of North Americans? At his opening address of the Royal Hawaiian Agricultural Society, commissioned by Kamehameha III, American planter and consultant to the king, William Lee, remarked:

> Until within the last year the Hawaiian held his land as a mere tenant at sufferance, subject to be disposed at any time it might suit the will or caprice of his chief... I thank God that these things are an end, and that the poor kanaka [laborer] may now stand on the border of his little kalo patch, and holding his fee simple patent in his hand, bid defiance to the world.
>
> (Royal Hawaiian Agricultural Society 1850, 30)

This declaration represents a moment when the fundamental shift from the Hawaiian mode of production to one based on plantation capitalism took form. Hawaiians did not become yeoman farmers, but instead plantation contract laborers.

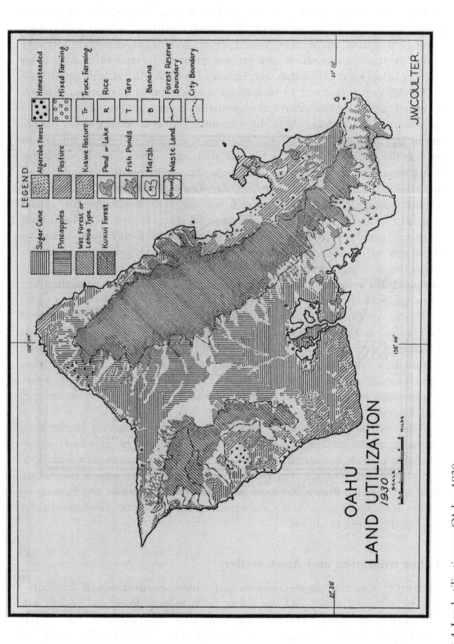

Figure 1.1 Land utilization on Oʻahu, 1930

Source: John W. Coulter, *Land Utilization in the Hawaiian Islands*, Research Publication No. 8 (Honolulu: University of Hawaiʻi, 1933, 37)

The rapid transition toward plantation agriculture at the hands of the immigrant North Americans and Europeans initiated a cascade of environmental events. Land in cane and pineapple shifted Hawai'i from subsistence production to production for export. Land, water, and forests were harnessed to the yoke of providing for human and production regimes on plantations. Stream diversion, through irrigation ditches that crossed several watersheds, delivered necessary water to open plantations in dry regions of Maui (central isthmus), O'ahu ('Ewa plains), Kaua'i (Kekaha), and Hawai'i (Kohala). All available land below 1,500–2,000 feet devoted to plantations was scraped of vegetation, planted, fertilized, and watered. Above the plantation zone, cattle ranches occupied non-forested lands. After 1900, the remaining forests of 'ōhia and koa (indigenous tree species) became forest reserves, managed by the government to protect the watershed necessary for plantation agriculture. Near-shore plantation coastal zones served as small landings for sugar mills that dumped their molasses and cane trash in the ocean. Erosion, especially from the vertically aligned pineapple fields, depleted rich volcanic soils. Fertilizer—first guano and then synthetic nitrogen—were a must for a productive crop. Feral pigs, goats, and cattle roamed the edges of the upland forests, their hooves disrupting the fragile relationship between soil and vegetation. Deforestation became a major threat to sugar production. Planters and the government organized forest re-vegetation utilizing eucalyptus and ironwood trees which, although fast growing, proved to be heavy water users and invasive.

By the 1940s, little remained of the native forests (dry and wet), coastal vegetation, and native grasses except in pockets at the interior of Kaua'i Mountains, near Maui's Haleakala crater, and on the slope of Hawai'i Island's Mauna Loa. All of these native outposts became protected parks. Otherwise, the Hawaiian landscape, devoid of most of its endemic species, became a mix of mammals, birds, insects, and vegetation from North America, Asia, Europe, and Australia.

The human communities, once organized by Hawaiian agricultural demands, transitioned into plantation villages surrounded by cane and pineapple fields. Densely populated, they became the hosts to diseases such as cholera, the plague, and typhoid, and required vigilant public sanitation campaigns. Remade, the Hawaiian Islands bore the mark of a plantation society landscaped by the demands of productivity and export markets, and populated by workers imported to work the fields.

Labor migration and Asian settlers

Hawai'i's plantation agroecosystem may have been designed by Euro-American capital which laid out fields, mills, railroad lines, and wharfs, but the work camps assumed their character with Chinese, Japanese, Portuguese, and Filipino workers in successive waves of immigration. Smaller groups of Okinawans, Puerto Ricans, and Koreans also came to work on the plantations. For over one hundred years, Asians (and a small group of Portuguese)

Table 1.1 Immigration of plantation laborers

Ethnic group	Dates	Total immigration
Chinese	1852–1899	57,720
Japanese	1868–1924	213,752
Portuguese	1868–1913	25,000
Filipino	1909–1946	125,917

Source: Compiled from Eleanor Nordyke, *The Peopling of Hawai'i, Second Edition* (Honolulu: University of Hawai'i Press, 1989)

populated the landscape of this plantation society. Their churches and temples, schools, gardens, and cultural practices made Hawaiian plantations distinct communities All told, plantation-bound worker–immigrants from these disparate cultures eventually totaled nearly 239,000.[9] By 1920, Hawai'i was a plantation society of migrants, many of whom became settlers and eventually citizens. This third wave of Asian migration made sugar capitalism and its environment, dictated by plantation production, possible. It also reshaped the non-plantation environment.

Anthropologist Eric Wolf (1985, 355), who writes about the rise of a global system of capitalism, connects mobility and migration with the needs of capital when he writes: "The essence of capital is the ability to mobilize social labor by buying labor power and setting it to work [....] The working classes, entering industry or plantation agriculture [...] constituted a new phenomenon in the world." Hawai'i was not alone in the global sugar trade with its demand for imported labor that worked rapidly industrializing plantations. In the Oceanic Pacific alone, in addition to migrants bound for Hawai'i, large numbers of Chinese, East Indians, and South Sea Islanders migrated to other sugar districts in Fiji and Australia.

Chinese were the first to be recruited by Hawai'i's sugar planters after 1850, when it became clear that the number of Hawaiian workers would not be adequate for cane cultivation and harvesting. After the Reciprocity Treaty increased plantation capital investment, the Hawaiian government sought an agreement with Japan to allow migration of men for plantation fieldwork. By 1900, Japanese migrants constituted nearly 40 percent of island population. At that time, 63 percent of Hawai'i's total workforce was agricultural, mostly composed of Asian immigrants. The 1924 US Immigration Act ended Japanese immigration, which supplied sugar plantations with the majority of their workforce for over thirty years. As a result, the Hawaiian Sugar Planters' Association brought in Filipino workers who were considered nationals since the Philippines was a US territory at the time. By 1940, Asians (primarily Japanese, Filipino, and Chinese) made up over half of Hawai'i's population.

Starting in 1850, the Hawaiian government legalized and enforced a contract labor system which was abolished in 1900 when Hawai'i became a US territory. For fifty years, planters signed workers to three to five-year contracts, enforced by the county sheriff. Runaways were caught, returned, and fined. In addition, plantation stores allowed workers to draw upon future wages, thus making it difficult to leave plantation employment at the end of a contract. Once free from their contracts, many of the Asian immigrants stayed in Hawai'i, others returned to their homeland, and a number moved on to California. We know that about 40,000 Japanese returned to Japan or moved on to California. Those remaining settled into plantation work as free wage workers, sent home for wives and family members, and educated their children. Many planned futures as small farmers or skilled workers in towns such as Honolulu, Hilo, Wailuku, and Lihue.

When Chinese, Japanese, and Portuguese families left plantation work, they were replaced by Filipino immigrants (mostly men). A snapshot from 1930 in Table 1.2 shows the emerging structure of ethnicity in plantation communities. The total plantation workforce (all skill levels) numbered 52,700. Of the 30,000 unskilled workers, 24,000 were Filipino. The remaining 12,700 skilled workers and overseers (*luna*) were largely Portuguese, Hawaiians, and other Caucasians. Even at the skilled level, the workforce was segmented: Portuguese were *lunas*, Hawaiians were generally transportation and wharf workers, and other Caucasians were managers. Table 1.2 shows a labor force segmented by class and race (Lind 1938, 324).

The plantation created a rural landscape of cultivated fields, dense settlements of barracks and houses, and transportation networks driven by the seasonal clock of cane cultivation and milling. Created out of whole cloth, this new environment introduced non-native vegetation, human diseases, and a myriad of human cultural practices as new groups settled into the landscape. Agricultural districts monopolized the lowland shoreline of all the major islands up to about 1,500 feet elevation in all but the driest regions. Human, plant, and animal communities that served the plantation section replaced the native Hawaiian environment. Human settlements were organized by work regimes. Plantation managers kept each cultural group separated in work camps that dotted the plantation fields—creating a segmented labor force. Amenities were minimal. Single men and some families were housed in barracks. After a wave of diseases such as the plague, cholera, and typhus swept the islands in the early 1900s, the Hawaiian Sugar Planters' Association promoted the establishment of centralized villages near the mill. They designed villages that included indoor kitchens and running water in separate family cottages (see Figure 1.2). Villages had gardens for worker families to cultivate, social halls for gatherings and films, and baseball teams. But the ethnic labor segmentation persisted well into the twentieth century through separated villages and job classifications.

The rapid alteration of Hawai'i's landscape after annexation can be partly attributed to the developing conflict between an increasingly organized and capitalized planter class and a growing labor movement. For plantation workers, the admission of Hawai'i as a territory into the US acted as a check on the power of the planters in three important ways. First, contract labor was abolished in favor of wage labor and release of plantation workers from their

Table 1.2 Number of persons employed by Hawaiian sugar plantations by social–economic class and race

Classes	Races									
	Hawaiian	Portuguese	Puerto Rican	Other Caucasian	Chinese	Japanese	Korean	Filipino	Others	Total
Professional	17	59	0	177	8	96	1	33	4	395
Proprietary and luna	77	395	23	238	11	286	14	152	20	1,216
Clerical	30	113	4	233	36	357	9	86	2	870
Skilled	99	319	36	136	57	804	16	266	15	1,748
Semiskilled	227	614	384	23	149	2,602	38	4,287	21	8,345
Contract farmer	4	42	36	1	110	2,227	134	7,193	1	9,748
Unskilled and farm labor	179	666	516	22	385	4,053	308	24,122	57	30,308
Other	2	11	1	0	1	78	0	2	1	96
Total	635	2,219	1,000	830	757	10,503	520	36,141	121	52,726

Source: Reproduced from Andrew Lind, *An Island Community* (New York: Greenwood Press, 1938, Appendix F, 324)

Figure 1.2 HSPA model plantation home, 1930s
Source: Courtesy of the Bishop Museum, Hawai'i

contracts with the right to leave the islands or seek out better employment. A mobile labor force forced the sugar industry to create better housing and wage practices to keep their workers on the job. Second, the US Bureau of Labor kept a watch on plantation labor practices for nearly two decades, conducting regular inspections and producing reports on wages and working conditions. Congress, too, kept an eye on what it perceived to be a central threat of Hawaiian entry into the union: monopolistic practices of large sugar corporations and a growing Asian population. A third check on the power of the sugar industry was the growing number of Asian citizens (children of immigrant workers), who began to vote in large numbers in the 1920s. Within twenty years of annexation, Hawai'i had become a settler society which benefited from education and citizenship, and whose plantation workers agitated for labor rights.

After 1900, Japanese workers organized the Higher Wage Association and, through individual plantation strikes, pressured the Hawaiian Sugar Planters' Association (HSPA) to raise wages and issue bonuses, and achieved some improvements with strike actions in 1909 and 1920. The sugar and pineapple workers did not achieve collective bargaining rights until the 1940s through the International Longshoremen and Workers' Union (ILWU); Hawai'i's labor history is an Asian story. The vast majority of workers in this plantation economy were unskilled Japanese and Filipino in the 1920s to 1940s. The power of the "Big Five" corporations that controlled sugar and pineapple production, all shipping and support industries made it difficult to organize. But by the 1920s a growing number of Japanese–American children reached the age to vote and, educated in public English-speaking schools, assumed a role in civic life in urban and rural districts. The HSPA responded with a program to entice the youth to seek out vocational education and remain in plantation employment, but it failed. Aspirations were high and Japanese youth went to high schools and then on to college. HSPA then focused upon Filipino immigration, bringing in men to the islands rather than families. After World War II, US law allowed more open immigration from the Philippines and workers brought in wives and families. In the 1950s and 1960s, a large Filipino settler class populated the plantations as well as urban centers.

The impact of Asian labor migration to Hawai'i also had consequences beyond the labor movement. Asian settlers in the islands created a demographic plurality that penetrated occupations and locations other than the plantation. Ex-sugar workers along with Native Hawaiians became the backbone of diversified agriculture, establishing small enterprises that fed the island population. Chinese introduced rice cultivation in wet valleys previously occupied by taro fields. Japanese entered the fishing industry in large numbers, soon outnumbering Hawaiian fishermen in provisioning the islands with fish and shellfish. Japanese who left plantations opened up coffee farms in the Kona district on Hawai'i Island. Many *nisei* and *sansei* (second and third generation Japanese) in the islands opened businesses in towns such as Hilo, Lihue, and Wailuku nearby plantation districts. Those who went to college became teachers and civil servants in the new state government after Hawai'i's admission to statehood (Kimura 1988; Tamura 1994; Jung 2006; Ogawa 2015).

Of significance to Hawai'i's ecology and landscape is the migration of plantation workers away from their contracts, choosing not to "reship," and instead invest their skills and capital into diversified agriculture. Japanese *Issei* (first generation immigrants) planted a number of different vegetable crops for local markets, and developed the coffee industry. In the 1890s some of the earliest Japanese immigrants began to settle in Kona on Hawai'i Island, leasing land from the Bishop Estate and setting up family ventures. By 1909 there were 273 Japanese coffee growers in Kona, and on the eve of World War I, 80 percent of the coffee crop produced by Japanese. The Kona-grown coffee has endured and by the 1980s the second and third generation of the original owners continued production (Kimura 1988, 106–109).

After 1900 the Hawaiian-dominated fishery industry gradually became Japanese dominated. Immigrants from the coastal areas of Japan turned to fishing, coinciding with the 1899 arrival of Gorokichi Nakaji and his thirty-two foot long and six foot wide boat, especially constructed for deep-sea tuna fishing. The influx of Japanese plantation workers increased the demand for fish that surpassed the capability of the Native fishermen to supply. Deep-sea fishing, made possible by the fishing techniques and wooden boats from Japan, transformed the fishing industry. During the 1930s the Japanese had a monopoly on the then $2 million industry, with 1,000 engaged in the business and more than 140 fishing vessels. Both Chinese and Japanese controlled the fish markets in Honolulu and Hilo. A tuna canning industry emerged in 1916 by a *haole* (White) businessman who employed Japanese fishermen. Some Japanese immigrated especially to develop fishing businesses, such as Matsujiro Ōtani, who arrived in Hawai'i in 1908 and by 1920 had founded the Otani Seafood Company, importing seafood from Japan and the US. He won the contracts to supply seafood to the US military at Pearl Harbor and Scholfield Barracks on O'ahu. During World War II no fishing occurred in the Hawaiian Islands and Ōtani was interred in a concentration camp (while his son continued the business) and all Japanese fishermen became enemy aliens.[10] After the war, Ōtani could not convince *nisei* and *sansei* Japanese to become fishermen, but was successful in securing the immigration of Okinawan fishermen into the Hawaiian industry (Kimura 1988, 109–121).

Other smaller industries arose under Japanese and Chinese ownership, but persisted for shorter periods. By the early 1900s Japanese had begun small independent pineapple operations on Maui and Kaua'i to supply the Caucasian-owned canneries. They numbered 3,000 by 1930. The Depression, however, sent many of them back to the sugar plantations where income was higher (Kimura 1988, 102–106, 109). Japanese also entered the hog-raising industry, which had been a Chinese monopoly during its early years. By the 1930s, the industry (located primarily on O'ahu) was dominated by Okinawans. An important part of the plantation food system, commercial hog farms were also considered essential to the World War II food supply for the military and civilians. As a result, these operations continued well into the 1960s, continuing under Okinawan ownership (Kimura 1988, 109).

Rice farming, another essential component of the plantation food system, was an important industry between the 1860s and 1920. Chinese who left plantation contracts found ready employment by Chinese companies that planted and harvested rice fields primarily in the wet valleys of O'ahu and Kaua'i. Using loans from Chinese financiers in Honolulu, Chinese farmers leased old taro fields from Hawaiians, planted rice, milled and exported it, and by 1910 made rice the second largest industry in Hawai'i. After 1920 the rice market in Hawai'i shifted toward the preferred short grain rice produced in California, reflecting the large numbers of Japanese plantation workers. Within a few short years, the rice fields disappeared and many rice farmers moved on to California or returned to China (Coulter and Chun 1937). When rice fields disappeared, only a few Hawaiians replanted taro in once vast fields that had fed the Hawaiian population. Taro, still a Hawaiian staple, fed only a small fraction of people when Asian settlers became a plurality of island population.

The off-plantation migration of Asian workers who settled in the islands into agriculture and fishing played an important role in the food system and in populating non-plantation districts and towns. Added to this was the immigration of Chinese and Japanese businessmen and professionals from the Chinese and Japanese homeland. Since the early 1800s during the sandalwood trade, Chinese entrepreneurs arrived in the islands, bringing their sugar master skills and financial wealth to set up business in Hawai'i. Many married Hawaiian women and, as a result, gained ownership over Hawaiian land through marriage well before the American missionaries. In the Hilo region, a number of sugar plantations commenced in the very early era of plantation production (1840s and 1850s) under the ownership and financing of Chinese (Kai 1974). Japanese physicians, dentists, and midwives arrived soon after Japan and Hawai'i signed an agreement to monitor and protect the health of Japanese immigrants in 1886. Buddhist and Shinto priests followed, as did language school principals and teachers, to serve the Japanese plantation camps and villages. Eventually lawyers, newspaper publishers, and storeowners settled in locations that serviced plantations on each island, towns such as Lihue, Honolulu, Wailuku, and Hilo (Kimura 1988, 122–127). The children of plantation workers, armed with a public school education and voting rights, swelled the ranks of the towns as teachers, civil servants, and professionals.

The mark of Asian migration to the Hawaiian Islands during the sugar era (1850–1946) changed the demography, landscape, and culture of island life permanently. Immigration policies beginning with the kingdom and into the territorial period attracted and settled a plantation labor force which, within a generation or two, cemented the position of the plantation agro ecology until the late twentieth century. By the 1980s, when plantation agriculture began its decline in favor of a tourist and military-based economy, all land from forests to seas had assumed the role of a plantation support system. The population had grown to over a million people. Only 23 percent *haole* and 20 percent Hawaiian, the migrants from the earlier era were in the minority. The descendants of Asian immigrants dominated island population at 40 percent (Nordyke 1968,178–179).[11] Today, with over 1.4 million, Hawai'i's people reflect intermarriage among Hawaiians, whites, and Asians in a post-plantation society. Asians (part or full) constitute 56 percent of the total population; Hawaiians and Pacific Islanders (part or full), 26 percent; whites (part or full), 44 percent.[12]

The plantation landscape is now gone from the Hawaiian Islands, but the mark of industrial sugar production and settlement of the children of Asian workers into diversified agriculture, fishing, and more urban occupations has left their mark on today's environment. As the fiftieth state in the US, Hawai'i reflects the three waves of migrants who arrived relatively late in human history, settled one of the most remote regions of the world, and transformed its character and landscape.

Conclusion

Using the lens of layered migrations into an isolated non-human landscape over a short one thousand years allows for a unique view of the relationship between migrations and environment. Set apart from continents and nearby island landforms, Hawai'i offers what noted Pacific archaeologist Patrick Kirch (2010, 4) argues is a "model system" for study of development of archaic states. His concept can be extended to the role of human migration beyond Polynesian voyaging to include Euro-American and Asian immigrants who arrived in successive waves and to the transformation of an archaic state into a nation state. At the heart of state development and transformation is the environment – its resources and changing landscapes – and human migration and settlement. One cannot isolate the extensive impact of Japanese, Filipino, and Chinese immigration to Hawaiian plantation communities without understanding the earlier formation of capitalist plantation agriculture resulting from European and American merchant houses and missionary settlers. Nor can the success of a minority wave of Europeans and North American settlers in the establishment of a plantation society be understood without knowledge of Hawaiian settlement and intensification of agriculture and aquaculture that led to island states before contact.

Hawaiian colonization of these island landforms without interference for seven hundred years created the basis for a powerful kingdom, resilient through the nineteenth century of Euro-American colonization in the Pacific. Their agriculture, aquaculture, and water use regimes formed a base upon which European and American planters adapted an export-oriented plantation system using Hawaiian land and labor released from chiefly control. Missionary settlers introduced a political economy that simultaneously empowered the Hawaiian king in the Pacific trade and eroded the sovereignty of the Hawaiian people. Asian contract workers and their children populated the islands to work in sugar and pineapple plantations grown from the wealth of missionary settler descendants and Euro-American investors. Third and fourth generation Japanese and Filipino families spread their influence into towns and other agricultural districts that fed the plantations and later the urbanization of O'ahu. The struggles of their parents to unionize the plantation fields and wrest control from the large corporations that controlled the islands in the 1950s resulted in the rise of a liberal democratic system of governance after statehood in 1960. Hawai'i's environment bears the imprint of the successive waves of migrants and their agricultural pursuits, settlement on the landscape, and their transformation of these volcanic high islands into a natural and urban world unrecognizable to the first Polynesian travelers.

Notes

1 Two noted scholars differ over the estimate of the original population. Eleanor Nordyke (1989) estimates it at 270,000, while David Stannard (1989) puts the estimate at 800,000. This remains a contentious debate, but it may be reasonable to conclude an estimate at European contact of at least 400,000, as does archaeologist Patrick Kirch (2010, 130). He utilizes more recent GIS-analysis of irrigated and dryland production capacities, and argues that a more refined paleodemographic is needed to resolve this issue.

2 Using improved radiocarbon dating techniques, archaeologist Patrick Kirch (2011) has published new settlement dates for the Hawaiian Islands. Originally, archaeologists determined settlement of Hawai'i to be about AD 300–600.

3 Recent treatments of early Hawaiian state formation make convincing arguments for Hawai'i as one of the last archaic state formations. Patrick Kirch's (2010, 2012) two books weave decades of archaeological research in Hawai'i

and Hawaiki (the Hawaiian homeland in central Polynesia) with linguistics, oral traditions, genealogies, and documents from the earliest Europeans to arrive in the islands. Robert Hommon (2013) develops a model of the ancient Hawaiian state that is applied elsewhere in Polynesia—to Tonga.

4 Marshall Sahlins (1992) provides a detailed account of these changes on Oʻahu during the early decades of the nineteenth century, using archaeology, historical documents, and missionary reports to chronicle the decline of Hawaiian agriculture and the impacts of *aliʻi* trading demands on the *makaʻāinana*.

5 By the time Portuguese immigration ceased in 1911, a total of 16,000 individuals had migrated to Hawaiʻi. Unlike early Chinese and Japanese single male immigrants in the nineteenth century, sugar planters brought in Portuguese families to plantation communities (Schmitt 1968, 74–75).

6 On plantations see Thrum 1885, 14, 38–40. On number of laborers see Schmitt 1968, 77.

7 See MacLennan (2014) Chapters 3 and 4 for a discussion of the rise to economic power of settler missionary families and their descendants through five major corporations that controlled most plantation and ancillary company assets.

8 The total Caucasian population in 1920 included Puerto Rican, Spanish, and a large Portuguese plantation labor component. These groups are factored out in the numbers presented here (Schmitt 1968, 120).

9 Derived from immigration statistics reported in Nordyke (1989), 65, 44–45, and 223–224.

10 On the US mainland, most Japanese families were placed in concentration camps during World War II. In Hawaiʻi, only Japanese professionals, priests, and businessmen were placed in a local internment camp at Honolulu on Oʻahu. Japanese sugar workers and the families of professionals were left in place during the war because they were an essential workforce on plantations. Japanese fishermen, however, were labeled as "enemy aliens" and prohibited from fishing in Hawaiian waters because of active naval operations in the islands.

11 Population is in 1986 numbers. Japanese ethnicity accounted for 23 percent of the total population.

12 These figures are 2014 estimates, released from Hawaiʻi Department of Business, Economic Development, and Tourism in 2015.

References

Allen, J. 1997, 'Pre-contact land transformation and cultural change, Oʻahu,' in P. Kirch and T. Hunt (eds), *Historical ecology in the Pacific Islands: prehistoric and environmental landscape change*, Yale University Press, New Haven, Connecticut.

Athens, J.S. 1997, 'Hawaiian native lowland vegetation in prehistory,' in P. Kirch and T. Hunt (eds), *Historical ecology in the Pacific Islands: prehistoric and environmental landscape change*, Yale University Press, New Haven, Connecticut.

Coulter, J.W. and Chun, C.K. 1937, *Chinese rice farmers in Hawaiʻi*, Research publication no 14, University of Hawaiʻi, Honolulu, Hawaiʻi.

Cuddihy, L.W. and Stone, C.P. 1990, *Alteration of native Hawaiian vegetation: effects of humans, their activities and introductions*, University of Hawaiʻi Cooperative National Park Resources Studies Unit, Honolulu, Hawaiʻi.

Hawaiʻi Department of Business, Economic Development, and Tourism, 'Latest population estimate data: 2014 estimates,' Honolulu, Hawaiʻi, viewed 30 May 2016, http://census.hawaii.gov/home/population-estimate/.

Hommon, R.J. 2013, *The ancient Hawaiian state: origins of a political society,* Oxford University Press, New York, NY.

Jung, M.K. 2006, *Reworking race: the making of Hawai'i's interracial labor movement,* Columbia University Press, New York, NY.

Kai, P. 1974, 'Chinese Settlers in the Village of Hilo before 1852,' *Hawaiian Journal of History,* vol. 8, pp. 39–75.

Kimura, Y. 1988, *Issei: Japanese immigrants in Hawaii,* University of Hawai'i Press, Honolulu, Hawai'i.

Kirch, P. 2007, 'Like shoals of fish: archaeology and population in pre-contact Hawai'i,' in P. Kirch and J.L. Rallu (eds), *The growth and collapse of Pacific Island societies: archaeological and demographic perspectives,* University of Hawai'i Press, Honolulu, Hawai'i.

Kirch, P. 2010, *How chiefs became kings: divine kingship and the rise of archaic states in Hawai'i,* University of California Press, Berkeley, California.

Kirch, P. 2011, 'When did the Polynesians settle Hawai'i? a review of 150 years of scholarly inquiry and a tentative answer,' *Hawaiian Archaeology,* vol. 12, pp. 3–26.

Kirch, P. 2012, *A shark going inland is my chief: the island civilization of ancient Hawai'i,* University of Hawai'i Press, Honolulu, Hawai'i.

Lind, A.W. 1938, *An island community: ecological succession in Hawaii,* Greenwood Press, New York, NY.

MacLennan, C.A. 1995, 'Foundations of sugar's power: early Maui plantations, 1840–1860,' *Hawaiian Journal of History,* vol. 29, pp. 33–56.

MacLennan, C.A. 2014, *Sovereign sugar: industry and environment in Hawai'i,* University of Hawai'i Press, Honolulu, Hawai'i.

Nordyke, E. 1968, *The peopling of Hawai'i,* University of Hawai'i Press, Honolulu, Hawai'i.

Nordyke, E. 1989, *The peopling of Hawai'i,* 2nd ed., University of Hawai'i Press, Honolulu, Hawai'i.

Ogawa, M. 2015, *Sea of opportunity: the Japanese pioneers of the fishing industry in Hawai'i,* University of Hawai'i Press, Honolulu, Hawai'i.

Royal Hawaiian Agricultural Society (RHAS) 1850, *Transactions,* Honolulu, Hawai'i.

Sahlins, M. and Kirch, P.V. 1992, *Anahulu: the anthropology of history in the kingdom of Hawai'i, Volume 1 Historical Ethnography,* University of Chicago Press, Chicago, Illinois.

Schmitt, R.C. 1968, *Demographic statistics of Hawai'i, 1778–1965,* University of Hawai'i Press, Honolulu, Hawai'i.

Stannard, D. 1989, *Before the horror: the population of Hawai'i on the eve of western contact,* University of Hawai'i Press, Honolulu, Hawai'i.

Tamura, E.H. 1994, *Americanization, acculturation, and ethnic identity: the nisei generation in Hawai'i,* University of Illinois Press, Urbana, Illinois.

Thrum, T.G. 1885, *Hawaiian Almanac and Annual for 1884,* Black & Auld Printers, Honolulu, Hawai'i.

Wolf, E.R. 1985, *Europe and the people without history,* University of California Press, Berkeley, California.

2 European immigration and changes in the landscape of southern Brazil

Eunice Sueli Nodari and
Miguel Mundstock Xavier de Carvalho

Abstract

From 1824 to 1914, thousands of German and Italian immigrants settled in Rio Grande do Sul and Santa Catarina, the southern states of Brazil. The areas where the government and colonization companies settled them were covered by forests. These regions were completely different from what the European immigrants knew, imagined or had been told about when encouraged to settle there. Therefore, they tried to adapt and reshape the environment to their benefit. This model of colonization was responsible for many anthropic changes to the nature of the Atlantic forests and for the ecological crisis it created. Today less than 10% of the areas are still covered by forests.

Introduction – Europeans in the forest

This chapter addresses the European occupation and the consequent devastation of the Mixed Ombrophyllus Forest (MOF) and Temperate Deciduous Forest (TDF) in the states of Rio Grande do Sul and western Santa Catarina. In the name of colonization and progress, extensive deforestation was undertaken, while preservation and reforestation were ignored. Until the early nineteenth century, the MOF, known also as Araucaria Forest because of the visual impact of a rare conifer (*Araucaria angustifolia*), occupied around 250,000 km² of the higher altitudes of southern Brazil (500 meters and above) (Castella and Britez 2004; Medeiros 2004). The TDF, previously known as Subtropical Forest of the Uruguay River, comprised an area of approximately 47,000 km² located in lower altitudes in the Uruguay River basin (Leite and Klein 1990, 128). The settlers called the TDF "White Woods" as opposed to the "Black Woods," their term for the Araucaria Forest.

These two forest typologies are part of the *Mata Atlântica* (Atlantic Forest), a rich mosaic of tropical and subtropical forests whose previous area stretched from the northeast to the south of Brazil, northeast Argentina and eastern Paraguay. The process of European colonization in Rio Grande do Sul and in the west of Santa Catarina occurred in the MOF and TDF areas. The forests were regarded as one of the major economic attractions for them, because of the fertile soils of the little-disturbed ecosystems and the possibility of industrializing and selling the vast amount of timber growing there.

European visions of the forest and the settling

Father Roque Gonzales, S.J. (1576–1628) made perhaps one of the earliest descriptions of the MOF in southern Brazil that leaves us with a portrait of a disappeared pre-colonial landscape:

> Plains stretch as far as the eye can see, revealing extensively varied land-scapes and ripping through horizons of dilated amplitude. They alternate with playful valleys, which adorn the fragrant and slender yerba *mate* tree, while high above on the mountain the dark-green pine forest with round canopies darken the land, powerful in its nearly religious silence under the muffled light, where their arms are lifted towards Heaven, as in silent sup-plication, a thousand giant candelabra, formed by the slender and powerful Araucarias (Brazilian pines).
>
> (Teschauer 2002, 87).

A couple of centuries later, John Muir (1838–1914) traveled to Brazil visiting several regions including the Araucaria Forest (Muir 2001, 80). According to Donald Worster,

> the golden fleece of Muir's travels, however, was not to be found in the Amazonian basin. He was looking for a genus of evergreen coniferous tree, the *Araucaria*, that were living fossils dating back to the Mesozoic age. [....] One of the American species, *A.angustifolia* (formerly *braziliensis*), grew in southern Brazil and had become the dominant timber tree of the country.
>
> (Worster 2008, 443)

Muir's dream came true with a one-week trip through the Araucaria Forest in southern Paraná and northern Santa Catarina (by then Paraná). It seems that he spent nearly all the daylight hours of the week in the forest that he fondly described as "a place according to my heart." He wrote in his journal on October 24, 1911 that it was the "(most) interesting forest I have seen in my whole life" (Muir 2001, 88).

The forests of southern Brazil, particularly the one where Brazilian pine (*Araucaria angustifolia*) is predominant, attracted the attention of naturalists, visi-tors and immigrants, as mentioned in several reports. German physician Robert Avé-Lallemant (1812–1884) visited the three southern Brazilian states in 1858, where he made the most extensive notes about human population, fauna, and flora. Upon returning to Europe, his impressions were published in book form, therefore making them accessible to German readers in nineteenth-century Europe. The author praises the Araucaria Forests of Santa Catarina and Rio Grande do Sul, as follows:

Everything is covered with dense Araucaria forest. In this plateau, these vigorous columns rise from deep gorges by the millions, climbing the steepest slopes up to the heights of steep grassy hills – a dark, quiet, serious forest that I could properly call black forest. Only far below, on the mysterious gorges, is there noise. There, among the pines, fountains burst, streams murmur, rivers foam in sandstone boulders: thus the Pelotas river is born, the real Uruguay, called Uruguai-Mirim.

(Avé-Lallemant 1980, 58–59)

One aim of his mission was to search for suitable sites to settle German colonies, by visiting well-established settlements and lands not yet occupied by Europeans. In this sense, although Avé-Lallemant knew how distinct Brazilian forests were from the Black Forest, he preferred to stress the supposed similarities between the two terrains. The fact that these forests were completely different from those in Europe, almost impossible to enter because of the dense vegetation, was not even mentioned. After all, this would have never attracted any immigrants.

This strategy of hiding the ecological differences and emphasizing similarities was especially strong in the publications produced by the federal or state government, or private companies in order to attract immigrants. During that period there are numerous descriptions of nature in southern Brazil, particularly its forests, considered by many to be still untouched. The fact that indigenous groups had lived for centuries in those forests was ignored. Nonetheless, it was known that indigenous people moved towards the Brazilian pine forest during the season of the Araucaria seeds' ripening and dispersal, since those seeds served as their food for several months.

The process of attracting immigrant families from northern Italy and Germany was made by recruiting agents, who acted on behalf of the federal or state government, or on behalf of private companies, depending on the type of colonization. Forest areas were already described in the advertisements about the region. When Italian and German immigrants arrived in the states of Rio Grande do Sul and Santa Catarina during the nineteenth and twentieth centuries, this was the environment they found—an intricate forest, radically different from those they had left in Europe. Discourses on the beauty of the landscape and the importance and necessity of preserving forests were insufficient to prevent the large-scale devastation that immigrants have inflicted upon these two forest typologies.

In comparison to European forests, the interior of Brazilian tropical and subtropical forests was seen by Europeans as disorder on the verge of chaos. In 1879 the German land surveyor Maximilian Beschoren wrote: "In order to transform the 'white forest,' only a strong machete can open the path in this chaotic vegetation. The bushes make the forest inaccessible; what immense vegetation opposes us!" (Beschoren 1989, 104). He made his expedition to the Upper Uruguay River, in Rio Grande do Sul state, for topographical surveys of future colonies for European immigrants.

In the nineteenth century, in an attempt to find a way of belonging and create a relationship with their homeland, immigrants imagined nature reflecting the model they were familiar with. Thus, they tried to transform and adapt what they found according to what they knew. Learning about the land meant thinking of it as something familiar. This was the vision that scientists or travelers tried to convey to their European readership. The exotic tropical world was referenced, but the reports always tried to create some connection, such as mentioning places that had at least some similarities to their homeland. In the case of Germans, the idea of *Heimat* was associated with their concept of nature, especially of forests. This was probably the single similarity with their homeland, even if it was a subliminal one.

The Germans settled in Rio Grande do Sul, mainly in the valleys. German immigration started in 1824, with the first colony of São Leopoldo, followed by Montenegro, Santa Cruz do Sul, Lajeado, Estrela, Taquari, and São Sebastião do Caí. The state of Rio Grande do Sul received between 45,000 and 50,000 German immigrants (De Boni and Costa 1984, 37), roughly half the number of Italian immigrants.

The main influx of Italian migration to the state of Rio Grande do Sul occurred between the years of 1874 and 1914 with the settlement of around 100,000 immigrants (De Boni and Costa 1984, 68). The region chosen by the government for their settlement was mainly in the mountain range areas, principally in the colonies of Caxias do Sul, Antonio Prado, Bento Gonçalves, Garibaldi, Alfredo Chaves and Guaporé.

Family immigration was encouraged and desired in both groups, since settlers would become small farmers, as the amount of land granted would be 25 hectares each. From the beginning, the Italians established their vineyards, and also grew wheat and corn. The latter was a Native American plant, and probably one of the most important staple foods, as it served to make *polenta*, bread, and feed the animals.

The arrival of immigrants destabilized traditional indigenous communities and *caboclo*[1] inhabitants, who had lived there until then. As they possessed no ownership documents, these traditional groups were removed by the state or colonization companies from their lands, in favor of the establishment of settlers. The change from indigenous and *caboclo* occupation to European settlements generated drastic alterations in nature as a whole, throughout the nineteenth and twentieth centuries. One example is that the *caboclo* communities, who engaged in subsistence farming and raising pigs, lost access to the forest. Under the *caboclo*'s more sustainable management of natural resources, pigs were easy to raise, requiring little management – it was enough to simply leave them in the forest, where they grew and grew fat, feeding mainly on Brazilian pine seeds, which were abundant in the fall, as well as other fruits and seeds. In addition, forest usage was also important for harvesting honey from native bees, certain vines to extract wool dyes and medicinal plants, as well as for hunting (Brandt 2012, 181–194). Moreover, because of the settlements of

Europeans, the *caboclo* populations came to be seen as intruders in their own land. They were targets, not only for expropriation, but also of disqualification of their forms of access (i.e. mostly no ownership documents were involved) and use of the land, because they favored a more semi-nomad subsistence-oriented farming instead of a more sedentary and market oriented one (Brandt and Nodari 2011, 89). However, the alteration of landscapes in the so-called colonial areas had rather distinct stages in relation to the *caboclo* people, with the inclusion of European immigrants and their descendants into the forests.

The relationship with the *caboclo* people was very complicated, because while the immigrants struggled to maintain their cultural traditions from Europe – of which the survival of the mother tongue through several generations is the most prominent feature – and at the same time depreciated the *caboclo* way of life, the *caboclo* ecological knowledge was too essential for their survival to be neglected. Thus, from the beginning the Europeans incorporated the "strange" indigenous and *caboclo* crops into their diets, such as native beans (*Phaseolus vulgaris*), sweet potato (*Ipomoea batatas*), cassava (*Manihotesculenta*), as well as the practice of collecting food resources from the native forests itself, like *palmito* (*Euterpe edulis*), *butiá* (*Butia capitata*) and *pinhão* (Araucaria seeds). And not only the crops, but the *caboclo* and indigenous farming method itself, the *coivara*, a slash and burn agriculture followed by a fallow period, was extensively used by the immigrants (Waibel 1949). It is interesting to note that despite the strong influence of European immigration to the culture of the present states of Rio Grande do Sul and Santa Catarina, the names of rivers, plants, animals and places (cities, districts etc.) are indigenous, which suggests the importance of the ecological knowledge of the native or previous inhabitants.

The colonial context challenged the identity of settlers in many ways, and signs of identity became important for demarcation of their spaces. The forest could become one of these identity signs, but settlers had to learn how to work and live with it in order to do so. In this respect, there are countless reports made during the nineteenth century about the difficulties they found:

> We did not know how to prepare the land, cutting low vegetation first with a sickle and then the trees [....] We threw ourselves into the forest as towards an enemy, attacking it with all the tools at our disposal, machetes, hatchets, axes, and saws, swinging it left and right without method, cutting bushes, ferns, small and large trees, in disordered sequence.
>
> (Stoltz 1977, 25)

That same forest meant survival for many immigrants. The narrative of a Polish immigrant written in 1891 shows his initial contacts with Brazilian nature:

> For the first time, we breathed the pure air of the virgin forest. [....] Around the trees, the floor was full of Brazilian pine seeds, some half-eaten,

some intact. No one dared to eat one as we were afraid that the Brazilian pine seeds could be poisonous. That day, none of us could imagine that only a few days later that pine seed would save us from hunger.

(Stoltz 1977, 61)

The immigrants knew little about the environments in which they settled. This generated tensions, but also offered opportunities for learning.

The government and colonization companies chose to settle the immigrants in the valleys and mountain ranges, areas the government deemed to be without large populations prior to that, as indigenous groups were not considered. This view was also conveyed by an immigrant who in 1884 wrote to his family in Italy:

> In the field (of the Indians), 7 years ago there was not anyone besides the Indians, and wild men who had fled. Now there are 1,400 Italian and Tyrolean inhabitants and there are even thoughts of forming a new Italy. [....] The wine is made in February."

(Stoltz 1977, 103)

The importance of having familiar seeds for planting was an important factor in trying to recreate their European world. Italian immigrants brought with them "all the necessary tools to work the land and all kinds of seeds and grapevines." (Stoltz 1977, 98).

Occupation by immigrants in Rio Grande do Sul, particularly Germans and Italians, extended into the first half of the twentieth century. Since the 1920s, the west of Santa Catarina received waves of settlers coming mostly from Rio Grande do Sul and some from Europe. The colonization companies owned by Rio Grande do Sul entrepreneurs had become the main organizations responsible for the settlement of western Santa Catarina. Their responsibilities included implementing directed migration to specific groups that fit the standards set by the state government and the companies themselves, that is, people who would colonize and populate the region in an orderly fashion and would till the land beyond the mere subsistence level. The target audience was the German and Italian descendants established in Rio Grande do Sul, where they had already demonstrated their ability to colonize (Nodari 2009).

Concerns of deforestation and sawmills

Deforestation and the possibility of soil exhaustion linked to it were matters of concern already within a few decades after the settlement of the first immigrants. Humberto Ancarini, consular agent of Italy in the region of Caxias do Sul and Bento Gonçalves, Rio Grande do Sul, described the colony of Caxias in a report issued in 1905, calling attention to the farming method adopted by settlers, considered rudimentary and without any concern for the future: "The clearing was done by ax, mattocks and fire. There was no concern with replenishing the fertility of the soil. Everyone cuts trees and no one thinks about reforestation, and three fifths of the forests have been devastated" (Ancarini 1983, 54).

It is evident that the devastation of the forests in Rio Grande do Sul was already far advanced. In the early twentieth century, there was a new migratory wave by descendants of these first settlers due to numerous factors, including the size of land holding, population growth, and soil depletion. These migrants left the older colonies for other forested areas of the Upper Uruguay River, "occupying lands of the former municipalities of Lagoa Vermelha and Passo Fundo" (De Boni and Costa 1984, 70). The relationship between the European occupation and deforestation was very clear. In addition, we find that a good number of these lumber industries came to western Santa Catarina later.

The industrial census of 1920 shows, among other data, the distribution of timber industries, such as sawmills and factories of boxes, crates, and cooperages. The state of Rio Grande do Sul had 365 companies, followed by Santa Catarina, with 246 units. Furthermore, Miguel Carvalho recalls that one must be careful with data analysis, considering that the timber industries were not only located in a specific type of forest (Carvalho 2010, 118–119). It is important to highlight that, although our study focused on the TDF and the MOF, there were other forests within the Atlantic Forest biome in southern Brazil, where timber industries were established. There was also the practice of moving the sawmills, placing them in the center of the forest for a period of time and then moving to another region, as shown in records of the Legislative Assembly of Rio Grande do Sul in 1945 (Tedesco and Sander 2002, 215).

The economic census of 1940 recorded a total of 1,060 timber establishments located in Rio Grande do Sul, of which 296 were in the municipalities of Passo Fundo and Carazinho (Wentz 2004, 24). These two municipalities had received a large number of immigrants from the former colonies.

With the relative depletion of forests in Rio Grande do Sul, the deforestation process gained momentum in western Santa Catarina. Economic interests were at stake in all phases of devastation in which forests were perceived as a potential source of capital. Interest groups ranged from small local and regional timber loggers to large corporations. The former followed colonization companies which needed to have a "clean" area to settle the colonies, while the latter were branches of large companies, as was the case of the Southern Brazil Lumber and Colonization Company. In western Santa Catarina, the devastation process was particularly intense, as these interests were compounded by colonists who saw the forest as an obstacle to planting their future crops. Significantly, most of these colonists who settled in the region were descended from first to third generation immigrants (Nodari 2009, 23–64) and had already gone through the process of colonization in Rio Grande do Sul, either personally or with their parents.

It should be noted that in areas within railway reach for timber transportation, the process was much faster than in areas where this means of transportation was not available. When it was impossible to construct railways, they were substituted by waterway transportation through major rivers such as the Uruguay.

Statistics are always an issue for researchers when working with different types of sources. For example, it is difficult to reach a consensus on the number of existing sawmills in the south of Brazil. Previous surveys performed by researchers showed that not all of them were registered. There were also clandestine establishments which supplied timber to legalized sawmills. After 1943, when registry and records began to be required by legal regulation, data became more reliable. Owners who did not keep any records were prevented from selling their products to other states and, more importantly, from exporting to other countries.

In the industrial census of 1920, Rio Grande do Sul had a greater number of timber companies than Santa Catarina, as the establishment of colonies in western Santa Catarina had only started. The picture changed gradually in the decades from 1940 to 1970. In the databases used to compose the figure below (Figure 2.1), the Brazilian pine sawmills appear as one category, hardwood as another, mixed timber as a third category, and the last category is wood for local consumption. The three first categories were for timber exportation, while the fourth category of sawmills was for local purposes, the trade of all kinds of woods, including Brazilian pine and hardwood.

According to Figure 2.1, in 1947 Santa Catarina had 2,284 sawmills while Rio Grande do Sul had 1,688. In Santa Catarina, 736 of these were dedicated to cutting Brazilian pine wood, while 1,076 did the same in Rio Grande do Sul. Another aspect that stands out is that the number of sawmills for local

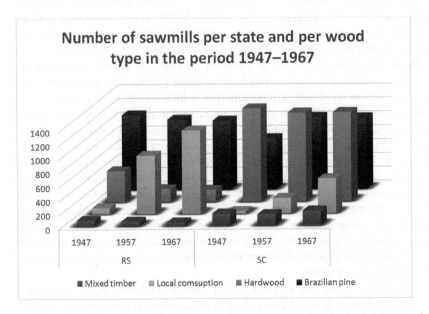

Figure 2.1 Number of sawmills and types of woods in Rio Grande do Sul (RS) and Santa Catarina (SC), in the period from 1947 to 1967

Sources: Anuário Brasileiro de Economia Florestal (1949, 1958, and 1968)

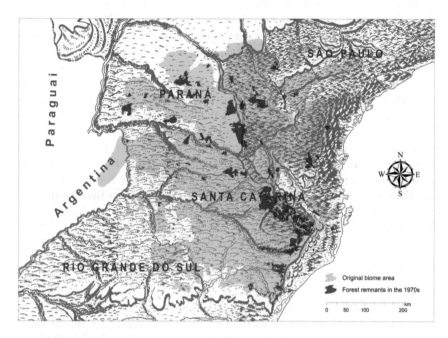

Figure 2.2 Araucaria Forest Domain in southern Brazil and remnants in the 1970s

Source: RADAM Brasil/IBGE and WWF. Map developed by Diogo de Carvalho Cabral, Coordination of Geography, IBGE

consumption is always larger in Rio Grande do Sul, during the period under analysis. Needless to say, most of these sawmills were established by the most economically successful immigrants, such as merchants, who little by little were accumulating enough capital to buy more sophisticated equipment and survive in the market.

The depletion of forests in Rio Grande do Sul occurred earlier than in Santa Catarina for historical issues of immigration and early colonization. The occupation of forest areas in Rio Grande do Sul by Italian and German immigrants occurred during the nineteenth and early twentieth century, which caused the transformation of a great deal of the land into small farms with subsistence crops. In contrast, many areas in Santa Catarina were settled only in the first decades of the twentieth century, which means that the virgin forests were more profitable for the lumber industry and also that technology and capital accumulation were higher in this new frontier.

According to RADAM project data, a large-scale radar scan of Brazil's natural resources done during the military government, the area of Araucaria Forest in the mid-1970s was already reduced to about 8 percent of its original size. This reduction detected in inventories, along with greater control to guarantee compliance with forest legislation by governments at the federal and state level, has led to the progressive decrease in the number of sawmills (Diretoria 1973).

After 1970, the causes and the forms of deforestation were different from those observed during the nineteenth century and the first half of the twentieth century. At this point, the major cause of deforestation became the expansion of exotic tree plantations, such as *Pinuselliotii* and eucalyptus, carried out by timber and cellulose companies (Moretto 2010).

The expansion of agricultural activities by these European descendants and others, now under the Green Revolution technologies, continued to cause deforestation and fragmentation in the remaining forests. The rapid formation of an industrial grain-oilseed-livestock complex, as well as heavy government investments in credit and infrastructures like paved roads and ports, stimulated the region to become a major exporter of agricultural commodities in Brazil, putting significant pressure on native forests. Arguably, the deforestation could be even more complete in southern Brazil if the terrain in some areas was not hilly, and thus impossible to harvest with machines like tractors and harvesters.

Conclusions

It is currently estimated that the TDF is one of the most devastated ecosystems in Brazil (Ruschel et al. 2003). TDF comprises solely 3.25% out of a total of 4.16% remaining native forest in Rio Grande do Sul. In Santa Catarina, recent surveys indicate that there is less than 3% of TDF in the form of very small fragments, which are subject to constant human pressure. The MOF currently has around 2 to 5% of its original area in Brazil, a "derisory 0.7% of which could be considered as primitive areas, the so-called virgin forests" (Campanili and Schaffer 2010, 146), placing it among the most threatened typologies within the Atlantic Forest biome (Mähler Junior and Larocca 2009, 245).

European settlement in forest areas has reached its short-term objectives under the socioeconomic aspects analyzed. The forests praised in travelers' reports of the past, and seen as obstacles by immigrants, have given way to industry and commerce in the villages that became cities; in rural areas, agriculture and intensive livestock production have further changed the landscapes. Future prospects were not considered at the time, with preservation and sustainability set aside. After the 1960s, with agricultural modernization, many immigrant descendants had to sell their small properties and move to the cities, and the rural landscapes became dominated by monocultures of soybean, corn, wheat, pastures, vineyards, and homogeneous plantations of exotic tree species (particularly eucalyptus or Pinus). Still others, given the depletion of forests and lack of available cheap land in southern Brazil, were attracted to moving to the Amazon from the 1970s onward: a new frontier landscape where many of the herein described patterns of interaction with the forest have been repeated.

In the last decades of the twentieth century alternatives already known to farmers have been resumed and new ones, especially in Rio Grande do Sul, have helped shift the economic power of the region, including for small to medium farmers. The viticulture in the regions where the first Italian immigrants were settled in the nineteenth century may be cited as an example. Nowadays, there are small farmers, family vineyards, and also medium to large companies. The region has become the largest producer of wine and sparkling wine in Brazil. Currently, in addition, their respective cities present high Human Development Index levels. Unlike during the extractive period, when timber sale profits went to entrepreneurs who were not often resident in the area, the model currently established in the Vineyard Valley (*Vale dos Vinhedos*) brings benefits to a large segment of rural and even urban populations and is more compatible with a sustained form of development in the long run.

Acknowledgments

Eunice Nodari thanks CNPq for the Post-doctorate scholarship at Stanford University, US, and Miguel Carvalho thanks the Federal University of Southern Frontier for a leave period abroad at the University of Guelph, Canada, a valuable time to prepare this book chapter. The authors also thank Stuart McCook, from the University of Guelph, Canada, for his careful reading and suggestions to improve this text.

Note

1 The term is used in the same way as did Paulo Pinheiro Machado in his work entitled *Contestado Leaderships*, that deals with the *caboclo* involvement in the Contestado War (1912–1916) in south Brazil. Although "there is no ethnic connotation in this word, often the *caboclo* was brown skin, often black. But the main feature of this word is that it distinguishes a social and cultural condition, i.e. poor peasants with no ownership documents, shifting cultivators, and/or landless workers in cattle ranches. Later, with the first waves of immigrants from Germany and Poland, from the second decade of the nineteenth century, also these immigrants turned to *caboclo* way of life, acquiring many habits and customs of that population, such as farming methods" (Machado 2004, 48).

References

Ancarini, H. (1983) Relatório: A colônia italiana de Caxias in De Boni, L.A. (ed.) *A Itália e o Rio Grande do Sul IV*, EST, Porto Alegre, Brazil
Avé-Lallemant, R. (1980) *Viagens pelas Províncias de Santa Catarina, Paraná e São Paulo (1858)*, Ed. Itatiaia/Ed. da Universidade de São Paulo, Belo Horizonte/São Paulo
Beschoren, M. (1989) *Impressões de viagem na província do Rio Grande do Sul*, Martins Livreiro, Porto Alegre, Brazil
Brandt, M. (2012) *Uma História Ambiental dos Campos do Planalto de Santa Catarina*, Unpublished PhD Thesis Graduate Program in History, Universidade Federal de Santa Catarina, Brazil
Brandt, M. and Nodari, E.S. (2011) Comunidades tradicionais da Floresta de Araucária de Santa Catarina: territorialidade e memória, *História Unisinos* 15 80–90

Campanili, M. and Schaffer, W.B. (2010) *Mata Atlântica: patrimônio nacional dos brasileiros*, Ministério do Meio Ambiente, Brasília

Carvalho, M.M.X. de (2010) *Uma grande empresa em meio à floresta: a história da devastação da floresta com araucária e a Southern Brazil Lumber and Colonization (1870–1970)*, Unpublished PhD Thesis Graduate Program in History, Universidade Federal de Santa Catarina, Brazil

Castella, P.R. and Britez, R.M. (2004) *A Floresta com Araucária no Paraná: conservação e diagnósticos dos remanescentes florestais*, Ministério do Meio Ambiente, Brasília

De Boni, L.A. and Costa, R. (1984) *Os Italianos do Rio Grande do Sul*, EST/EDUCS/Correio Rio Grandense, Porto Alegre

Leite, P.F. and Klein, R.M. (1990) *Geografia do Brasil: Região Sul*, IBGE, Rio de Janeiro

Medeiros, J. de M. (2004) *Floresta com Araucárias: um símbolo da Mata Atlântica a ser salvo da extinção*, Apremavi, Rio do Sul, Brazil

Machado, P.P. (2004) *Lideranças do Contestado: a formação e a atuação das chefias caboclas (1912–1916)*, Editora da UNICAMP, Campinas, Brazil

Mähler Junior, J.K. and Larocca, J.F. (2009) Fitofisionomias, desmatamento e fragmentação da Floresta com Araucária in Fonseca C.R. *et al* (eds) *Floresta com Araucária: ecologia, conservação e preservação*, Holos Editora, Ribeirão Preto, Brazil

Moretto, S.P. (2010) *Remontando a floresta: a implementação do Pinus e as práticas de reflorestamento na região de Lages (1960–1990)*, Unpublished Master Thesis, Graduate Program in History, Universidade Federal de Santa Catarina, Brazil

Muir, J. (2001) (edited by Branch, M.P.) *Last journey. South to the Amazon and East Africa*, Island Press, Washington

Nodari, E.S. (2009) *Etnicidades renegociadas:práticas socioculturais no Oeste de Santa Catarina*, Ed. da UFSC, Florianópolis, Brazil

Diretoria da Cooperativa Madeireira do Vale do Uruguai Ltda (1973), Relatório (Report of the Board of Directors), Acervo Arquivo do Centro de Memória do Oeste de Santa Catarina – CEOM (Archive of the Memory Center of the west of Santa Catarina), Chapecó, 24 de março

Ruschel, A.R., Nodari, E.S., Guerra, M.P. and Nodari, R.O. (2003) Evolução do uso e valorização das espécies madeiráveis da Floresta Estacional Decidual do Alto-Uruguai, *Ciência Florestal* 13 153–166

Stoltz, R. (1977) *Cartas de imigrantes (italianos, poloneses e alemães)*, EST Edições, São Leopoldo, Brazil

Tedesco, J.C. and Sander, R. (2002) *Madeireiros, comerciantes e granjeiros:lógicas e contradições no processo de desenvolvimento socioeconômico de Passo Fundo (1900–1960)*, UPF Editora, Passo Fundo, Brazil

Teschauer,C. (2002) *História do Rio Grande do Sul dos dois primeiros séculos* 2nd ed. volume 1, Editora Unisinos, São Leopoldo, Brazil

Waibel, L. (1949) Princípios da colonização europeia no sul do Brasil, *Revista Brasileira de Geografia* 2 159–222

Wentz, L.I.M. (2004) *Os caminhos da Madeira:região norte do Rio Grande do Sul 1902–1959*, UPF Editora, Passo Fundo, Brazil

Worster, D. (2008) *A passion for nature: the life of John Muir*, Oxford University Press, New York

3 Migrants and the making of the American landscape

Marco Armiero

Abstract

In this chapter I will explore how migrants have adapted, fought with, and reshaped the environment they moved into, changing themselves and nature at the same time. Their tools, skills, knowledge, even their ethnic identities and solidarity, interacted with the local natural resources. Immigrants have looked at nature with different eyes; sometimes they saw natural resources where others could not see anything (for instance, in the case of urban commons); they adapted themselves or fought against the landscape they arrived in (as in the case of Southern plantations in the Mississippi Delta or the making of California's agricultural landscape); their bodies became part of the capitalistic ecologies of industrial and mining production transforming both the external and the internal nature. While in the classical narrative pioneers entered, settled, and coped with a natural environment they heroically tamed, in this chapter I argue that immigrants' environments were never only "natural." Those were racialized landscapes, where class, law, and property rights were influential at least as much as soil, climate, viruses, or wild animals. Therefore, rather than speaking of how immigrants shaped or adapted to the "natural" environment, it seems more appropriate to analyze the metabolic relationships between immigrants and the socionatures in which they settled. I will do so employing several examples from the history of various immigrants' groups, especially Italians, in the United States.

Migrants' metabolism

Stressing the stratification of ethnic landscapes in the Monterey Bay area, the economist James O'Connor wrote: "Each [group] had their own more or less unique ways of doing things, which they superimposed on the local environment, which resembled closely or in broad outline their respective natures back home" (O'Connor 1998, 77). Indeed, each migrant group saw nature differently, perceived beauty and ugliness according to its system of values, and positioned itself in the geographical and cultural space where it arrived. According to James O'Connor—inspired by Karl Marx—work was the mediation between the ethnic cultures and the environment. The immigrants' skills, techniques, and knowledge were their access keys through nature. In their backyards and in the city's streets, in the forests and in the fields, in the sweat-shops and in the tenements, the entire world around them acquired new meanings. Migrants saw the environment not only with their eyes but through their whole body. It was not only an issue of seeing, rather of a metabolic relationship which affected both the immigrant's body and the environment.

In this sense the American landscape is much less American than one generally realizes. Blended with its soil, rocks, and plants is the work of generations of immigrants. The best approximation of this immigrants' landscape is what historian Thomas Andrews has labeled "workscape":

> [Workscape is] not just an essentially static scene or setting neatly contained within borders, but a constellation of unruly and ever-unfolding relationships—not simply land, but also air and water, bodies and organisms, as well as the language people use to understand the world, and the lens of culture through which they make sense of and act on their surroundings. [....] Going beyond the hoary dualisms that separate "man" and "nature" in much of Western thought, the workscape concept treats people as laboring beings who have changed and been changed in turn by a natural world that remains always under construction.
>
> (Andrews 2010, 125)

Many times, together with hard work, immigrants kneaded the soil with seeds and plants from their own lands. Being acquainted with other climates and water regimes, immigrants had to adapt their tools and techniques to the environments they settled, reinventing both the land and their place in it. In the current age of rampant xenophobia and nationalistic revanchism, re-stating the obvious can be revolutionary: diversity is not only a political statement or an act of social kindness, but it is inscribed into the environment we live in. The cherished nations of the neo-nationalists have been materially made by people who did not belong, but nonetheless have left their mark in the land.

The ingenuity of immigrants, their ability to mobilize natural and cultural resources in order to make a living, but also to articulate their relationship to the environment, is the central pillar of this chapter. However, unlike the classical pioneers' tale, here I do not see heroic individuals taming the American wilderness, and with it its native inhabitants. Theirs were collective rather than individual enterprises; instead of a little house in the prairie, a tent camp in the field or a boarding house in the tenements seem to be the most adapted setting for their epic. Unlike the usual pioneers' tales, immigrants' stories do not end necessarily with successes, but might well just be failures, lost traces in an elsewhere which never became home. Obviously, defining what success means is always controversial, even more as one wishes to consider the ecological and not only the social effects of immigrants' agency. I argue that the most relevant difference between my understanding of the immigrants' experience and the pioneers' tales regards the very notion of environment. While in the classical narrative pioneers entered, settled, and coped with a natural environment they heroically tamed, I argue that immigrants' environments were never only "natural." Those were racialized landscapes, where class, law, and property rights were influential at least as much as soil, climate, viruses, or wild animals. Of course, this is true for pioneers as well, but the narratives in which pioneers are embedded do not allow us to recognize it. Therefore, rather than speaking of how immigrants shaped or adapted to the "natural" environment, it seems more appropriate to analyze the metabolic relationships between immigrants and the socionatures in which they settled. I will do so employing several examples from the history of various immigrants' groups, especially Italians, in the United States. Focusing on the metabolic relationship and work, I will not address some themes in the environmental history of migrations which nonetheless are crucial. For instance, I am not assuming that immigrants knew nature *only* through work. As Colin Fisher has brilliantly demonstrated, leisure was also an important part of the immigrants' experience of nature (Fisher 2015). I will also omit analysis of the controversial relationships between some strands of conservationism and immigrants which, as Betsy Hartmann, Adam Rome, Louis Warren, Peter Coates, and Lisa Sun-Hee Park and David Naguib Pellow have uncovered, were not immune to xenophobic sentiments (Warren 1997; Coates 2006; Rome 2008; Hartmann 2010; Park and Pellow 2011). Finally, an environmental history of migrations and migrants should consider the class, race, and gender dimensions, or, in other words, it should avoid treating migrants as a cohesive group of humans in relationship to "nature." In this respect, I refer to Connie Chiang's path-breaking work on inter-ethnic conflicts related to natural resources in the Monterey Bay area of California (Chiang 2009). Failing comprehensiveness, I hope that this chapter, as well as the entire collection, could be considered as a contribution to spark a renewed interest in blending migration, social, and environmental history.

Nature in a stranger mirror

When the Japanese arrived in Sutter, Yuba, Colusa, Glenn, and Butte counties, in California, they found nothing more than a "waste land" covered with a layer of "hardpan." However, they were also able to see something different, since within a few years those areas became home to intensive rice plantations. By 1918 the Japanese immigrants had added 25,000 acres of rice to California agriculture (McWilliams 1978 [1935], 109). Evidently, their acquaintance with water placed Japanese and other Asian migrants into the landscape as powerful agents of transformation. In fact, the "natural" features of the Sacramento, San Joaquin, Santa Clara, and Imperial Valleys have been the result of the hard work of those immigrants who reclaimed the land. Recognizing their agency does not imply erasing the inequalities and power relationships in which immigrants' interventions upon the land were imbricated. McWilliams spoke of 3,000 Japanese who died draining Fresno County alone (McWilliams 1978 [1935], 114). In the footsteps of McWilliams, Don Mitchell has uncovered how "the shape of the landscape is a compromised product of the multitudinous relations of power that structure and are created out of the workings of the political economy" (Mitchell 1996, 121).

In the San Joaquin Valley, the Chinese community employed its traditional technique of irrigation—"a series of wooden paddles affixed to a strip of canvas which conveyed the water through a rectangular wooden trough" (Minnick 1988, 47)—to transform a portion of arid land into vegetable gardens. The importance of the Chinese immigrants in the making of western agriculture was even recognized by some contemporaries. John Faragher and Robert Hine, addressing the issue of Chinese relevance in developing intensive methods of cultivation, quoted an article published in 1869 by the *Overland Monthly*:

> The descendants of the people who drained those almost limitless marshes on either side of their own swiftly-flowing Yellow River, and turned them into luxuriant fields, are able to do the same thing on the banks of the Sacramento and the San Joaquin.
>
> (quoted in Hine and Faragher 2000, 359)

Building levees and draining the land, the Chinese rearranged the Delta area by backbreaking work, as Sylvia Sun Minnick wrote in her history of the area (Minnick 1988, 25). According to Carey McWilliams, the transition from wheat to fruit acreage was made possible by the Chinese who "taught their overlords how to plant, cultivate, and harvest orchards and garden crops" (quoted in Minnick 1988, 70). The Japanese colony of Cortez, California, presents another story of immigration and transformation. Vineyards and orchards conquered sandstorms and voracious jackrabbits as the Japanese used the land to produce a seasonal cycle of different crops (Matsumoto 1993, 46).

The same stories can be told for other immigrant groups. The Italians in California, for instance, left a significant mark on the landscape. A book published in 1909 defined Secondo Guasti, the leader of the Italian Vineyard Co., as a man who had "faith in the desert" (quoted in D'Amico 1986, 17). Evidently the author was referring to Guasti's investment in a land which did not seem well suited to being farmed. Nonetheless, things are more complicated than a heroic pioneer's tale which simply substitutes the Ingalls family[1] with the Guastis. Mine is not a narrative of bold Italians taming California's desert, but rather a story of a capitalistic industrial farming enterprise, ethnically marked, nonetheless exploitative of other immigrant workers, especially Mexicans, who did most of the hard work under worse living and working conditions than the Italians. As the Italian historian Simone Cinotto has written:

> Secondo Guasti was careful to draw lines between Piedmontese workers, on the one hand, and Asian and Latino migrants when it came to distinctions in wages or benefits. [...] a differentiated distribution of rights

and resources and a systematic, symbolic structuring of everyday life thus offered Italian workers the feeling of social superiority.

(Cinotto 2012, 142–143)

Looking at how immigrants transformed the land should not mean obliterating class, race, and gender inequalities, ignoring the complicated socioecological relationships among groups and with the environment. The immigrants' landscape was not a peaceful one and the struggle was not primarily with "nature"; as Don Mitchell has clearly demonstrated for California, the "struggle over the shape of the land" was truly the spatial embodiment of class struggles (Mitchell 1996, 193).

Italian wine production required a major transformation of the landscape. To create its famous vineyard plantation, the Italian Swiss Colony in Asti, California, had to clear the pre-existing vegetation of manzanita, scrub oaks and brush (Florence 1999, 44). In his inquiry on the wine making industry published in 1900, the Italian agronomist Rossati described the area of the Asti colony: "It lies in a wavy valley on the Russian River, protected by high mountains from winds and weather, with a volcanic soil where vineyards, olive and orange trees grow as in the best Italian regions" (Rossati 1900, 189). However, the landscape described by Rossati was less natural than he imagined; originally, the entire area (1,800 acres) had been covered by woods, above all oak trees which had been cleared by the Italians. At the beginning of the twentieth century, the vineyard covered 1,200 acres, while the rest of the land was cultivated with fruits and other vegetables. In the first years of its life, the colony had many troubles, some related to the market, that is, the monopoly of winemaking companies, and others directly connected to ecological issues. The Russian River, which was so important for irrigation, was also a source of problems with its frequent floods, perhaps caused by the huge environmental transformations introduced in the area for the grape culture. Even the most relevant ecological event in the California grape culture, the Phylloxera bio-invasion, can also be understood through ethnicity. According to Rossati, due to its Italian character, the Asti colony was much more exposed to the disease; their Italian grape understocks reacted quite badly to the invasion, while hybridization with native plants produced better results. The Italian contribution to the grape culture and wine making industry is well known.[2] The United States Immigration Commission divided California's wine makers into "whites" (43%) and Italians (40%) (Fichera 1981, 254). In 1913 250,000 acres of Californian land were devoted to grapes (Smith 1913, 258).

Vineyards were the most obvious sign of immigrants' presence on the land but were not their only environmental transformation. From over 560 acres of land obtained by the Italians in the San Francisco area, no more than 300 were ready to be farmed (Fichera 1981, 244). Within a few years, the immigrants had transformed the sand hill dune of Outer Mission into fields of lettuce, cabbage, and artichoke (Gumina 1978, 33). These tales are not limited to the Golden State. In 1913, celebrating the contribution of the new immigrants to America, Leila Allen Dimock quoted the cases of Poles and Bohemians. The narrative is almost the same; immigrants were able to see opportunities in the land where others, namely Anglo-Americans, did not. Hence, in the Connecticut Valley were the Poles who discovered that the thin soil higher up the river was worth cultivating with certain crops, while until their arrival agriculture had been concentrated only in the rich lands closest to the river (Allen Dimock 1913, 41). The Italian Committee for Immigration, trying to persuade people to avoid the overcrowded cities of the East Coast, praised the natural opportunities in the South. The convergence between the ecological heritage of plantations and the social changes caused by the Civil War seemed to free a large portion of land, only apparently exhausted, but actually ready to be farmed following the typical Italian intensive style (Bollettino dell'emigrazione italiana, hereafter BEI 1904 (4), 17–19). Soil depleted by the cultivation of cotton or still covered by pines yielded strawberries and other vegetables in Independence, Louisiana (BEI 1904 (4), 22). There the Sicilian immigrants showed their skills in coping with water, draining the land when it was too wet, and digging ditches and canals when it was too dry (Giordano 1979, 127). Where the traditional white pioneers could not handle the condition, Sicilians succeeded (BEI 1904 (4), 74–75). According to the Dillingham Commission[3] "the success of many of the farmers in the Italian colony around Independence [a town in Louisiana with strong Italian presence] has been due largely to care in drainage" (quoted in Baiamonte 1990, 51).

Accepting environmental risks seems to have been one of the main strategies adopted by the Italian immigrants in their efforts to gain ownership of the land. Such was the case, for instance, of Brazos Valley, Texas. There, continuous floods had reduced the price of land, but Italians decided to gamble with the environment and bought land which no one wanted (Institute of Texan Cultures 1973, 13). Obviously, a low price has always been more enticing than environmental constraints, but our knowledge of the facts is not thorough enough to determine whether those Italian immigrants had just obliterated nature or rather had been able to cope with it. In other words, it is difficult to evaluate the environmental effect of this Italian agricultural colonization. Some data seem to confirm the immigrants' success. Between the 1890s and 1905 Brazos County and its main center, Bryan, registered a high percentage of Italians, among the largest in rural America, although in these same years the area was affected by a series of dramatic floods. Evidently, the Italian approach to hydrological problems was not successful in ecological terms, but the story seems to demonstrate their resilience to this environmental stress. According to the historians Mangione and Morreale, the tools they adopted were more social and cultural than technological. To face floods and a situation of permanent risk the Italians had to cooperate, sharing work, animals, resources, and skills (Mangione and Morreale 1992, 186). Less contradictory seems the Italian impact on at least two other Texas areas. In Montague County the immigrants' work covered sandy land with vineyards, orchards, and vegetable farms in the twenty years from the 1880s to the 1900s. When in the 1930s the oil industry appeared in the Dickinson area, the economy was based essentially on the production of figs, introduced by Italian immigrants (Institute of Texan Cultures 1973, 24).

While planting vineyards and introducing rice were rather massive transformations, immigrants also articulated their relationships to nature on a more micro-scale, which nonetheless spoke of broader socio-ecological patterns. What was, for instance, the otherness of Italian backyards, full of vegetables, rabbits, and chickens, if not the evidence of a different relationship to the land and another vision of the urban nature? Visiting Minneapolis in the 1910s, the Italian writer and journalist Amy Bernardy stressed the strange oxymoron of urban and rural which characterized the Italian neighborhood: "The life in the tenements is not even suburban; we might say it is rural. The zoology of the backyard is composed by chickens, ducks, etc. There are also a few goats, and countless dogs and cats" (Bernardy 1913, 53, my translation).

After all, as the historian Rudolph Vecoli has written, in the 1880s Goatsville was the nickname for West Englewood, one of Chicago's Italian neighborhoods (Vecoli 1986, 296–297). In the first decades of the twentieth century, Italians were still raising rabbits and chickens in their yards in the Excelsior district of San Francisco (Cancilla Martellini n.d.) or were moving to the Bronx in New York looking for more land to grow their vegetables and breed their goats (Glazer and Moynihan 1963, 187). In his PhD research on Italians in San Francisco, Thomas Arthur Pedemonte wrote that in the 1910s they terraced even the slopes of Telegraph Hill to make room for their gardens (Pedemonte 1971, 51).

The fact that the Italians had a different vision about how to relate to each little spot of land is unquestionable. Where the Anglo-Saxon residents had the inevitable lawn, often Italians, instead, grew vegetables and raised small livestock (Siciliani 1922, 30). Recollecting her experience of moving from New York to Detroit, Clementina Todesco stressed her joy at having finally a small backyard where she immediately planted a garden (Mathias and Raspa 1985, 279). As she said, "everything grows there" (279)—indeed, an odd coupling of an urban space with a rural quality.

On several occasions Italians' skills in truck farming and grazing small animals, that is, their other way of seeing and using nature just around the corner, became the shock absorber which enabled them to endure hard times. Remembering the Depression years in the Delta, many people pointed out that Italians were better equipped to face the crises, thanks to their vegetables and animals—first of all the hogs (Canonici 2003, 49). It was the same during the frequent strikes occurring in the mining communities when the Italian families could survive better thanks to their self-sufficiency (Taylor and Williams 1992, 87). This was neither an exclusive prerogative of Italian immigrants nor something occurring only in the US. A Serb immigrant recounted that in 1912 everyone in the Slavic community of Chisholm, Minnesota, had gardens with vegetables and animals (Holmquist, Stipanovich, and Moss 1981, 389). The writer Patricia Klindienst (2006) has illustrated the centrality of gardening in the making of ethnic identities in almost all migrants' groups in the US. Sue Bruley (2010) has researched the role of women in the provision of free food during the 1926 coal controversy in South West, Australia, while Carla Iacovetta pointed out that during harsh times Italian women in Toronto contributed to the survival of their families by growing vegetables (Iacovetta 1987, 8). In both cases, it seems evident that the environmental history of migrations—or better off, of migrants—should not obliterate the gender dimension.

While we already have some notions about diversity in immigrants' backyards, there is still much to be researched about their ability to activate the urban commons. It is clear that our understanding of the immigrants' ways of seeing and accessing nature depend to a large degree on our comprehension of those urban commons. We might discover that at the beginning of the twentieth century immigrants could see in the urban streets of a New Jersey town things practically invisible to others, as, for instance, the carpet of leaves useful to breed their animals (Fogg Meade 1909, 56–57). According to the environmental historian Ted Steinberg, garbage piled up in the streets was a strategic resource for the immigrant communities which used it as an urban

Figure 3.1 Elwood City, Pennsylvania, 1920s. Alice Nardini and her son in their
    backyard

Source: Courtesy of the Fondazione Paolo Cresci

common resource. Their animals, especially their pigs, roamed through it, transforming rubbish into cheap protein, at least until the policies of sanitization ended this practice, which had indeed been a way to gain access to an urban common (Steinberg 2002, 811). In his vivid descriptions of the misery in which immigrants were living in New York, the writer and social reformer Jacob Riis mentioned the large number of goats grazing unattended around the tenements, apparently even becoming a threat for the safety of the most vulnerable inhabitants, the children and elders (Riis 1890, 313–318). The sanitary city, to use the telling expression of environmental historian Martin Melosi (2000), severed this metabolic connection between immigrants and urban commons. This was the case, for instance, of the chicken coops in San Francisco, studied by Joanna Dyl. At the beginning of the twentieth century San Francisco was home to some 16,000 domestic chicken yards; the birds were strategic for the subsistence of poor families. Hence, it was a disaster when the 1908 sanitization policies following the plague outbreaks of 1907 made it prohibitively expensive to continue to have birds in the city (Dyl 2006, 48–49). Garbage, activated by migrants, was the most used among urban common resources. Indeed the rag collector has been one of the "classical" images of immigrants, proving the poor conditions of a large portion of them. It would be interesting to think of that activity also in ecological terms, as an example of the practices through which immigrants activated urban commons. In San Francisco, as scavengers and gardeners, Italians exploited the opportunities of both identities. If as farmers they had the right skills to cope with scarce water supply (digging wells), as scavengers they had access to garbage as a free resource for shaping the soil, both on the surface (leveling it) and in its internal chemistry composition (fertilizing it) (Nicosia 1960, n. p.). So, it was not by chance that the sanitation policy following the 1907 plague specifically targeted the Italians and their double business in truck farming and manure collection (Dyl 2006, 50). According to Amy Bernardy, in Saint Paul, Minnesota, the Italian colony was materially built on the waste and debris from the city:

> The impressive height difference between the river's shore, known as the Upper Leeve, and the anything but pleasant small valley marked with the railroads has been filled with the debris and waste coming from the city, materials that the industrious immigrants headed off competing with each other in order to make their own soil.
>
> (Bernardy 1913, 52)

Through their bodies

"Not only have humans mixed their labor with nature to create hybrid landscapes; nature—already a mixture of human and nonhuman elements—has intermixed with human bodies, without anyone's consent or control, and often without anyone's knowledge" (Nash 2006, 209). With these lines historian Linda Nash introduces a different perspective on the environmental history of mass migration which moves beyond the classical Turnerian Frontier thesis which depicted bold white pioneers taming wilderness and conquering nature. Migrants themselves have been nature on the move. Their bodies have interacted with the new environment which was not simply raw material for the making of their dreams. Healthy or sick, strange as it may seem, migrants understood the environment through those categories (Valenčius 2002, 2). As historian Coneverey Bolton Valenčius puts it, those categories referred to a different perception of the world, one in which the relationships between bodies and nature were much stronger.

In the migrants' experience, environment and the body, space of work and space of living were not separated by rigid barriers; rather they overlapped, both metaphorically and materially. Due to endemic illnesses the land could be unhealthy and dangerous to settle. Difficult to see from the outside, but extremely evident to those who struggled with adversity, malaria and yellow fever were the main hidden features of the new landscape. The relevance of the health of the land emerged from several sources. In 1875 the Secretary of Agriculture stated that immigrants avoided Michigan due to its reputation as a place of malaria and wolverines (Michigan State Board of Agriculture 1876, 309). In his book *Where to Emigrate and Why*, published in 1869, Frederick B. Goddard considered malaria and other diseases among the main variables in choosing a place; if Minnesota seemed particularly healthy, "exempt from malaria and consequently the numerous diseases known to arise from it" (Goddard 1869, 238), the new, warm, and highly fertile areas were listed as not healthy to an unacclimated person. As Goddard wrote: "The northern emigrant runs some risk of undergoing a seasoning course of chills and fevers" (1869, 498). Indeed, in the Southern states and in California malaria was the face of nature for immigrants. Mosquitoes were the main actors in the colonization of the Mississippi Delta. All the sources speak about the impact of this disease on the immigrant communities. As illustrated by historians Martellini (1999) and Whayne (1993), malaria was the main cause for the failure of the Sunnyside Italian colony in Arkansas. The immigrants, who were driven there by an agreement between the American entrepreneur Corbin and the Italian landowner and politician Ruspoli, did not find the fertile lands and hospitable conditions promised to them, but marshes, contaminated waters, and malaria (BEI 1904 (4), 34–35). Already in 1898, the Italian official Guido Rossati stated that in the absence of improvement Italians should have left the colony, an impression confirmed a few years later by the Italian consul in New Orleans, who found Sunnyside submerged by floods and attacked by fevers and gastroenteritis (BEI 1905, 17). The same conditions can be listed for other communities in the Delta area. Analyzing the gravestones in the old cemetery in New Gascony, Arkansas, local historian Paul V. Canonici has discovered a high percentage of children among the dead, a circumstance confirmed by one of his informers who remembered the frequent funerals caused by malaria (Canonici 2003,126–129).

Beside the Mississippi Delta, California was also a focus of concern about malaria. In the 1910s, it was common to say that California was the most malarial state in the country. The same advancement of agriculture seemed to have unwanted effects on the diffusion of malaria, above all with the expansion of rice (Nash 2006, 87–121). California was also one of the places in which land and race met in the immigrants' bodies. In an escalation of xenophobia and racism, instead of mosquito infestation, the immigrant was considered the vector for malaria. In a publication in 1917 we can read:

> Part of the price we paid for finding gold in California was introduc-ing malaria into our beautiful valleys. Dr. Ebright has shown how our immigrant laborers and our present citizens brought in this infection from different parts of the world and it is those carriers that we keep introducing and redistributing throughout California that make a large part of our problem.
>
> (Transaction 1917, 12)

Immigrants were blamed not only for malaria. At the end of the nineteenth century, physicians attributed the spread of hookworm in the California min-ing camps to Austrian, Italian, and Spanish workers (Nash 2006, 123). The historian Alan Kraut (1994) has done extraordinary research on the connec-tions linking nativism, immigrants' health and diseases. Just to give some exam-ples: the 1832 cholera epidemic was attributed to the Irish; Chinese were the scapegoat for several outbreaks in San Francisco, from 1870s smallpox to 1900 plague; in 1907 Italians were blamed for a polio epidemic and in 1915 for the typhoid infection in Philadelphia; for a long time tuberculosis was defined as a Hebrew disease. The most common accusation against immigrants was their supposed poor hygiene. According to some health officers, immigrants loved to live in filth, as Michael M. Davis reported in his 1921 book (112). On the other hand, several physicians and social workers advocated a different expla-nation for the racial distribution of diseases and morbidity. Dr. Antonio Stella for the Italians and Dr. Maurice Fishberg for the Jews tried to demonstrate that the poor health of those ethnic groups in America was the by-product of the environmental and social conditions they met in the New World, rather than of bad behavior or genetic deficiency. Again, land, race, and work merge in the immigrant experience. According to Dr. Stella and Dr. Fishberg, it was not the immigrant who brought diseases to America; on the contrary, the new environment and its ways of living and working were detrimental, destroying the health of the newcomers. In 1910 the Italian official publication on emigra-tion confirmed that many Italians died by tuberculosis after three years in the US (BEI 1910 (13), 87).

Employing the findings from the Federal Writers' Project, the historian David Steven Cohen has confirmed the connections between the spreading of diseases among immigrants and their poor housing conditions:

A description of a Polish boardinghouse in Newark in 1890 informs us that there were either families or several men living in each of its eighteen rooms. There were five toilets in the backyard and no indoor plumbing. Pitchers of water were brought into the room by the boarders to wash themselves, and sometimes several people used the same water. Most of the rooms had oil lamps, although a few had gas lights. The result of these unsanitary conditions was that diseases such as tuberculosis and pneumonia were rampant.

(Cohen 1990, 3)

Apparently six months in an American workers' neighborhood were enough "to transform the strong young man from Calabria, the stocky Sicilian fisherman, and the vigorous women from Abruzzo and Lucania into the weak, sickly, and ricketed creatures we see in the New York and Chicago streets" (BEI 1905, 30). According to a survey on Johnstown, Pennsylvania, the rate of mortality rose with the overcrowding in housing conditions (Davis 1921, 83). Too many people living in one room increased the chances of infection, while the lack of sanitary services, mainly water supply, made it impossible for them to clean themselves and the environment. With the authority coming from its official status, the Dillingham Commission stated that thousands of immigrants had become sick in the US under unusual conditions of climate, food or hazardous working (Dillingham 1911, 24). Several records confirmed the immigrant tendency to respiratory diseases. In Lowell, Massachussets, the Greek community was so affected by tuberculosis that in 1906 the Board of Health printed a notice for the Greek section of the city, stating the causes of illness and the means of its prevention (Fairchild 1911, 145). The statistical data are unable to give an exact count of the spread of tuberculosis and other diseases among Italian immigrants because, as Dr. Stella remarked, once sick, they preferred to go back to Italy. Of 81,412 Italians returning to Italy in 1906, about 450 were affected by advanced stage tuberculosis (Stella's data, in Davis 1921, 55).

Housing conditions were just part of the problem. Actually, for immigrants working was a dangerous task. Exploited in the factories and farms, immigrants mixed their bodies with their work, paying a high price to the capitalistic discipline of labor. One of the first workers interviewed by the pioneer founder of occupational health, Alice Hamilton, was V.O., an Italian immigrant; the fact that he was an Italian was central to his experience of factory hazards, performing the worst job and with minimal English incapable of understanding what he was doing (Kraut 1994, 176). Jacob Riis quoted the case of the Boemian workers who became sick inhaling tobacco fumes in cigarette factories (Riis 1890, 139). Outside of factories, immigrants still needed to deal with highly risky jobs. Mines, of course, were graves for so many of them. The historian David M. Emmons has studied the health hazards in the Irish mining community of Butte, Montana, recording a rate of fatalities five times higher than that of Czarist Russia in the same period (1896–1906) (Emmons 1998). Historian Thomas Andrews has uncovered the permanent state of danger in which immigrant miners worked in the coalfields of Colorado (Andrews 2010).

Other kinds of occupations could also be fatal for immigrants. Clearly, comparing rural life, supposedly safe and healthy, to the urban environment, evil and sick, was just a rhetorical expedient, useful more to weaken the social force of the town workers than to improve their living conditions. Indeed, working on the land was anything but safe or healthy. Apart from malaria and other diseases, more prevalent in the countryside than in the city, working in the field could also be a dangerous task. The forests were called widow makers because of the high percentage of death accidents linked to lumbering (Gage 1951, 87). Even the Mediterranean landscape of a California lemon plantation could hide a bitter reality; as Alamillo describes in his book, the Mexican laborers "experienced frostbitten hands, gas poisoning from chemical and pesticides, sprained backs and broken arms from ladder falls and a host of other injuries" (Alamillo 2006, 40). As well known, the impact of pesticides on farm workers became crucial from the 1960s onwards, and especially in the 1980s, launching a protest campaign led by the union leader Cesar Chavez and United Farm Workers who were able to bridge consumers and producers in a campaign for the safety of both (Gottlieb 2005, 313–317; Pawel 2009; Bruns 2011).

Indeed, the immigrants' environment cannot be understood only as an ecological fact; rather it has to be seen as a political ecological fact. The theme of an environmental history of migrations is not the plain meeting of immigrants with new environments, but the moving of people who entered the ecologies of labor, exploitation, and resistance. Pesticides were not a natural feature of California's fields to which immigrants had to adapt; pesticides were part of the capitalistic ecology organizing people and nature for the enrichment of the few. Immigrants were part of that ecology, suffering from its injustice, but also resisting and shaping it, as for instance in their boycott of grapes, which revolutionarily bridged the space between production and consumption in one ecology of safety for all.

As in the fields, so in the factories immigrants blended their bodies with the capitalistic ecologies of transformation of nature, production of goods, and exploitation of labor. The sweatshop has not always been included among the classic environmental history places of exploration; the effects of factories on the environment may be themes for urban environmental historians, much more than the factories per se. In this sense, an environmental history of migrations should converge with those lines of research stressing the centrality of work and workers' experience in the understanding of socio-ecologies, especially of the capitalist one (Barca 2014; Sellers 1997; Montrie 2008).

On 25th March 1911 a huge fire started at the Triangle Shirtwaist Factory in New York.[4] 146 garment workers were killed; the youngest was 14, the oldest 45. The fire doors were all locked because the owners of the factory wanted to avoid petty theft from the workers. A firefighter who arrived at the fire location during the disaster said in court: "The first thing I saw was a man's body crashing down. The bodies were hitting all around us." Just a year before the fire, the garment workers were on strike; many of them went to jail and their working conditions did not improve. Instead nobody went to jail for the death of 146 workers. At the trial the jury found the owners of the factory not guilty. Most of the victims were immigrants, many Italians. The fact that they were mostly immigrants was not an accident; it was a structural part of the ecology of that capitalistic organization of production. An environmental history of migrations should look into the ashes of the Triangle Shirtwaist Factory, with the doors closed to protect private property, workers trapped inside, and bodies hitting the streets of New York City. That is also an ecology of migration.

Conclusion

Working on the environmental history of mass migrations might reassemble the work of archaeologists. In both cases, the researcher is engaged in an excavation aiming to uncover what has been buried under layers of past epochs. However, when studying the landscape of migrations those layers are not so much disposed in strata but intertwined and blended the one with the other. They might look like the strange mix of Roman ruins and new buildings so common in many Italian cities. In this sense the metaphor of the excavation might not work so well. While it does deliver the idea of making visible what has been hidden, it also implies a well delimited succession of strata which does not correspond to the reality of the hybrid landscapes created by immigrants. Actually, individuating an Italian, Chinese, or Serbian landscape might contradict the whole point of thinking in terms of metabolic relationships and socionatures. How much were the vineyards Italian in California, in the face of the Phylloxera bio-invasion, of the challenges coming from local soil and Russian River, or of the work of the Mexican laborers who prepared the land? Or how much was an immigrant landscape the coalfields of Colorado and Pennsylvania, where the hard work of miners, mostly immigrants, capital investments and interests, energy policies and technological shifts shaped the land and the bodies of people working and living there? The same could be asked of the urban environment where the marks of various ethnic communities—Little Italies or Chinatowns, for instance—spoke at the same time of immigrants' agency in the city and their metabolic relationships with broader dynamics of urban political ecology such as land rent, zoning, and gentrification. More than sealed layers in a succession, it seems a bricolage where what matters is the relationship among pieces, even more than the figure obtained through the assemblage. And, of course, the power and the resistance at play in the very making of that bricolaged landscape.

Maybe the best metaphor to describe the kind of work the environmental history of migrations should do comes from the experimental volume produced by Pulido, Barraclough, and Cheng, *A People's Guide to Los Angeles* (2012). In the introduction they propose the image of the haunted landscape to describe the hybrid blend of invisible presences which peopled the places we live in: "Los Angeles is filled with ghosts—not only of people, but also of places and buildings and the ordinary and extraordinary events that once filled them" (2012, 4). This metaphor of the ghosts gives back the sense of the immigrants' presence/absence into the landscape. As those ghosts, immigrants haunt the landscapes where they settled with traces which are embodied in the place even when they are completely gone. Many times those traces are stories, because ghosts' stories are what actually haunt the places.

The immigrants I presented in this chapter haunt the US landscapes as ghosts. Their presence is in the shapes of the California farmlands, embedded into the energy systems fuelling the industrial and post industrial societies, cooked with food, inscribed in the urban texture, mixed with blood, dust, and sick cells in the bodyscapes of exposures and exploitation which are also part of that history. The figure of the ghost can also help us to overcome binary opposition between culture and nature or material and immaterial. Immigrants literally built the environment where they settled, making soil out of waste but also understanding the environment around them in ways that no one had done before. An environmental history of migrations and migrants should make peace with the fact that the environmental and the social are never apart. With the right jargon, one might say that they are mutually constituted in socionature formations. But I prefer to say that they haunt each other, never leaving a place, a story, a landscape, a body alone.

Acknowledgments

Research for this paper has received funding from the European Union's Horizon 2020 research and innovation programme, under grant agreement No. 700385 CLISEL, and by the Swiss State Secretariat for Education, Research and Innovation (SERI) under contract number 16.0038. It has also benefited from ITN Marie Curie Program Enhance, grant agreement No. 642935.

Notes

1 The Ingalls embodied the prototype of the pioneers' tale in the book series *Little House on the Prairie*, written by Laura Ingalls Wilder, and popularized around the world by the NBC television series of the same name.
2 A history of the Italian wine making industry in California can be found in Cinotto 2012.
3 The so-called "Dillingham Commission" was a special committee of the US Congress created with the purpose of studying the causes and effects of immigration in the United States. The committee operated from 1907 to 1911 and was instrumental in promoting restrictive policies, especially in relation to Southern European immigrants.
4 The information and quotes about the Triangle Shirtwaist Factory fire are from http://trianglefire.ilr.cornell.edu/story/introduction.html.

References

Alamillo, J.M. 2006 *Making lemonade out of lemons. Mexican American labor and leisure in a California town 1880–1960*, University of Illinois Press, Chicago
Allen Dimock, L. 1913 *Comrades from other lands. What they are doing for us and what we are doing for them*, Fleming H. Revell Co, New York

Andrews, T.G. 2010 *Killing for coal: America's deadliest labor war*, Harvard University Press, Cambridge

Barca, S. 2014 Laboring the earth: transnational reflections on the environmental history of work, *Environmental History* 19.1: 3–27

Baiamonte, J.V. Jr. 1990 *Immigrant in rural America. A study of Italians of Tangipahoa Parish, Louisiana*, Garland Publishing, New York

Bernardy, A. 1913 *Italia randagia attraverso gli Stati Uniti*, F. Bocca, Turin

Bollettino dell'emigrazione italiana (BEI) 4 1904 La colonizzazione agricola negli Stati Uniti in rapporto all'immigrazione italiana. Relazione del Prof. A. Ravaioli addetto commerciale a Washington

BEI 17 1905 Gli Italiani nel distretto consolare di Nuova Orleans. Relazione del Regio Console Cavalier Fara Forni

BEI 20 1905 Notizie sul servizio sanitario di bordo delle navi addette al trasporto degli emigranti durante l'anno 1904. Relazione del tenente colonnello medico della Regia Marina Cavaliere Ufficiale dottore A. Montano

BEI 13 1910 Avvertimenti e consigli per gli immigrati italiani negli Stati Uniti

Bruley, S. 2010 *The women and men of 1926: a gender and social history of the General Strike and Miners' Lockout in South Wales*, University of Wales Press, Cardiff

Bruns, R. 2011 *Cesar Chavez and the United Farm Workers Movement*, Santa Barbara, ABC-CLIO

Cancilla Martellini, P. no date An urban village in San Francisco. Unpublished. Deposited at the Italian American collection, San Francisco Public Library

Canonici, P.V. 2003 *The Delta Italians: their pursuit of "the better life" and their struggle against mosquitos, floods, and prejudice*, P.V. Canonici, Madison, Mississippi

Chiang, C.Y. 2009 *Shaping the shoreline: Fisheries and tourism on the Monterey coast*, University of Washington Press, Seattle

Cinotto, S. 2012 *Soft soil, black grapes: the birth of Italian winemaking in California*, New York University Press, New York

Coates, P. 2006 *American perceptions of immigrant and invasive species: strangers on the land*, University of California Press, Berkeley and Los Angeles

Cohen, D. S. (ed.) 1990 *America, the dream of my life: selections from the Federal Writers' Project's New Jersey Ethnic Survey*, Rutgers University Press, New Brunswick

D'Amico, R.A. 1986 La comunità italiana di Guasti: esempio di una felice integrazione nella società americana. Unpublished thesis submitted in partial satisfaction of the requirements for the degree of master of arts in Italian, University of California, Los Angeles

Davis, M.M. 1921 *Immigrant health and the community*, Harper and Brothers, New York

Dillingham Commission or United States Immigration Commission 1911 Brief Statement of the Immigration Commission with Conclusions and Recommendations and Views of the Minority, Washington, D.C., USA: Government Printing Office, available at http://site.ebrary.com/lib/stanfordimmigrationdillingham/Doc?id=10006604&ppg=11, last accessed on 3rd January 2016

Dyl, J.L. 2006 "The war on rats vs.the right to keep chickens: plague and the paving of San Francisco, 1907–1908" in Isenberg, A.C. (ed.) *The nature of cities*, University of Rochester Press, New York, 38–61

Emmons, D.M. 1998 "Safe and steady work: The Irish and the hazards of Butte" in Luebcke, F.C. (ed.) *European immigrants in the American West*, University of New Mexico Press, Albuquerque, 91–107

Fairchild, H.P. 1911 *Greek immigration to the United States*, Yale University Press, New Haven

Fichera, S. 1981 The meaning of community: a history of Italians of San Francisco. Unpublished PhD dissertation, Department of History, University of California, Los Angeles

Fisher, C. 2015 *Urban green: nature, recreation, and the working class in industrial Chicago*, University of North Carolina Press, Chapel Hill

Florence, J.W. Sr. 1999 *Legacy of a village. The Italian Swiss Colony winery and people of Asti*, Raymond Court Press, Phoenix

Fogg Meade, E. 1909 "Gli Italiani nell'agricoltura" in Sheridan, F.J. and Colajanni N. (eds) *Gl'Italiani negli Stati Uniti*, Biblioteca della Rivista popolare, Roma

Gage, J.H. 1951 *The Beckoning Hill,* The John C. Wiston Company, Philadelphia

Giordano, P.A. 1979 *The Italians of Louisiana: their cultural background and their many contributions in the field of literature, the arts, education, politics, and business and labor*, University Microfilms International, Ann Arbor, Michigan

Glazer, N. and Moynihan, D.P. 1963 *Beyond the melting pot; the Negroes, Puerto Ricans, Jews, Italians, and Irish of New York City*, MIT, Cambridge

Goddard, F.B. 1869 *Where to emigrate and why*, The People Publishing Company, Philadelphia

Gottlieb, R. 2005 *Forcing the spring: the transformation of the American environmental movement*, Island Press, Washington, D.C.

Gumina, D. Paoli 1978 *The Italians of San Francisco 1850–1930*, The Center for Migration Studies, Staten Island, New York

Hartmann, B. 2010 Greenwash: nativists, environmentalism and the hypocrisy of hate, Southern Poverty Law Center, available at *http://climateandcapitalism. com/2010/08/31/the-greening-of-hate-an-environmentalists-essay/*, last accessed 3rd January 2017

Hine, R.V. and Faragher, J.M. 2000 *The American West. A new interpretative history*, Yale University Press, New Haven

Holmquist, J.D., Stipanovich, J., and Moss, K. 1981 *The South Slavs: Bulgarians, Croatians, Montenegrins, Serbs, and Slovenes*, Minnesota Historical Society Press, St. Paul

Iacovetta, F. 1987 Trying to Make Ends Meet: An Historical Look at Italian Immigrant Women, the State and Family Survival Strategies in Post-War Toronto, *Canadian Woman Studies* 8.2: 6–11.

Institute of Texan Cultures 1973 *The Italian Texans*, University of Texas at San Antonio, San Antonio

Klindienst, P. 2006 *The earth knows my name: food, culture, and sustainability in the gardens of ethnic Americans*, Beacon Press, Boston

Kraut, A. 1994 *Silent travelers: germs, genes, and the "immigrant menace,"* Basic Books, New York

Mangione, J. and Morreale, B. 1992 *La Storia: five centuries of the Italian American experience*, HarperCollins Publishers, New York

Martellini, A. 1999 *Fra Sunny Side e la Nueva Marca. Materiali e modelli per una nuova storia dell'emigrazione marchigiana fino alla Grande Guerra*, Franco Angeli, Milano

Mathias, E. and Raspa, R. 1985 *Italian folktales in America: the verbal art of an immigrant woman*, Wayne State University Press, Detroit

McWilliams, C. 1978 (1st edition 1935) *Factories in the field. The story of migratory farm labor in California*, Peregrine Smith Inc., Santa Barbara

Matsumoto, V. J. 1993 *Farming the home place. A Japanese American community in California 1919–1982*, Cornell University Press, Ithaca

Melosi, M. 2000 *The sanitary city: urban infrastructure in America from colonial times to the present*, John Hopkins University Press, Baltimore

Michigan State Board of Agriculture 1876 Fourteenth annual report of the secretary of the state board of agriculture of the state of Michigan for the year 1875. Lansing: W. S. George and C.

Minnick Sund, S. 1988 *Samfow. The San Joaquin Chinese legacy*, Panorama West Publishing, Fresno

Mitchell, D. 1996 *The lie of the land: Migrant workers and the California landscape*, University of Minnesota Press, Minneapolis

Montrie, C. 2008 *Making a living: work and environment in the United States*, University of North Carolina Press, Chapel Hill

Nash, L. 2006 *Inescapable ecologies: a history of environment, disease, and knowledge*, University of California Press, Berkeley and Los Angeles

Nicosia, F.M. 1960 *Italian pioneers in California*, Italian American Chamber of Commerce of the Pacific Coast, San Francisco

O'Connor, J.R. 1998 *Natural causes: Essays in ecological Marxism*, Guilford Press, New York

Park, L. S-H. and Pellow, D.N. 2011 *The slums of Aspen: immigrants vs. the environment in America's eden*, New York University Press, New York

Pawel, M. 2009 *The union of their dreams: power, hope, and struggle in Cesar Chavez's farm worker movement*, Bloomsbury Press, New York

Pedemonte, T.A. 1971 Italy in San Francisco: "Old Wine in New Bottles." Unpublished Thesis (M.A. in History), California State College

Pulido, L., Barraclough, L.R. and Cheng, W. 2012 *A people's guide to Los Angeles*, University of California Press, Berkeley and Los Angeles

Riis, J. 1890 *How the other half lives*, Charles Scribner's Sons, New York

Rome, A. 2008 Nature wars, culture wars: immigration and environmental reform in the Progressive Era, *Environmental History* 13.3: 432–453.

Rossati, G. 1900 *Relazione di un viaggio d'istruzione negli Stati Uniti d'America fatto per incarico del Ministero*, Tip nazionale G. Bertero, Roma

Sellers, C.C. 1997 *Hazards of the job: From industrial disease to environmental health science*, University of North Carolina Press, Chapel Hill

Siciliani, D. 1922 *Fra gli Italiani degli Stati Uniti d'America. Luglio Settembre 1921*, Stabilimento Tipografico per l'Amministrazione della Guerra, Roma

Smith, J.R. 1913 *Industrial and commercial geography*, H. Holt and Co, New York

Steinberg, T. 2002 Down to earth: nature, agency, and power in history, *The American Historical Review* 107.3: 798–820

Taylor, D.A. and Williams, J.A. 1992 *Old ties, new attachments: Italian American folklife in the West*, Library of Congress, Washington D.C.

Transaction of the Commonwealth Club of California 1917, vol. xi, San Francisco

Valenčius, C.B. 2002 *The health of the country. How American settlers understood themselves and their land*, Basic Books, New York

Vecoli, R.J. 1986 The formation of Chicago's Little Italies, in Glazier, I.A. and De Rosa, L. (eds) *Migration across time and nations. Population mobility in historical contexts*, New York, Holmes and Meier

Warren, L.S. 1997 *The hunter's game: poachers and conservationists in twentieth-century America*, Yale University Press, New Haven

Whayne, J.M. 1993 *Shadows over Sunnyside: an Arkansas plantation in transition, 1830– 1945*, University of Arkansas Press, Fayetteville

4 Making the land Russian?

Migration, settlement, and environment in the Russian Far East, 1860–1914

Mark Sokolsky

Abstract

This chapter examines migration to the Russian province known as Primor'e between 1860 and the First World War in the context of the Great Siberian Migration, the late-nineteenth century movement of Russians and other peoples from the European part of the tsarist empire to the east. It contends that Russian settlement of Primor'e was not an instance of "ecological imperialism," nor did it involve the easy transfer of biota between ecologically similar regions. Russian subjects populated the territory despite significant ecological barriers, due mainly to their flexibility and interdependence with migrants from China and Korea.

Introduction

Many scholars are familiar with the emigration of millions of Russian subjects from the tsarist empire to the Americas during the late nineteenth and early twentieth centuries. Less well known is what historians have called the "Great Siberian Migration," the movement of some 5.5 million people, mostly peasants, from European Russia to Siberia and the Russian Far East during the half-century before the First World War.[1] Russian peasants, particularly those native to northern Russia, had over the course of the seventeenth through mid-nineteenth centuries trickled into the Urals, western Siberia, and the fertile foothills of the Altai Mountains. After the emancipation of Russia's serfs (1861) and state peasants (1866) migration to the east became more frequent. Finally, with the advent of direct state assistance for migrants and the construction of the Trans-Siberian railroad, migrants flooded to the east, with most traveling between 1905 and 1914 (Coquin 1969; Marks 1991; Treadgold 1957).

This chapter examines one part of this broader eastward movement, focusing on the territory known today as *Primorskii krai* (the Maritime Territory), or simply Primor'e, between 1860 and 1914. Primor'e, centered around the port city of Vladivostok, was one of the principal destinations of migrants to the Far East during the late tsarist era. It was also one of the most unusual; although contiguous with the rest of Russian territory, the region was—and remains—environmentally quite distinct. Its climate has a more moderate, maritime character than elsewhere in Siberia and the Far East, and is strongly influenced by the East Asian monsoon. As a result, the majority of the region's precipitation falls during the summer months, while winters are dry and cold. Its flora and fauna are a unique amalgam of boreal (northern) and temperate species. Thus, pine, larch, cedar, and fir trees grow alongside Manchuria oak, cork trees, and wild grapes; elk, moose, sable, and brown bears share the region (though not necessarily the same habitat) with sika (spotted) deer, raccoon dogs, Himalayan black bears, Amur tigers, and leopards. Primor'e's waters also contain a great diversity of organisms, including chum and pink salmon, sturgeon, sea cucumbers, and various mollusks. In addition, its main river, the Ussuri, as well as its largest internal waterbody, Lake Khanka (see Figure 4.1), serve as stopping points for thousands of migratory birds. One early twentieth century visitor, observing the bewildering mixing of wildlife in the region, called it "either a riddle or a joke of nature" (Ossendowski 1924, 93).

Given Primor'e's temperate climate and abundance of natural riches, Russian officials were initially optimistic about the prospects for settlement and economic development (particularly agriculture) in the territory, and even spoke of "making the territory Russian": populating Primor'e with peasants and Cossacks, and making the land more cultivable and habitable. The result, however, was considerably more complex. Instead of making Primor'e Russian, migration to the territory resulted in a kind of ecological and economic compromise in which Russian settlers were forced to adapt to local conditions and become interdependent with Chinese and Koreans, who migrated to the territory in smaller but significant numbers at the same time.[2]

Alfred Crosby has called Siberia a "neo-Europe manqué," because although colonized at roughly the same time as the Americas, is was ecologically very similar to the rest of Eurasia; only a difficult climate, he argues, impeded the movement of Neolithic crops, livestock, and peoples (Crosby 1986, 36–39). Primor'e was certainly not a world apart; its environment was not utterly alien to migrants from Russia and Ukraine. However, it was different enough to impede the transfer of biota from west to east, and not simply because it was too cold. Migrants from Russia and Ukraine encountered major environmental hurdles in Primor'e, challenging their ability to import crops, livestock, and forms of cultivation. They enjoyed epidemiological advantages vis-à-vis the indigenous peoples, but their livestock suffered from zoonotic diseases imported from Chinese Manchuria and Korea. Migration did not result in a replication of the agricultural lifeways of European Russia, nor did it mean a wholesale remaking of Primor'e's ecosystems.

Nevertheless, Slavic settlers made do. They adapted to the new territory, modified their household economies to be less dependent on farming, and became economically interdependent with their East Asian migrants. Instead of Russian dominance, the result was a complex mix of peoples, cultures, and economic relations. Together, migrants from Russia, China, and Korea

Figure 4.1 The Russian Far East in 1860

Source: Adapted from Kimitaka Matsuzato, "The Creation of the Priamur Governor-Generalship in 1884 and the Reconfiguration of Asiatic Russia," *Russian Review* 71, no. 3 (July 2012), 367. (Used with author's permission.)

changed Primor'e's landscapes in many ways, but the territory did not come to closely resemble the villages of Ukraine and European Russia. The success of Russian and Ukrainian settlers owed much to negotiation, flexibility, and interdependence with East Asian migrants, not ecological imperialism or intentional manipulation of the landscape.

Migration to Primor'e: an overview

Russia acquired Primor'e through the Treaty of Peking in 1860. In 1858, in the face of Russian and European encroachment, Qing China had granted Russia the lands along the upper Amur River, together with the north bank of the Amur below the Ussuri River (see Figure 4.1). The area south of the Amur and east of the Ussuri—known as the South-Ussuri region or Primor'e—was to be a joint Russo-Chinese possession. By 1860, however, Russian diplomats had secured this region as well (Paine 1996; Stephan 1994; Vlasov 2005). At the time, there were only a handful of Chinese subjects in Primor'e, in large part because the Qing government had restricted migration to the northeast to preserve its cultural heritage. In addition, there were perhaps an estimated 9,000 to 11,000 indigenous people—the Nanai, Udeghe, Nivkhi, and Ul'chi—living in the territory. Though independent, these peoples had long-standing cultural and economic ties to Beijing, and Chinese influence remained strong even after Russian annexation (Lee 1970; Paine 1996; Reardon-Anderson 2005).

To secure the territory, Russian officials sought to direct settlers to Primor'e. Even before Russia acquired the territory, the Governor-General of Eastern Siberia, Nikolai Murav'ev, implanted peasants and Cossacks in the Amur valley and Ussuri valleys. His successor, M.S. Korsakov, believed that holding the new territories would only be possible when the military could "rely on the population," and gain ready access to "manpower [and] provisions"; Korsakov and other officials immediately began to encourage settlement to this end.[3] Because of its relatively mild climate, Primor'e seemed well-suited to agricultural settlement. Rear Admiral Kazakevich, the first military governor of the territory, believed that the Far East could be made Russian only "through its settlement by native Russian farmers," who could turn its wilds into the "granary [*zhitnitsa*] of the whole region."[4] Other travelers in the Far East enthused that even on this distant periphery, the humble Russian peasant would "make Russia" (Aliab'ev 1872, 88; Przheval'skii 1947, 70).

Russian settlers—many of whom were Ukrainian—came in three increasingly large waves. Because of the strategic importance of populating Primor'e, the tsarist government offered numerous incentives to would-be settlers, including subsidized transportation, land allotments, and temporary exemption from military service and some taxes. The first wave, between 1860 and 1882, was largely comprised of peasants traveling overland from Siberia, many of them religious dissidents. In total, about 17,800 Russian subjects settled in the Maritime *oblast'* (which included the entire Pacific littoral, along with Primor'e) during the first two decades after annexation (see Figure 4.1). Because of the slow pace of settlement, beginning in 1882 the state began to fund sea transportation between Odessa and Vladivostok. As a result, between 1882 and 1907, nearly 100,000 settlers from Ukraine and southern Russia migrated to Primor'e by sea. Finally, the Trans-Siberian and Chinese Eastern Railroads facilitated another burst of settlement, bringing an additional 164,000 migrants between 1907 and 1917, more than tripling Primor'e's population, which reached 485, 735 inhabitants by 1914 (Kabuzan 1998, 1985; Stephan 1994; Vashchuk et al. 2002).

Russian settlement occurred alongside migration from neighboring China and Korea. There were probably between 1,000 and 3,000 Chinese subjects living permanently in Primor'e in 1860 (Kabuzan 1973, 51). In addition, tens of thousands of Chinese hunters, trappers, and foragers traveled to the province seasonally to collect furs, deer antlers, ginseng, mushrooms, seaweed, and numerous other products. According to the empire's first full census (in 1897) there were roughly 38,144 Chinese, Korean, and Japanese subjects in Primor'e, but estimates for the total number of non-subjects from neighboring countries vary a great deal. One Chinese source put the population of their co-nationals in Primor'e at 20,000 already in 1885, while Russian estimates were closer to 13,000 (Lee 1970, 90; Sorokina 1999, 29–37). Russian government statistics in 1910 assessed the total foreign population (including temporary workers) in Amur and Maritime *oblasts* at 133,500, while unofficial estimates were much higher (Babrenko 2003; Pozniak 2006, 50; Vashchuk et al. 2002, 12). Ironically, given Russian concerns, the Qing began to encourage settlement of Manchuria in large part because of Russian encroachment. The relaxation of migration restrictions in China, combined with a high demand for labor in the new Russian territories, led to the rapid increase of Chinese in Manchuria and, indirectly, in Primor'e (Paine 1996, 10–12).

Koreans also migrated to Primor'e, beginning in 1864. Russian authorities initially welcomed Koreans, who they believed would be productive agriculturalists and loyal subjects. Koreans received land, tax exemptions, and Russian subjecthood (if they arrived before 1884). During the 1860s and 1870s, many settled near Primor'e's southern border, while others moved north toward Lake Khanka. In some parts of southern Primor'e, Koreans formed the majority of the rural population in the 1870s and 1880s. In the early 1900s, they too migrated to the territory on a temporary basis as laborers; in 1914, there were an estimated 61,000 in the Maritime *oblast'*, many of them in Primor'e (Babrenko 2003; Kim 2013; Petrov 2001, 163; Vlasov 2005). Thus, while Russians and Ukrainians constituted the bulk of migrants to Primor'e during the late tsarist era, they came to inhabit a space that was very ethnically and culturally diverse.

Typhoons, bugs, and tigers

Slavic settlers, particularly those who originated in the dry steppe and forest-steppe regions of southern Russia and Ukraine, encountered a number of difficulties in establishing new lives in Primor'e's unique environment. Winters were cold and dry, with little snow cover to insulate seeds planted in the autumn. Monsoon winds and late-summer typhoons brought heavy rains, fog, and humidity that frequently ruined crops and, in some cases, threatened life and limb. In addition, wild animals, insects, and zoonotic diseases complicated the task of raising livestock. Though these challenges were not insurmountable, they did slow the development of agriculture among Cossacks and peasant settlers, whose biological portmanteau offered few advantages in the new territory.

In Ukraine and European Russia, both peasants and Cossacks generally relied on a handful of grains for the bulk of their caloric intake: rye, spring and winter wheat, oats, barley, buckwheat, and potatoes. Most supplemented this with vegetables grown in kitchen gardens, along with fruit, dairy products, and occasionally meat. Those living in more southerly latitudes might also grow melons, pumpkins, and other heat-tolerant plants. Foods acquired through fishing and foraging, such as mushrooms and berries, were also an essential part of peasant livelihoods. In addition, most households kept a small number of livestock (mainly horses, cattle, chickens, and pigs), which were one of the few ways Russian and Ukrainian peasants accumulated wealth (Moon 2000, 1999; Pallot and Shaw 1990; Robinson 1949).

Although traditional Russian crops and livestock fared quite well in much of southern Siberia, adapting them to Primor'e proved more difficult. Primor'e's mountainous topography, rocky soils, and—most of all—its dampness complicated the introduction of Russian-style grain farming. Foggy springs and humid summers encouraged the growth of fungi, which damaged crops adapted to dryer conditions. From the 1860s on, peasants and Cossacks complained of "drunken grain," a form of stem rust that spoiled the harvest and led to widespread illness (not drunkenness). According to peasants in affected villages, "drunken grain" was a nearly annual occurrence.[5] Sergei Khudiakov, the grandson of settlers who had come to Primor'e from Siberia in the 1870s, wrote that the fungus frequently rendered their wheat inedible for either people or animals (Khudiakov 1989, 40).

Flooding, usually a result of late-summer typhoons, was probably the greatest hazard. In the 1860s, floods struck some of the earliest settlements in the Amur and Ussuri valleys and along Primor'e's southeastern coast, washing away crops and livestock and killing many settlers. In 1868, the head of the military post at St. Olga Bay, northeast of Vladivostok, reported that as a result of "nearly continuous rains for half a month and driving, tropical downpours," floods had swept through a nearby valley, destroying settlements and killing a number of peasants.[6] In the marshy plain around Lake Khanka, one village was forced to relocate its fields 24 kilometers away from their original settlement after repeated inundations (Aliab'ev 1872, 89–90). Along the Ussuri, flooding washed away houses in 1861, 1863, 1872, and 1879, even those that stood on relatively high ground (Timonov 1897, 85). Disastrous flooding continued into the early twentieth century, incurring heavy losses, necessitating state assistance to settlers, and driving many newcomers from Primor'e altogether. In 1909, a third of all migrants who abandoned the Far East cited rain, floods, and difficulty working the soil as their main reasons for leaving.[7]

Besides rains and humidity, a more exotic hazard lurked in the forest: Amur tigers. Though attacks on humans were rare, tigers frequently killed livestock, which were in short supply in Primor'e during the early years of settlement. Stories of tigers rampaging through villages were legion in reporting on the territory. According to one account, in 1869 a tiger killed 22 head of cattle and horses in a single village. Dogs were also a frequent target; one village reportedly lost 25 dogs in 1866 alone (Aliab'ev 1872, 77; Atkinson 1860, 375–376). Michael Iankovskii, a Polish exile who eventually became known as an expert tiger hunter, claimed that in his first 15 years in Primor'e he lost over 50 horses to tigers, along with dozens of dogs, pigs, and smaller livestock (Yankovsky 2007, 10). One finds less fantastic but basically similar accounts in state records.

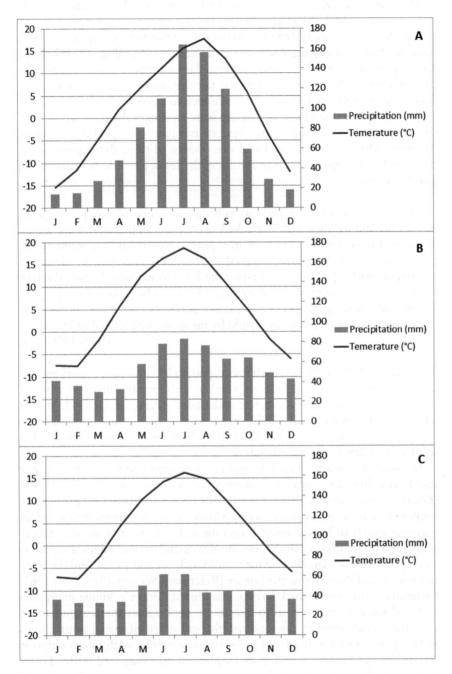

Figure 4.2 Average monthly precipitation and temperatures in Vladivostok (A), Tver' (northeastern Russia) (B), and Kharkhov (eastern Ukraine) (C)

Source: Pogoda i klimat, 2016

In 1869, for instance, a local official in the Lake Khanka district, the curiously named Captain Melville (*Mel'vill'*), wrote his superiors requesting shot and powder for local peasants, who needed to defend themselves against a (white?) tiger that had been making frequent appearances in their village.[8] Similarly, in 1878 a peasant on the lower Amur requested permission to move his family to the neighboring Amur *oblast'*, citing the fact that, besides damage inflicted by floods and drought, he had lost all his livestock to tigers.[9]

A more prosaic but ubiquitous hazard were swarms of flying insects, collectively known as *gnus*, which were a general nuisance and especially dangerous to horses. One of the most colorful descriptions of these flying pests comes from the first European visitor to Primor'e, the Jesuit priest de la Brunière. Of *gnus* he wrote:

> I have not words to express to you the multitude of mosquitos, gnats, wasps, and gadflies which attacked us at every step. Each of us, armed with a horse's tail fixed on an iron prong, endeavoured to strike them, and this weak defence only served to render the enemy more vicious in his attacks [...] if, at times, I raised my hand to my face, I crushed ten or twelve with one blow. Two wretched horses, which carried the baggage and occasionally our persons, lay down panting in the midst of the grass, refusing to eat or drink, and could by no means be induced to march.
>
> (James 1888, 425)

The explorer Nikolai Przheval'skii found *gnus* no less irritating, remarking that the "mosquitoes, flies, and gadflies [were] in such quantity that one who has not seen it with his own eyes cannot understand" (Przheval'skii 1947, 56). As a result of these insects, what little horse-breeding did occur in Primor'e was confined to the shoreline, where sea breezes kept insects at bay, though cattle seem to have fared somewhat better.

Because of shortages, Cossacks and peasants imported horses from China and Korea, but these small breeds often carried diseases across the border (*Obzor po konnozavodstu* 1911). Zoonotic diseases exacerbated the problem of keeping livestock, particularly among Cossacks, whose duties demanded an adequate supply of horses. Insect bites caused infections, and diseases such as hoof-and-mouth disease, rinderpest, anthrax, glanders, and rabies were common. These diseases largely originated in Manchuria and Korea, and the trade in cattle spread them across the border (Veterinary Section 1913).[10] In 1883, for instance, rinderpest struck livestock in central Primor'e, killing many animals and forcing veterinarians to quarantine or slaughter the remainder.[11] A veterinarian employed by the local resettlement office estimated annual losses at 11.4 percent (3,420 head) for the *oblast'* as a whole, with rates as high as 30 percent in some areas, and in many places deaths outpaced births. Losses to zoonotic diseases were not always devastating, but even minor losses could exacerbate poverty among migrants. As one local official observed, the loss of a single horse or oxen could be disastrous to new settlers.[12] Vulnerability to zoonotic diseases was one of several ways in which Russians' biota fared poorly in Primor'e.

To be sure, epidemic human diseases did contribute to a decline in the population of Primor'e's indigenous peoples, the Nanai, Udeghe, Nivkhi, and Ul'chi. Their numbers fell rapidly after 1860 and only began to recover in the early 1900s (Startsev 2005). While the decrease in indigenous populations bears resemblance to the fate of colonized peoples elsewhere in the world, it did not greatly facilitate the influx of migrants. Russian and Ukrainian colonists seldom competed with indigenous peoples for land, nor did they enjoy preferential treatment from the imperial state, which was quite concerned with protecting indigenous peoples (especially from Chinese traders) (Startsev 2005; Stolberg 2004).

As a result of these various difficulties, peasants and Cossacks had a difficult time adapting their traditional crops and agricultural practices to Primor'e. The Ussuri Cossacks, among the first to settle in the territory, were dismally poor throughout the 1860s and 1870s, and managed to survive only because of emergency grain supplies from the army. The explorer Nikolai Przheval'skii wrote that in Cossack settlements grain grew well in the spring, "and it brings joy to the heart," but "in summer either water floods it or rain crushes it, or worms eat it, and you barely collect anything for all your labor" (Przheval'skii 1947, 44). Cossack settlers had been assigned lands in areas vulnerable to summer flooding, leading to the destruction of crops, hayfields, and livestock. Even without flooding, agricultural output was low. According to the battalion commander, yields ranged from 3:1 for winter rye to less than 1:1 for wheat and barley. Gains in one year might be upset by calamity the next; the 1876 harvest, for instance, was good, but in 1877 the commander again reported that his unit needed assistance, having lost crops and roughly a third of their hayfields to flooding, dampness, and parasites. Disease had also claimed many settlements' horses, while official duties had kept many Cossacks from their fields during the planting season.[13]

Peasants, for the most part concentrated around Lake Khanka and near Vladivostok, were generally more successful than the Cossacks, producing modest grain surpluses within a few years of settlement, despite having less land per person. However, winter wheat grew poorly, due to lack of snow cover in the winter, and most peasants abandoned the crop almost entirely. The share of rye in peasant diets also diminished. Although some crops, such as potatoes, fared quite well, others did not. One settler wrote in 1864 how Russian rye—a key crop in northern and central Russia—grew well initially but turned to straw under the influence of fog blowing off the sea, while there was simply "no hope for barley and wheat" (Agafonov 1995; Petrov 2003, 429). One resettlement official, A.A. Rittikh, wrote that Russians were simply unable to farm effectively in southern Primor'e due to excessive dampness.[14]

To be sure, barring flooding or some other catastrophe, Russian settlements could be fairly productive. In 1876, for example, a local peasant supervisor reported his district had produced roughly 1,820 tons of grain during the previous

Figure 4.3 Mixed forest, Shkotovo region, Primorskii Krai, Autumn 2013
Source: Author's photograph

year, yielding a 3:1 return not inferior to many areas of European Russia. In the 1890s, official statistics for the same region saw yields as high as 9:1 for many crops, albeit in an especially good year (Goncharova et al. 2009, 37–39, 102–103). Good local yields, however, did not necessarily translate into regional prosperity. In the 1870s, three-quarters of the grain requirements for the Maritime oblast' still came from Russian stores on the Baltic Sea. The situation was similar in the 1890s. Military units still imported much of their grain—some 6,200 tons over three years—from European Russia, along with 12,000 head of livestock, largely from Manchuria.[15] The region as a whole remained dependent on imported food throughout the tsarist era (and into the early Soviet period) (Mandel 1944).

Compromises, adaptations, and cooperation

Despite the many difficulties that Russian settlers faced in Primor'e, they adopted a number of strategies that enabled them to survive and even thrive in the unfamiliar environmental conditions. First, many diversified their house-hold economies. In a territory rich in fish, game, and other resources, with difficult access to markets, complete reliance on agriculture was unnecessary and often imprudent. Nearly all settlers hunted and fished to varying degrees, and many participated in the lucrative trade in forest products, such as ginseng and furs. Facing mediocre harvests, the Khudiakov family, for instance, supplemented their diet with other forms of sustenance, including fruit (which grew wild), boar, and deer. The eldest Khudiakov sons worked at a local lumber mill, where they were paid cash to supply workers with ducks and pheasants, and the family also sold deer antlers to local Chinese merchants. Although agricultural ventures did not always thrive, wage labor and hunting could fill the gap (Coquin 1969, 672–673; Khudiakov 1989, 36–44). While it may not have fed Primor'e's military garrisons, the peasants' approach probably yielded a more interesting and varied lifestyle than had they relied on grain-farming for subsistence.

Second, settlers quickly became economically interdependent with Korean and Chinese migrants, both those residing permanently in Primor'e and those who sojourned in the territory on a seasonal basis. In the nineteenth century, Cossacks and peasants relied on the Chinese for staples like millet, tea, and tobacco, trading fur, silver, crafts, and other items in exchange. There was also a bustling trade in alcohol and opium, imported from China, along the border. In addition, Koreans and Chinese supplied cities and military posts with produce from their gardens. Indeed, according to A.F. Fel'dgauzen, the military governor of Vladivostok (1880–1886), Chinese farmers supplied crops to the Vladivostok fortress itself (Kutuzov and Ivanov 2003, 45–47; Petrov 2003, 426).

While Slavic migrants achieved only middling gains in terms of agricultural productivity, East Asian migrants who took up farming thrived, producing far more per person (and per unit of land) than Russian and Ukrainian settlers. East Asians shared some crops with their Russian neighbors—such as potatoes and cabbage, for instance—while there were others (such as foxtail millet, corn, and soybeans) that they alone raised. Even those crops that all groups shared, however, tended to grow better on Chinese and Korean farms. Chinese wheat and millet, for instance, were better suited to Primor'e's cool, damp planting season than variants brought from Siberia or European Russia. The Chinese, accustomed to humidity and heavy summer rains, tended to plant their crops in raised beds, a labor-intensive method but one better able to protect seeds from rot and rain, and they were also careful to avoid areas prone to flooding (Petrov 2003, 427–428).

Strangely, Russian and Ukrainian migrants rarely adopted the methods of their East Asian neighbors. In the 1890s, the agronomist Nikolai Kriukov contrasted Russians' farms with those of local Koreans, observing that Korean farming methods were an "unattainable ideal for our peasants" (Kriukov 1893, 49). Observing colonists' failure to adapt to local conditions, one agronomist even spoke of the "Russian peasant's complete inability for colonization." It is possible that settlers adopted Chinese or Korean crops and methods, but if they did so they left little evidence of such experimentation (Coquin 1969, 671).

The experience of one Cossack family illustrates both the rarity of adopting East Asian agriculture and the potential returns in doing so. In 1898, a

Cossack officer named Savinskii and his family settled a plot of land in northern Primor'e. Initially, the Savinskii family relied on "Russian labor and Russian crops," but with a shortage of workers they began to hire Koreans, who introduced different crops and their system of planting in raised furrows with seed drills. In the early years of the Savinskii homestead, a small amount of arable precluded the possibility of fallowing, leading to soil depletion. They also had difficulty keeping livestock, particularly horses, sheep, and goats, which suffered from insects. However, according to Ol'ga Savinskaia, the introduction of "superior Asian crops" and methods had revolutionized the farm. Russian crops on virgin soil had produced yields of 7–8:1, whereas Asian crops regularly yielded an output of 20:1 or 30:1 for beans, or even more for foxtail millet. Some "European" crops, such as potatoes and buckwheat, grew well, Savinskaia said, while rye, wheat, and barley were more fickle. The Savinskiis combined Asian and European crops but relied exclusively on furrow-planting and the use of seed drills. Her family's experience seems to have been the exception that proved the rule: most settlers were reluctant or unwilling to follow the example of Primor'e's Chinese and Korean farmers (Savinskaia 1913).

There were good reasons for Russians' reluctance to take on new agricultural practices. First, Chinese and Korean methods were labor-intensive, requiring meticulous cultivation of raised furrows and constant weeding. As T.N. Sorokina has pointed out, Russian labor was worth more than twice that of East Asians'; adopting such methods would be a poor use of resources, particularly when other work (in forestry, fishing, or railroad construction, for instance) was available. Moreover, by the early 1900s, Manchurian grain was plentiful in Primor'e, dissuading settlers from growing surplus grain for the market (Sorokina 1999, 57–58).

Second, because Slavic migrants had privileged access to land, they could often rent their holdings to Chinese and Koreans. Only Koreans who could prove long-term residency could acquire the lands they worked as property. Russian and Ukrainian settlers, in contrast, were granted plots by the local branch of the Resettlement Administration, and in practice they often simply occupied the lands they wanted, even if East Asians or indigenous peoples were already living there (Babrenko 2003). As a result, it had become common practice by the early 1900s for Russian and Ukrainian peasants to lease part of their allotments to Chinese and Koreans. One study estimates that in some parts of Primor'e, 98 percent of the East Asian population rented land (Vashchuk et al. 2002, 40). Some Cossacks and long-time settlers were able to live solely off rents, like petty landowners, giving them time for other pursuits, such as hunting, fishing, logging, or, in the case of Cossacks, military service (Gluzdovskii 1917, 72; Kutuzov and Ivanov 2003, 46; Sorokina 1999, 58–60).

Even settlers who arrived after 1900, who had smaller land allotments, rented land to non-Russians. In February 1908, a tsarist official reported that in one village, new settlers wanted the local Chinese—recently evicted by state authorities—to stay because they had agreed to rent land.[16] These transactions did not produce written contracts, but observers found that Slavic settlers, with their near-monopoly on legitimate land-holding, could charge Chinese and Koreans twice as much as their compatriots (Gluzdovskii 1917, 82; Vashchuk et al. 2002, 40). It is a testament to the productivity of Chinese and Korean agriculturalists that they were able to pay such high rents while maintaining their own livelihood. Settlers also gave forested areas to Koreans rent-free on the condition that they undertook the backbreaking work of clearing and de-stumping the land. They could then farm the more easily worked soil themselves, or continue to lease it out (Petrov 2001, 161–162).

Another important source of income for Slavic settlers, particularly in the early 1900s, was opium. Contemporary accounts suggest that opium was widely cultivated in Primor'e by the end of the nineteenth century. Already in 1881, Vsevelod Krestovskii, who had served with the navy in the Far East, noted that the Chinese grew opium in Primor'e and observed that Russian peasants had also taken up the crop.[17] In 1887, an envoy from the Governor-General's chancellery found opium among Chinese in the Ulakhe Valley.[18] Because the opium trade was largely clandestine, it is difficult to estimate the scale of the trade, but it was likely very widespread by the First World War. One local official estimated in 1913 that in his small coastal district alone peasants rented 16,350 ha. to Chinese migrants, who in turn devoted about a fifth of this land to opium.

Attempts to halt opium production illustrated the close interdependence between Slavic settlers and their Chinese and Korean tenants. In May 1915, the Council of Ministers banned the planting, import, selling, and possession of opium; soon afterward Primor'e's foresters set about deporting Chinese and Koreans engaged in the trade, characterizing these groups as "depraved foreigners."[19] However, the law soon prompted local resistance. In June 1915, a Cossack woman petitioned the local administration, arguing that with her husband at the front, she had been forced to rent land to Chinese farmers, who planted opium because flooding had damaged the grain crop. She claimed that over 18,000 ha. of land in her district were sown with opium poppies, and that removing them would render her and her community destitute.[20]

Revolution, civil war, and foreign intervention precluded any further anti-opium campaigns for several years. The close interdependence of Slavic and East Asian migrants, however, continued throughout the revolutionary period and the 1920s, ending only with the forced deportation of Chinese and Korean populations in 1937–1938. Faced with the challenges of adapting agriculture to an unfamiliar environment, Russian migrants adopted a variety of strategies for making ends meet, even if this meant dependence on their non-Russian counterparts.

Conclusion

Primor'e's natural world presented opportunities and challenges to the migrants who flooded into the territory in the late nineteenth and early twentieth centuries. With its temperate climate, fertile soils, and plentiful precipitation, conditions for settlement here seemed considerably more propitious than elsewhere in Russia's Asian domains. However, for settlers from European Russia and Ukraine the results were decidedly mixed. The grain harvest was fickle, pests, disease, and predation carried off or weakened livestock, and flooding was an ever-present threat. Although not exactly hobbled by their biological "portmanteau," Russian colonists enjoyed few ecological advantages.

Yet over the long term they were able to survive and even thrive, suggesting that while environmental factors placed limits on European expansion— as in the tropics, for instance—as Crosby (1972, 1986) suggested, having an "ecological" edge was not always necessary for the creation of permanent colonial settlements. In this regard, colonization in Primor'e bears some similarity to the settlement of the Caucasus—another unfamiliar environment—by religious sectarians, and suggests that success of Russian expansion depended in large part on persistence and flexibility more than biological hangers-on (Breyfogle 2005, 87–127).

The interdependence among Slavic, Korean, and Chinese migrants that developed in Primor'e during the late tsarist era was strikingly at odds with contemporary rhetoric among Russian officials, which was extremely anti-Asian by the early 1900s (Li 2010; Schimmelpenninck van der Oye 2001; Siegelbaum 1978; Stolberg 2004). Given local conditions, however, and the territory's historical connections to the Sea of Japan region, the fact that such an "in-between" space prevailed in Primor'e should not come as a surprise. That it was also a sort of ecological compromise between Asian and European biota points to the fact that although the Russian Empire was territorially contiguous, its vastness and diversity meant that migration from one part to another was no simple matter.

Notes

1 Although often conflated in popular discourse, Siberia and the Russian Far East are administratively, geographically, and historically distinct regions that scholars (particularly in Russia) generally have examined separately. Administrative divisions have varied over time, but generally speaking Siberia refers to the area between the Ural Mountains and Lake Baikal, while the Far East refers to everything further east, including Yakutia, Chukhotka, Kamchatka, the Amur Valley, and Primor'e.
2 I use the expression ecological compromise to denote an "in-between" space in which no single culture or political authority was hegemonic. For examples of other "in-between" spaces see White 1991 and, for the Russian context, Barrett 1999 and Breyfogle 2005.
3 Russian State Naval Archive (RGA VMF), Fond (collection) 410, opis' (inventory) 2, delo (file) 4178, ll. (pages) 27–28. Fond 410 is the Chancellery of the Ministry of the Navy (1836–1918).
4 RGA VMF, F. 909, op. 1, d. 44, ll. 16–17, 26. Fond 909 is Administration of Pacific Ports (1856–1887).
5 Russian State Historical Archive of the Far East (RGIA DV), F. 1, op. 4, d. 846, ll. 3–5. Fond 1 is Primorskaia Provincial Administration (1818–1917).
6 RGIA DV, F. 1, op. 4, d. 121, 1–2, 10–11, 26, 83; RIGA DV F.1, op. 4, d. 38, ll. 1–3.

7 Russian State Historical Archive (RGIA), F. 391, op. 3, d. 270, ll. 40–41. Fond 391 is Resettlement Administration (1867–1918).
8 RGIA DV, F. 1, op. 4, d. 137, l. 3.
9 RGIA DV, F. 1, op. 5, d. 283, l. 11.
10 RGIA DV, F. 5, op. 1, d. 55, ll. 1–15, 58–80. Fond 5 is Primorskaia Provincial Statistical Commission (1887–1917).
11 RGIA, F. 391, op. 1, d. 24, ll. 63–64.
12 RGIA, F. 391, op. 4, d. 1288, l. 11.
13 RGA VMF, F. 401, op. 2, d. 4179, ll. 8–13, 24, 98; RGIA DV, F. 1, op. 4, d. 136, l. 1; RGIA DV, F. 1, op. 4, d. 465, ll. 1–20.
14 RGIA, F. 1273, op. 1, d. 409, ll. 20–24. Fond 1273 is the Committee for the Siberian Railroad (1892–1906).
15 RGA VMF, F. 909, op. 1, d. 44, l. 12; Russian State Military-Historical Archive (RGVIA), F. 99, op. 1, d. 87, ll. 21–22.
16 State Archive of Primorskii krai (GAPK), F. 1, op. 1, d. 33, l. 67.
17 RGA VMF, F. 401, op. 2, d. 4046, l. 249.
18 RGIA DV, F. 1, op. 5, d. 661, l. 3.
19 RGIA DV, F. 94, op. 1, d. 49, ll. 20, 40–41. Fond 94 is Primorskaia Provincial Forest Inspector (1888–1920).
20 State Archive of the Russian Federation (GARF), F. 102, op. 2, d. 33, ll. 1–3. Fond 102 is the Department of Police (of the Ministry of Internal Affairs) (1880–1917).

References

Agafonov, O. 1995 *Kazach'i voiska Rossiiskoi imperii.* Moscow; Kaliningrad: AOZT Epokha: Russkaia kniga; Iantarnyi skaz

Aliab'ev, N., 1872 *Dalekaia Rossiia: Ussuriiskii krai,* Obshchestvennaia pol'za, St. Petersburg

Atkinson, T., 1860 *Travels in the Regions of the Upper and Lower Amoor, and the Russian Acquisitions on the Confines of India and China,* Hurst and Blackett, London

Babrenko, Ia.A., 2003 Otnosheniia russkikh krest'ian i koreiskikh pereselentsev na iuge Dal'nego Vostoka vo vtoroi polovine XIX – pervoi treti XX vv. *Oikumena,* 8 (2003): 17–23

Barrett, T.M., 1999 *At the edge of empire: the Terek Cossacks and the North Caucasus Frontier, 1700–1860,* Westview Press, Boulder, Colorado

Breyfogle, N.B., 2005 *Heretics and colonizers: forging Russia's empire in the South Caucasus,* Cornell University Press, Ithaca

Coquin, F.-X., 1969 *La Sibérie: peuplement et immigration paysanne au XIXe siècle,* Institut d'études slaves, Paris

Crosby, A.W., 1986 *Ecological imperialism: the biological expansion of Europe, 900–1900,* Cambridge University Press, Cambridge, New York

Crosby, A.W., 1972 *The Columbian Exchange: Biological and Cultural Consequences of 1492,* Greenwood Press, Westport, Connecticut

Gluzdovskii, V.E., 1917 *Primorsko-Amurskaia okraina i severnaia man'chzhuriia,* Dalekaia Okraina, Vladivostok

Goncharova, E.M., Gorchakov, A.A., and Troitskaia, N.A. (eds), 2009 *Iz istorii zaseleniia khankaiskogo raiona: dokumenty i materialy,* Rossiiskii gos. istoricheskii arkhiv Dal'nego Vostoka, Vladivostok

James, H.E.M., 1888 *The Long White Mountain, or A Journey in Manchuria,* Longmans, Green, and Co., London and New York

Kabuzan, V.M., 1998 *Emigratsiia i reemigratsiia v Rossii v XVIII – nachale XX veka*, Nauka, Moscow

Kabuzan, V.M., 1985 *Dal'nevostochnyi krai v XVII – nachale XX vv.: istoriko-demografich-eskii ocherk*, Nauka, Moscow

Kabuzan, V.M., 1973 *Kak zaselialsia Dal'nii Vostok. Vtoraia polovina XVII-nachalo XX v*, Knizhnoe izdatel'stvo, Khabarovsk

Khudiakov, S.A., 1989 "Avtobiografiia" (unpublished manuscript), University of Hawai'i at Manoa

Kim, A., 2013 On the preparation and conduct of the repression of Koreans in the 1930s Soviet Union. *Historian* 75, 262–282

Kriukov, N.A., 1893 *Ocherk sel'skago khoziaistva v Primorskoi oblasti*, Tip. V. Bezobrazova, St. Petersburg

Kutuzov, M.A., and Ivanov, V.D., 2003 "Kazachestvo na russko-kitaiskoi granitse." *Zapiski Obshchestva izucheniia Amurskogo kraia* 36, 2 (2003): 36–49

Lee, R.H.G., 1970 *The Manchurian Frontier in Ch'ing History*, Harvard University Press, Cambridge, Massachusetts

Li, E.L., 2010 "'Zheltaia ugroza' ili 'zheltii vopros' v trudakh Amurskoi ekspeditsii 1910 g." *Oikumena*, 3 (2010), 29–40

Mandel, W.M., 1944 *The Soviet Far East and Central Asia*, Institute of Pacific Relations Inquiry Series, The Dial Press, New York

Marks, S.G., 1991 *Road to Power: The Trans-Siberian Railroad and the Colonization of Asian Russia, 1850–1917*, Cornell University Press, Ithaca, N.Y.

Moon, D., 2000 Russia's Rural Economy, 1800–1930. *Kritika, Explorations in Russian and Eurasian History* 1, 679–689

Moon, D., 1999 *The Russian peasantry, 1600–1930: the world the peasants made*, Longman, London and New York

Obzor po konnozavodstu i konevodstvu v Primorskoi Oblasti: 1860–1910 g., 1911 Tipografiia V.K. Iuganson, Vladivostok

Ossendowski, F., 1924 *Man and mystery in Asia*, E.P. Dutton and Co., New York

Paine, S.C., 1996 *Imperial rivals: China, Russia, and their disputed frontier*, M.E. Sharpe, Armonk, NY and London

Pallot, J., Shaw, D.J.B., 1990 *Landscape and settlement in Romanov Russia, 1613–1917*, Clarendon Press; Oxford University Press, New York

Petrov, A.I., 2003 *Istoriia kitaitsev v Rossii, 1856–1917*, Beresta, St. Petersburg

Petrov, A.I., 2001 *Koreiskaia diaspora v Rossii: 1897–1917*, DVO RAN, Vladivostok

Pogoda i Klimat (Weather and climate), 2016 "Klimat Vladivostoka" (www.pogodaiklimat. ru/climate/31960.htm), "Klimat Tveri" (www.pogodaiklimat.ru/climate/27402.htm), and "Klimat Khar'kova" (www.pogodaiklimat.ru/climate/34300.htm), all accessed June 30, 2016

Pozniak, T.Z., 2006 "Politika rossiiskoi vlasti v otnoshenii immigrantov na Dal'nem Vostoke vo vtoroi polovine XIX – nachale XX v." in: *Dal'nii Vostok Rossii: problemy sotsial'no-politicheskogo i kul'turnogo razvitiia vo vtoroi polovine XIX–XX v.*, Trudy Instituta istorii, arkheologii i etnografii DVO RAN 13. Dal'nauka, Vladivostok, pp. 43–59

Przheval'skii, N.M., 1947. *Puteshestvie v Ussuriiskom krae, 1867–1869 g.* Gosudarstvennoe izdatel'stvo geograficheskoi literatury, Moscow

Reardon-Anderson, J., 2005 *Reluctant pioneers: China's expansion northward, 1644–1937* Stanford University Press, Stanford, California

Robinson, G.T., 1949 *Rural Russia under the old régime: a history of the landlord-peasant world and a prologue to the peasant revolution of 1917*, Macmillan Co., New York

Savinskaia, O.T., 1913 Khutor Ol'gin–Kut, in: Eggenberg, A.I., Zolotov, D.I. (eds), *Otchet o s'ezde sel'skikh khoziaiev Primorskoi oblasti 11–14 noiabria 1912 goda*, Tip. Kantseliariia Priamurskago General-Gubernatora, Khabarovsk, pp. 74–94

Schimmelpenninck van der Oye, D., 2001 *Toward the Rising Sun: Russian Ideologies of Empire and the Path to War with Japan*, Northern Illinois University Press, DeKalb, Illiinois

Siegelbaum, L.H., 1978 Another "Yellow Peril": Chinese Migrants in the Russian Far East and the Russian Reaction before 1917. *Modern Asian Studies* 10, 307–330

Sorokina, T.N., 1999 *Khoziaistvennaia deiatel'nost'kitaiskikh poddannykh na Dal'nem Vosoke Rossii i politika administratsii Priamurskogo kraia (konets XIX – nachalo XX vv.)*, Omsk State University, Omsk

Startsev, A.F., 2005 *Kul'tura i byt udegeitsev (vtoraia polovina XIX–XX v.)* Dal'nauka, Vladivostok

Stephan, J.J., 1994 *The Russian Far East: a history*, Stanford University Press, Stanford, California

Stolberg, E.-M., 2004 The Siberian frontier between "White Mission" and "Yellow Peril," 1890s–1920s. *Nationalities Papers* 32

Timonov, V.E., 1897 *Ocherk glavneishikh vodnykh putei Priamurskago kraia*, Tipografiia Ministerstva Putei Soobshcheniia, St. Petersburg

Treadgold, D.W., 1957 *The Great Siberian Migration: government and peasant in resettlement from emancipation to the First World War*, Princeton University Press, Princeton

Vashchuk, A.S., Chernolutskaia, E.N., Koroleva, V.A., Dudchenko, G.B., Gerasimova, L.., 2002 *Etnomigratsionnye protsessi v Primor'e v XX veke*, DVO RAN, Vladivostok

Veterinary Section of the Primorskaia *oblast'* administration, 1913 *Svedeniia o veterinarno-sanitarnomsostoianii Primorskoi oblasti*, Tipografiia Primorskago oblastnogo pravleniia, Vladivostok

Vlasov, S.A., 2005 *Istoriia Dal'nego Vostoka Rossii: Kurs lektsii*, Dal'nauka, Vladivostok

White, R., 1991 *The middle ground: Indians, empires, and Republics in the Great Lakes region, 1650–1815*, Cambridge University Press, Cambridge, New York

Yankovsky, V.G., 2007 *From the crusades to gulag and beyond*, Elliott Snow, Sydney, Australia.

5 Coal lives

Body, work and memory among Italian miners in Wallonia, Belgium

Daniele Valisena and Marco Armiero

Abstract

This chapter explores the link between environmental history and migration studies by analyzing the case of Italian miners in Wallonia after World War II. Employing an Environmental Humanities approach, we use novels and poems to analyze the ecological shift operated by the capitalistic organization of coal extraction and how this affected the socio-environmental structure of the Walloon landscape and its relationship with the people who inhabited it. We aim to demonstrate how workers' bodies are a key element of the interaction between nature and society, constituting a vantage point to access subaltern ecologies.

Introduction

An abandoned pit, followed by a rusty rail track half-covered by grass that drives the sight directly into the belly of a black, barren hill. Behind that, the shape blurred in the greasy rain, a rundown coal power plant silently awaits its fuel, probably on its way on a cargo ship coming from China. Emerging on the horizon is the outline of giant metallic spider claws which overwhelm the city of Seraing and its decaying factoryscape. Traveling today by train or car between Charleroi and Liège, everything still relates to the mines. Twenty-four years after the closure of the last mine, the past seems to have left no space for another present in the landscape which is lightly dotted by features of a new modernity.

Wallonia, the French speaking region of Belgium, lies at the very heart of the Coal Measures which originated in the medium Carboniferous era, embracing Europe from Great Britain to the Ruhr, Saar-Lorrain and High Silesia, and with the Franco-Belgian basin constituting the center of this underground geological system. Until the technological shift operated by the industrial revolution, the extraction of coal coexisted with the dominant agricultural nature of the region. Everything changed with the industrialization of coal mining, starting in 1720 with the introduction of the first steam engine. The entire landscape became a machine for coal extraction with canals, railways, and new roads, while the cultivated fields started to be drawn out by *terrils*, the coal waste hills that even now are the main feature of the region. In 1840 the annual coal production rate was around 2.6 million tons per year, with a workforce of 32,000 miners employed. In 1910 the production had risen to 22.7 million tons per year, with more than 140,000 workers (Michotte 1929). That was the beginning of a potent rise in Belgian coal production, which, due to the two World Wars, did not diminish until 1959. By 1961 200,000 Italian immigrants were living in Belgium, most of them employed as miners and coal workers (Canovi 2011, 3). Since then, coal has never stopped haunting landscape and memory in Wallonia. But as with every ghost, coal's heirloom is no longer visible to everybody.

Belgium is now perceived as a place for EU bureaucrats, tasty chocolate, and recently, a terrorist refuge, but no longer as a land of miners and coal. Nevertheless, coal and its legacy are still present everywhere, stratified within the landscape, and in the memories and bodies of miners (Bertucelli 2012). The Wallonia coal past and the histories of thousands of immigrants who worked there have disappeared from the public imaginary, but, as Don Mitchell (1996) would put it, they are still engraved within the landscape and the collective memory[1]. Mining is, after all, an underworld business, largely hidden, invisible to the majority of the population. Indeed, the mine was a foreign country where nature and people did not look like their counterparts on the surface. The Wallonia underworld was peopled by immigrants, many of them Italians, embodying in their skin, language, culture a radical otherness.

Figure 5.1 Wallonia
Source: Courtesy of Région Wallonne

Coal was the very foundation of Belgian capitalism, the engine of a broad metabolic circulation of mineral, humans, and money. Migrants were an essential part in this circulation, providing the cheap and disposable labor for an extremely risky and consuming job. In this sense, their migration to Wallonia implied a twofold alienation and adaptation: they had to cope with the violence of the mines' environment and the otherness and xenophobic space of the surface. In this chapter we aim to uncover these migrants' two-fold experience.

In the spirit of Environmental Humanities we think that in order to under-stand the socio-environmental processes and the memorial and corporeal ecologies in which migrants are entangled we need to broaden our objects of study. As we have argued elsewhere, we believe that "immigrants [...] are entangled in landscapes where social inequalities and power relations are sedi-mented [...] blending their bodies with new environments through work and social relationships" (Armiero 2010). In this sense, we are interested in the body of the miner as a site where bio-political practices of control, exploita-tion and commodification are played. At the same time, bodies are narrative and sensing corporeal apparatuses, through which work and the everyday life practices are understood and preformed. Finally, bodies are resistance and resil-ience instruments that enact complex and contradictory forms of opposition and adaptation to the labor discipline that miners withstood. In this way, the body becomes a methodological but also an epistemological site that widens the migration studies lens and bridges it with environmental history.

We also believe that identity processes are deeply entangled with the socio-environmental relations linking social actors to the land they live in; both physical and imaginary environments influence the construction of this self-recognition process. As Noiriel (2006, 45) points out, when it comes to iden-tity the challenge is to de-construct what Bourdieu call *reconnaissance* (Bourdieu and Passeron 1970; Bourdieu 1994). The French sociologist intended this concept as the process of unconscious interiorization of social constraints and norms that are a crucial part of every identity construction process. Institutions and powerful actors have driven this process towards a social hegemonic rela-tionship which can be framed as a form of symbolic violence exercised by a class or a social group over another. In the context of the Italian miners' communities, the metabolism of coal defined this social relation both materi-ally and socially. We aim to explore how this power relationship has shaped and signified the self-representation of Italian miners in Belgium and the role played in this process by the social and corporeal landscapes. Our hypothesis is that the de-construction of these self-representations, if analyzed in the frame of political ecology and environmental justice, shows the oppressive hegem-onic narratives that Italian miners withstood, but also the strategies of ecologi-cal resistance and the escape mechanisms used by Italian migrants to recreate and save their memory reservoir—that is, their stock of identity's memory and the spatial concretization of this will to remember—in the desolate mining landscape of Wallonia.

Indeed, migrants assumed the burden of creating and keeping alive an imaginary community of Walloon miners. Mining has been the main economic and socio-environmental process in the definition of Belgian and Walloon identities. Only miners' communities were able to inhabit, recognize and signify this socio-ecological memory through their labor and their everyday life practices. At the same time they were able to build a strong community around the struggle for rights, health and socio-environmental justice. The hinge around which all of these processes occurred was mining work. The closing of mines and the shift in the Belgian economic and social structure brought the region and its inhabitants into a still unsolved condition of anomie. What is the memorial and social meaning of this process?

Although deeply rooted in environmental history, we place our contribution within the rising field of the environmental humanities. With this, we aim to stress the multi-disciplinary approach employed in this article for which we have borrowed from history, ecocriticism, and political ecology. In particular, we have built upon Stacy Alaimo's (2010) transcorporeality and Erik Swyngedouw's (2003) metabolism. The analysis will focus mainly on fiction and non-fiction produced by Italians and Italians' descendants who grew up and lived in Belgian mining regions, experiencing the life and the imaginary of these communities. We will also briefly analyze some Belgian and French poems connected with the mining epic, in order to trace a brief outline of the collective imaginary at the time when Italians came. Our sources are fiction writings, all with some kind of autobiographical inspiration; nonetheless, they are largely reliable in terms of the information they provide on the conditions of the Italian miners in Wallonia. However, this is not our main point. Rather the narrative character of our sources is an asset as our aim is to unpack the ways in which Italian migrants understood and perceived their position within the metabolism of coal. The fact that we are employing (more or less) fictional narrative only proves that those landscapes and bodies are made of stories and memories at least as much as of coal, blood, and money.

The contested memory of Wallonia and the role of Italian miners

The mine had been for two centuries a defining place in the collective memory of Belgium: "*les champs noircis*" (the blackened fields) of Liège and the "*fumeux vallons*" (the smoked valleys) of Mons were celebrated in the national poem, "La gloire belgique," written by Le Mayeur in 1830. Also Paul Verlaine, in 1872, referring to the mining city of Charleroi in *Romances sans paroles*, chanted "the black grass where Kobolds go." However, the most important French-speaking poet of the mine is Jules Mousseron. Born in Picardie, Northern France, in 1868, he worked as a miner in the mining basin that lies across France, Belgium and Luxembourg. His most important poetic collections are *Fleurs d'en bas* (Flowers from below) and *Croquis au charbon* (Coal sketches). In those poems Mousseron exalts the bravery and the force of miners, before

Figure 5.2 Coal builds the wealth of the country

This poster by André Linglex (1950) is part of the collection of the Centre d'interpretation de l'Immigration en Région du centre of La Louvière. Coll. Blegny-Mine, courtesy of the owner.

whom *"everybody bends down."*[2] Schools and streets are still named after the poet, and children from Wallonia, today as fifty years ago, learn those words by heart. Coal was the blood running through kilometers of mines under the surface of Wallonia; the miners were the flesh mixing with that blood and making the tissue of the social body, eventually ending up sacrificing their very lives on the altar of this modern epic. For this very reason Wallonia became the richest and politically most influential part of Belgium. As a famous trade union poster, created by the Belgian artist Linglex, advertised, coal "built the wealth, the life of the Country."

Following the positivist narrative of technology and industrial development as a means of civilization and progress, Mousseron's words describe the heroic and Promethean effort of miners, struggling with the mean and tricky earth, the *grisou*[3] and the collapsing vaults, which, in the end, can be subjugated[4]. The misery and the socio-environmental inequalities that could be glimpsed through Mousseron's description of *corons*[5], from health conditions to the physical suffering of miners and their families, did not receive the same attention in the public celebration of his works. In Mousseron's verses the power relationships between workers and companies were informed only by paternalism, such as that which linked the poet with Lucien Jonas, entrepreneur and *patron de mines*, who helped Mousseron publish his poems and to whom the poet dedicated these lines: *"It's all black / our brave Country / due to its terrils and its efficient factories! / But you made it shine thanks to the consolatory image / of our courage and welcoming gifts reunited".*[6] According to this Christian paternalistic vision the virtuous worker was grateful towards his patron and piously eager to accept the suffering driven by the capitalistic and industrialist coal metabolism, which blackened the land and the body.

This celebratory narrative of coal, work, and capital fell into crisis with the new economic phase after World War II, which drastically changed the very foundations of Belgian identity. All of a sudden, what had been considered a glorious national fundament and a defining social heritage became an uncomfortable, derelict memorial. Oil had overthrown coal in nurturing the progress and the technological development driven by the post-war Economic Boom in Europe, obliterating also the essential role of Wallonia in the nation state narrative of Belgium. Flanders, for a long time seen mostly as a producer of a labor force, was about to become in a couple of decades the rich and modern region of the *Plat Pays*, with its chemicals factories, diamonds trade and service-oriented economy. Corporeal, exhausting, dirty work was the past, and the mining desolated landscape of Wallonia was transformed from a sign of prosperity into a physical and aesthetical wound for the country. Mining was no longer able to sustain the nation's wealth; on the contrary, it was the activity that brought silicosis into the public realm, affecting thousands of workers and the state's finances since after 1964 those sick workers had to be supported by the state (Geerkens 2009). Mining became a synonym for Marcinelle, the tragedy of Bois du Cazier, the worst page of Belgian labor and social history (Rwanda and asbestos were not yet on the scene). Polluted air, toxic animals, poisoned rivers, contaminated water basins, and tainted fields were the legacy of years of mining. The very miners' bodies bore in their torn flesh, in their clogged lungs, and in their finger stumps the wounds of an entire region. Mines needed to be forgotten.

In this climate of memorial shift and denial, there was no place for Italian immigrants, who had come to Belgium to fight the so-called "Coal Battle,"[7] believing that they were helping Europe and Italy to stand anew after the nihilistic destruction of World War II. Coal was what took them thousands of kilometers away from their home, their land, their family; coal was what they had seen, what they breathed, absorbed, ate, touched, worked, and had been immersed in every day for years; what they felt behind the rusty windows of their barracks and in the creases of their skin; what paid the rent and sustained their families back in Italy, allowing them to think of another future. Indeed, coal was what gave sense to their presence in Belgian society. Borrowing from Bourdieu, coal and mines were the social and physical frame where they found recognition, preventing them from falling into an anomic state of outcasts among the voiceless and faceless *lumpenproletariat*. For this reason Italians became the main actors in the creation and preservation of the memory of the Belgian mining past. Italians attempted to restore the dignity of miners in Belgian labor, political and social history, uncovering the inequalities brought by the "Coal Battle" and inserting their epic in the transnational narrative of the European Union with all its contradictions.

The novels we will examine have been written and conceived by Italian miners and second generation migrants who lived, worked, and merged their bodies and imaginaries with Belgian coal between the late 1950s and 1970s. We believe that these narratives can help scholars understand the capitalistic socio-environmental metabolism that miners withstood and experienced in Belgium, but also in other working sites in Europe and in the rest of the world. We could say that the mine was re-invented by the workers, mostly immigrants, who appropriated the collective memory of Wallonia through their labor, their socio-environmental struggles, and their narratives of all this. Novels, newspapers, popular songs and movies, but also trade unions and political parties, all concurred in producing a new narrative about the Italian migrants. Not anymore the dangerous, dirty and alien working "tools" they used to be, Italians became the strongest actors in the national struggle to defend the mining industrial and social heritage, as well as the subjects of the struggle for health and the recognition of silicosis as an occupational disease[8]. Without acknowledging this process it is almost impossible to understand how the Italian presence has been so paramount in the Belgian political and trade union scene in the last three decades. Also, these processes helped the Walloon mining basin to obtain the status of UNESCO World Heritage Site in 2012.

In the next section we will illustrate the transcorporeal landscape and the human ecology (Alaimo 2010) of Italian miners, showing the many physical interchanges between their bodies—conceived as permeable sites merged and transformed by the social and economical powers they were subjugated by— and the techno-capitalistic metabolism of coal that shaped their everyday life and the very space they inhabited. We argue that in order to grasp the miners' experience of the environment we need to analyze their bodily and memorial understanding of the metabolism of coal, that is, the human ecology they participated in and resisted and the material self they elaborated and perceived.

Peri-urban aesthetics and xenophobic spatialization

L'Étoile:

> was a vast coal sweep, an almost muddy soil, disseminated of strange and derelict constructions and all of them had something to do with the mine. Behind that, dominating everything, there was an immense mountain, so black that one could have guessed the sky was so dark because of that.
>
> (Santocono 1986[9])

These lines were written by Girolamo Santocono, the son of a Sicilian couple, a former barber married to a ruined *rentier*, who moved to Morlanwelz, a mining village just outside La Louvière, in 1953. He wrote his *Rue des Italiens* (Italians' street) in 1986, when he was 46, two years after the closure of the last mine of the coal basin of Wallonia. In that novel, Santocono describes the normalization of the presence of coal in everyday life. Coal, in its powerful and lumbering materiality, adds another dimension to the lives of Italians, another color to their landscape, becoming the undying *file rouge* that materially and ideally connected the working and private sphere of miners.

> [...] coal was everywhere in the Étoile, people lived in it. The terril, this coal mountain, overflowed through the streets, finding its way inside houses.
>
> (Santocono 1986)

Coal is turned into a geo-historical myth, a sort of identity mark that bonded humans, labor and land, defining the social and physical environment of Italian miners and their families. The metaphoric and physical immanency of coal is represented by *terrils*, the coal waste hills that still dominate the landscape of Wallonia and that most of the times lay next to the miners' villages. Huge, gloomy and dirty, their muddy gutters spread from the hillside on the frequent rainy days, entering houses and leaving black marks everywhere.

> Our home was some kind of a big building, colored in dirty yellow [...] La Cantine, an old cave for the Flemish workers who worked in the mines of Wallonia before the war. Two entrances, two stairs and twenty-four large families lived there, between the factory, the dump and the coal debris.
>
> (Santocono 1986)

Coal was a physical path within the human settlements, indicating clearly the place of the outcasts enslaved to the bottom of the earth. Coal was a social border, which separated clearly the "us" and "them," marking the bodies, the clothes, and the mental horizon of the ones who were bonded to it. Coal also occupied a strange space between the urban and the rural. In the city, coal embodied an idealized modernity, metabolized through ovens, stoves, heating systems and sacks. In the rural space, coal lost all its allure of modernity and comfort, becoming the marker of segregation. We can find this divide in Santocono's description of L'Étoile, the Italian slum in Morlanweltz, in the heart of Hainaut province:

> All those who weren't lucky enough to find an "apartment" in this gigantic hens cage, they found a place to live in the cement and wooden made barracks called Le Camps [...] L'Étoile was [...] well isolated at the border of the city and strictly compact like a ghetto, where, for great intellectual laziness, were put "all those who were of the same kind."
>
> (Santocono 1986)[10]

The very name of these settlements explains their nature of liminal zones, spaces of non-urbanity and yet not country. *Étoile* in French means star, but also a big roundabout where many roads meet: a passage, a *non-lieu* (Nora 1984–1992). On the other hand, *Le Camps* was the place where the German captives were forced to live and work after the end of the war. A real prison, where Italian miners were forced to stay due to the impossibility of finding or affording another place to live, controlled and segregated in the heteroclite space of the former segregation site.

The living maps: miners' economy of the body

This xenophobic spatialization[11], which, as in Morlanwelz, grouped most of the Italians' settlements in the sadly famous *corons,* was also a way to control the movement and the socio-economical mobility of Italian miners inside the urban space. Belgians did not want to rent houses to Italians, especially in the first decade after World War II, hiding xenophobic sentiments behind the excuse of health protection. In this sanitation narrative Belgians from the upper and working classes as well as health institutions represented Italians as "dirtier and less attentive to their personal hygiene" because of their "cultural difference" (Cumoli 2012). This cultural and corporeal feature was inscribed on their skin. The novelist Monica Ferretti (2003) evokes this stigma in her *Gueules Noires* (literally Black Snouts[12]), when she describes how the black of coal on miners' faces became a social and racial divide separating them from the rest of the society, which was conversely clean and sane.

> These scars are not like ours, barely visible: these scars are black and they seem to be designed with the tattoo print. They stood out on their skin like inerasable hieroglyphs of a dead language. Their color is black due to the powder that leaked in their wounds. There's not a centimeter of these bodies that don't bear the sign of the mine.
>
> (Ferretti 2003)

Raul Rossetti (1989), in his novel *Schiena di vetro* (Glass Back), also insists on how this visible mark of working with coal was experienced as a stigma.

> On those white faces one could descry signs black as tattoos. They were the scars of the mine, which never fade. They remain with you for your entire life.
>
> (Rossetti 1989)

What is interesting here is how the temporal and logical orders have been subverted by the cultural construction of the racially inferior Italian miners. The black signs were not perceived as the signs of the mines, but as marks "naturally" inscribed in the dirty immigrants from Southern Europe. The everlasting black marks that miners gained through their work in the bowels of the earth were turned into a natural characteristic of Italian immigrants. Using a common religious narration, shared by all the local Belgian Catholic community as well as with the Italian immigrants, this work mark was silently associated with a natural and divine sign of their diversity. And that diversity was turned into a sin, which was visible on their bodies. In this sense social and spatial exclusion of Italian miners from the local community could be justified and re-affirmed on a supposedly "natural" basis. In a similar way for centuries urban societies had stigmatized the stranger, the intruder in the social order, who easily became the anointer, the plague-spreader. Lazarettos gone, the mine and its apparatus of landfills became an easy surrogate for the new capitalistic outcasts. In this way a socio-political inequality, built around the constraint linking Italian miners with the mine through the mediation of the Belgian state and the control of mining companies (Morelli 1988; Cumoli 2012), was transformed into a "natural" feature of the foreign community in order to justify its otherness, hence re-affirming the identity and the different social and anthropological status of the local society.

This dominion of the mine over the body can be traced also by looking at the description of the working environment and how this job status required skills that deprived the miner of his humanity. Again, Ferretti, the daughter of an Italian miner who accompanied her father many times down the pits, is able to evoke and describe this animalization process in a very powerful way.

> Miners didn't walk, they crawled on their heels and elbows. In this position they broke rocks, they shoveled, took away and transported coal. All this while a never-ending wind slapped them in their faces, throwing against them powder, little rocks, debris...
>
> (Ferretti 2003)

Also Rossetti, who was himself a miner, explains how the working regime required many complicated techniques that forced miners to expose their bodies to continuous discomfort and danger:

> A foot and a half. Gran Vein mine was as tall as this down at 800 metres deep. It was so short that one had to work without hat and the lamp couldn't stand still. We had to work 80 quintals of coal lying aside on our bellies and hips, and the spade had no handle.
>
> (Rossetti 1989)

As Santocono explains, "year after year miners' bodies became living maps," shaped, consumed and forever marked and enslaved to mining labor. The signs of this enslavement were "[...] broken bones, missing fingers, and, obviously, scars of every kind [...]" (Santocono 1986).

The mine was a hostile environment. It took away strength, health, breath, light, but it also stole limbs, fingers, arms, legs, feet from the very bodies of workers. Accidents were the standard in the veins, where the security of the workers was not exactly a priority for the companies. Workers' bodies turned into gears, part of a complicated and huge mechanism created to extract out of the mines richness in the form of coal. If physically demanding jobs have always put workers under high risk, alienating them socially and corporeally from their body, for miners this regime was even more demanding. Miners were nothing more than "arms,[13]" biological extensions of shovels, picks and jackhammers. Their "expiration date" was calculated at around five years[14], an estimation made taking into account the physical and mental consumption as well as the "natural" turnover of new biological coal extractor "tools" from Italy. This assumption was also very well known among the miners. Rossetti puts these words in the mouth of a veteran of the mine who warns the author about the inescapable damage that every miner will get from working in the pits for a long period of time:

> It has been five years since I arrived and by now my bags (his lungs) are full. If one works for five years into the vein is finished, he has not much time left to live, so please go away […]
>
> (Rossetti 1989)

This huge transnational metabolism digested thousands of people, a large number of whom, after a "round" down into the veins, were already affected by silicosis or had lost a part of their bodies or their precious arms. On the other hand, miners could frame their experience as a sort of virile and hubristic challenge against the coal, where strength, technique and bravery would help them in mastering the element that cursed them. Rossetti explains this process as a sort of hubristic challenge between the miners and the very element that caused, in this simplistic reconstruction, all the migrants' physical suffering and troubles:

> After some time I was able to work the coal with the usual technique, but I didn't want to prove my power against it; I wanted to dominate it [….] Yes, now I was like a star. I could finish the five meters task one hour before the others. I worked laughing and crying. For God's sake, coal, you are mine.
>
> (Rossetti 1989)

An anthropocenic and anthropocentric view was developed from within the coal by the miners: they could develop strength, technique and a bodily knowledge of the mining environment, a knowledge that allowed them to control the matter they were facing and challenging, though in a deceptive and tricky way, as Rossetti continues to describe:

> As if to get its vengeance, [the coal] throw a stone at me, crushing two of my fingers. I licked the blood away and continued working and when I finished I allowed myself to feel the pain.
>
> (Rossetti 1989)

Mastering the job and dominating the coal could be understood as a way to exorcize the perennial sense of risk, the physical and labor danger as well as taking a personal, hysterical and useless revenge against the personification of all the socio-environmental and bodily threat that miners withstood on a daily basis. Danger, pain, disease could come from breathing, breaking, accidentally eating or falling into the coal, but also from the crumbling of a vault, a gas leak that could asphyxiate the workers or set the mine on fire.

> Coal dust—Rossetti explains—can enter in your throat, but it is so thin that you can walk as if there was none at all [....] You can fall mouth-opened, risking your skin and choking in the coal dust.
>
> (Rossetti 1989)

Characterizing the mine as a trickster, some sort of death deity or spirit that could trick you in every moment for no apparent reason, can be understood as a process similar to the personification of nature in traditional rural societies, where spirits and more than human entities enact the agency of nature and other forces threatening and opposing humans. Miners personified the mine, and this was a way to avoid addressing the real trickster, that is, the capitalist organization of coal extraction.

Following this rationale, miners' bodies, along with machines, tools and animals, were all part of the same extraction-destruction apparatus[15]. The poor Rossi, an Italian miner driven crazy by the mine and, in particular, by the machine he was supposed to supervise, is a dramatic example of this de-humanizing apparatus.

> Rossi had been there for five years and he had nothing left of his humanity. Gimbo [an American machine to move coal] was his enemy. It drove him crazy. Few knew of his madness, maybe the managers, but it didn't really matter as long as he could work [....] Rossi talked to Gimbo as if it was a Christian [a human being, in Italian] and when it didn't work, he bit it. Because of this, he had only a few chipped teeth left. He bit and cried, hated and loved.
>
> (Rossetti 1989)

On the other hand, some forms of corporeal resistance (Alaimo 2010, 37) were developed by the miners, in a peculiar and astonishing way. The capability to re-imagine themselves inside the new environment brought into the scene a peculiar and striking survival strategy through a carefully planned economy of the body, which consisted in its further de-humanization (the body turned into a mere instrument) and in a metaphoric and painful detachment of its physicality from the mental and social sphere. Miners started to cut their limbs, phalanx after phalanx. They did it methodically, studying the quickest, safest and most efficient way to stop the coal extracting machines that their bodies had become. Santocono describes this self-harm practice:

The finger-cutting mania showed up during the five years after, when people understood that they weren't ready to go back home. [...] It's not like men started to cut themselves so easily. Things needed to mature, to be prepared in order to reach the goal and not all [fingers] were paid the same amount of money. The ring finger, for instance, was easy to cut, but wasn't worth economically. The thumb instead was a good deal, but was dangerous to cut, because you risked losing the entire hand. One could also be satisfied with small finger pieces, for the bureaucrats evaluated the early cases establishing an amputation seriousness standard. They started to count finger parts [....] To endure the pleasure of the injury one only needed to put some onion juice on the wound, faking a never-ending heal-over process.

(Santocono 1986)

Being de-humanized by the technocratic and capitalistic discipline of labor, Italian miners were able to elaborate a drastic and shocking strategy to escape from this assembly line of exploitation of their bodies by renouncing parts of themselves. Because the body was the main concern of the mining companies, its efficiency was the most important thing. So by "stopping" it for a while with a little help from a comrade, miners were able to stay at home with their families, trying to survive with the disability checks that the company paid for a couple of weeks, a month or even more. This corporeal trade elaborated by miners could be understood as a form of resilience strategy. In the absence of any other forms of health and psychological care, Italian miners tried to temporarily escape from that work and its corporeal control by tricking the central gear of this mechanism: their own body. Of course, this strategy also shows how far the dehumanization process that miners withstood was deeply embodied and accepted by the very victims, who could not elaborate any structured or politically articulated form of resistance at the time when mining was the uncontested dimension of working and living in Wallonia.

Imaginary landscapes and alternative ecologies

The mine—Monica Ferretti writes in her novel—is a subterranean city, which expresses itself in a vertical dimension, in a completely symmetric way to a city full of skyscrapers. Footsteps descend deep underground for hundreds of meters, intersected by many galleries that continue to go deep down for kilometers. The continual activity goes on 24/7, divided in turns. There's a big movement of elevators [....] The mine is also a very noisy place: coal is broken by mechanic drills and their earsplitting sound is enforced by the carriage sand cages striding against the rocks; there are horses' and humans' voices; you can hear people swearing [...]

(Ferretti 2003)

Although so drastically apart from the surface, nonetheless the mine projected its shadows into the outside world. The landscape was made of coal and its remains. Coal not only covered the clothes of workers, but it penetrated under the skin, filling the lungs and tearing limbs apart. Furthermore, the violence of underworld re-emerged on the surface in the daily lives of miners' families. Several sources confirm this. For instance Olivia Slongo—an Italian woman born and raised in the Venetian countryside before moving to Belgium, where she married a violent miner—writes that when her husband

> [...] was tired; he had some bizarre reaction. For instance, when he came back, the soup needed to be already on the table and not too warm. One day he came home and nothing was ready: he destroyed a sheet that covered the bed, he smashed some oranges on the floor and he went away for hours. Another day, he kicked his hat because he couldn't find a hanger and he left slamming the door. In those moments I was afraid.
>
> (Slongo 1999)

Violence, in the form of hard consuming physical labor, was the norm in the mine. Also, violence permeated the social and power relationships that linked Italian miners and Belgian society. Violence was instilled through the xenophobic spatialization they were forced to experience and finally, violence was transferred also into the familiar sphere.

In contrast with this socialization of violence, Italian immigrants elaborated different strategies, rooted in the cultural and memory legacy coming from their life in rural Italy. Those cultural features played as a material knowledge apparatus that "talked a different language" compared to the capitalistic dystopic denaturalization mobilized by the dominant mining narration. It is not surprising that the focus on this different aesthetic of the non-working space comes from the narration of a woman who in the hegemonic gender division of society was the responsible one in the domestic sphere. This social particle, though highly merged with the coal metabolism, was conceived as a sort of archaic, pre-industrial space of affection, care and leisure. Because of this heterotopic frame, it was from the domestic, private and familiar sphere that alternative narratives and practices were able to emerge, coexist, and survive within the mining hegemony. In Olivia Slongo's words:

> In this space consecrated to industry the Étoile's inhabitants found a way to practice the art of land farming. Amongst waste ponds, between the terrils and the railway, where the land mixed with the coal, prevailing on it, some vegetable gardens appeared. One centimeter of free land: a lettuce plant comes up. A pot: a basil is growing [....] No flowers, just one or two, but chubby vegetables, good meaty green vegetables to be cooked in water or fried in oil, to garnish with lemon or tomato sauce, to eat raw with a slice of bread [...]
>
> (Slongo 1999)

This rural imaginary was a powerful recall for the Italian community which, in the large majority, was composed of ex-farmers and peasants' sons and daughters. Building up from that identity, the community created and shared a different relationship with the land and a special ecological sensibility. That ecological bond allowed the community to oppose an alternative interpretation of the landscape which, we argue, constituted an embryonic form of ecological resistance. In fact that interpretation opened up small alternative socio-ecological spaces within the otherwise coherent and ordered environment of the mines.

> Zì Giacomino chose [...] a ditch exposed to the sun just below the terril, transforming it into a real Eden. In the good season this ditch was able to provide up to half of the vegetables consumed at the Cantine.
>
> (Santocono 1986)

We understand those gardening activities and the places they created as producers of an alternative community's culture based on material knowledge and material and immaterial needs (food as well as the reproduction/reinvention of the motherland). As Santocono explains:

> First of all, the vegetable garden needs to be convenient. Let the aesthetic to the rich ones, because beauty lies within what we can eat: little beans, fava bean, onions, garlic, cabbage, radish [....] The Rital[16] is more proud of his garden than of his house.
>
> (Santocono 1986)

Vegetable gardens nurtured an alternative economy, in a space where everything was dominated—and owned—by the mining companies. It was hard and expensive to find fresh tomatoes, basil, lentils, fava beans, paprika, and other herbs that constituted the basis of Italians' diet. Bringing back to Belgium the flavor, the smell, and the material objects of their food culture, immigrated communities reinstated their peculiarity, derived from a centuries-long history of relationship with their land. While reclaiming their culture in a specific relationship to nature, these immigrants were also resisting the homogenization and violence of mining everyday life. We do not argue that those gardens could re-create some ancestral and positive connections with a lost land. The social-ecological relations which organized life and land in the Italian countryside were by no means a lost paradise, rather an equally violent and unjust environment. Reflecting on the reinvention of an Italian identity, Santocono writes:

> Sure, they had in common hope, the sun and overall, this mythical Country, l'Italia. Immaterial and symbolic Country, of which everyone had taken some different pieces [....] To talk about the Country was to talk about the village.
>
> (Santocono 1986)

The village dimension, this lost or invented rurality, was the imagined Italy they were all a part of. As many migration studies have demonstrated, the concept of "Italyness" or "Italianity" was a cultural construction that most migrants elaborated when they became strangers in the host countries[17]. Culture can also be a bodily and ecological matter. That is why vegetable gardens became so important in miners' everyday life, as a place where it was possible to overcome all these national cultural cleavages through a common reference to the land, its memorial value and its usages. Vegetable gardens functioned as "memory reservoirs" and spaces of ecological resistance; they were conceived as exclusive spaces, where only Italian miners were allowed to enter. Italians' linguistic codes, their cultural references and their sociability structures had the function of conserving an utopic, forgotten rural Italy and its social structure. Those gardens were a memory island, a space of belonging and defense of a questioned identity in a sea of otherness shaped by the capitalistic organization of labor and xenophobic spatialization.

Not surprisingly, the second generation did not share the same organization of space and memory. For those children, born and raised under the black sky of the coal mining region, the vegetable gardens did not remind them of any ancestral and yet lost homeland. Instead, the apparently hostile environment created by coal extraction was their familiar space, the one which connected them to their childhood. As Santocono sums it up:

> Since the Étoile was the Étoile, the terril had always been the center of our quarrels between the children gangs of the region. It was something that belonged to us. Up there we had our monster, our kings and from atop we dominated the region that lay below at our feet.
>
> (Santocono 1986)

The *terril* became a hybrid space, transformed by the ludic activities in an evocative place, savage and familiar at the same time. It was a sort of Polar Star in the constellation of the domesticated and capitalized space of the mine. In the generational shift, the *terril* was no longer an ugly and alien place, but the peculiar mark of their land. For those kids, the challenge was not to domesticate it into an idealized Italian vegetable garden, rather to enjoy its special wild. In Santocono's words:

> We set up a great fire, like the American Indians, we sat around to eat and to stay together for the rest of the evening. Apart from the few who were able to smuggle a piece of cheese or a half banana, the majority of the guys brought just bread: a big piece of bread to play the part of the bread and a smaller one to play the part of the cheese.
>
> (Santocono 1986)

This image evokes a new form of wilderness. Instead of animals and spirits evoked by Native Americans, here in the *terril* the "natural power," the totemic medium connecting the soul of the natives with their land, was made out of coal.

Conclusions

In her book *Bodily Natures*, Stacy Alaimo employs the "proletarian lung" in order to explain what she means by transcorporeality:

> Similarly, the "pancreas under capitalism" and the "proletarian lung" testify to the penetrating physiological effects of class (and racial) oppression, demonstrating that the biological and the social cannot be considered separate spheres [. . . .] The proletarian lung illustrates my conception of trans-corporeality, in that the human body is never a rigidly enclosed, protected entity, but is vulnerable to the substances and flows of its environments, which may include industrial environments and their social/economic forces.
>
> (Alaimo 2010, 28)

In this chapter we have explored the embodiment of the capitalistic metabolism of coal in both the bodies of the Italian workers and the landscape they lived in. Coal infiltrated into the bodies of Italian migrants, leaving distinctive marks which reinforced their "otherness." Sometimes those marks were visible on the surface of the body; at others they went deep inside, as in the case of the silicosis haunting a large part of the miners'community. Although so overwhelming in the ecologies of miners, it would be a mistake to see coal as the main agent. The self-harm miners inflicted on themselves or the psychotic relationships with machineries and rocks were not an effect of coal, rather a consequence of the capitalistic organization of coal extraction. Migrants, coal, and mining corporations were part of a capitalistic ecology which extracted surplus from humans and nature. An environmental history of Italian migrants in Wallonia cannot be "environmental" in a narrow sense, but it must incorporate labor and social relationships as well.

While uncovering the unequal burdens to which Italian miners were exposed, we do not want to obliterate their agency in the making of the Wallonia landscape. No doubt their relationship with the Belgian mining landscape was permeated by environmental and social inequalities, which, nonetheless, left some room for forms of socio-ecological resistance and sabotage. We have illustrated how the very body became a terrain of confrontation and sabotage, with the companies pushing workers to the extreme, assuming that in five years' time they would be useless, and the miners trying to sabotage their own bodies with planned self-mutilations.

On the surface, Italian miners tried to take control of the wasted space created by coal extraction, transforming a devastated environment into a garden of memory. In fact, even more than the vegetables, memory was the staple crop of those gardens. In cultivating the *terrils*, Italians were cultivating their own identities, negotiating their skills with the local ecologies. As the self-production of food was per se an act of sabotage of the capitalist ecologies of mines—everywhere the companies controlled the entire market of their communities—in the case of Italian migrants it also constituted an act of resistance against the imposition of a double negative identity over miners and mines' landscapes. Italian miners found themselves alienated not only from their work but also from the environment where they had emigrated. Struggling to reaffirm their identity, they fought in order to subtract the nature of their bodies and that of the environment around them from the totalitarian metabolism of coal capitalism. In creating vegetable gardens on the *terrils*, the Italian migrants proved that they were more than machineries for coal extraction and that their landscape could be more than a wasteland.

In 2012 the four major Walloon mining sites[18] became part of the World Heritage. The description provided by UNESCO to advertise these sites helps to understand the physical and ecological transformation that occurred in Wallonia during the industrial revolution. The Belgian landscape has been turned into a net of "industrial, urban and architectural ensembles highly integrated into the landscape" (UNESCO 2012). Like a giant spider weaving its net underneath, the capitalistic production of coal has formed its infrastructural web of waterways, roads, coal waste deposits, power plants, steel and chemical factories. This geo-historical feature still marks landscape, bodies, and memory, dominating the social and labor rationale of the region. The economy of coal might be dead in Belgium, but its ecology is still alive.

Notes

1 In this chapter we will use the concept of collective memory as a social process of identity construction and self-representation, as defined by Halbwachs in the social frame of memory theory. See Halbwachs 1950.

2 *"Devant ton fier courage, tous, nous nous inclinons / Et te montrant aux jeunes et futurs compagnons, / Nous leur disons: 'Comme lui, ayez confiance / Dans salutte sans fin, son guide c'est la foi / Qu'il ne cesse d'avoir en notre faible science, / Debout donc et crions: "Mineur, Salut à Toi!"'"(In front of your bravery, we bend / Showing to the young and to future comrades / we say to them: "Like him, be confident / in his never ending struggle, its guide is faith / the faith he does not cease to have in our weak science. / Let us stand still and cry: 'Miners, we salute you!'* "). Mousseron J. 1919 Salut au mineur, *Les Boches au Pays Noir*. For this chapter we have used the 1971 volume gathering together all of Mousseron's works (Mousseron 1971).

3 *Grisou* is firedamp, a mixture of hydrocarbons, mainly methane, found in coal mines. It is explosive when it comes into contact with the air.

4 *"L' câble, su l' bobine s' déroule, / Plonqu eel' cage dins l' puits béant, / L' manivell' tourney et randoulle / L' carcass' dé t' Moulin géant"* (The cable up the reel uncoil / dip the cage inside the cavernous pit / The handle turn and repeats / the wreck of your giant mill). Mousseron J. 1907 Machine et outils, *Au pays des corons*.

5 The *corons* (crowns) were the working-class houses, circularly developed around mining sites.

6 Mousseron J. 1929 *Autour des terris*, translation from Picard dialect by the authors.

7 Coal Battle is the name chosen by the Belgian Government to present the post World War II coal production increase that became a national, political and economic goal in the 1950s.

8 The silicosis struggle has been one of the most important political and trade unions battles of the post-war period in the country. We can say that this common struggle has strongly helped in changing the status of Italian miners from objects of the socio-economical sphere into subjects of a shared socio-environmental struggle and actors in the Belgian political and trade unions scene.

9 This quote, as well as those from Olongo's, Rossetti's and Ferretti's books, have been translated by ourselves from the original version in Italian and French. Since we have used the ebook version, there are no page numbers in the quotes.

10 Regarding Le Camps, this is the description that Santocono gives: "All around the Cantine there were some barracks. It was a prison camp from the last war, reconverted to an ensemble of living units. There lived the most part of migrants of Morlanwelz. Every family had its own barrack [...] wooden walls and cement roof. All of them were on the ground, with a cement layer as a floor [...] these things burned down with a yawn."

11 With this term we refer to the spatial and socio-environmental discrimination and marginalization withstood by ethnical, racial and social minorities in the urban context.

12 We decided to use this literal translation in order to preserve the neo-Latin usage, common also in Italian, to associate the word for an animal face (*geuele, muso*) with humans in an offensive way.

13 We are referring to the emblematic sentence the Swiss novelist Max Fritsch wrote about the Italian Gästarbeiter in Switzerland: "We wanted arms, but instead men arrived" (*"Man hat Arbeitskräfte gerufen, und es kommen Menschen"*) (quoted in Seiler 1965).

14 This was the standard length of the contracts that the future miners had to sign before moving to Belgium. The contract also stated that they could not change job or mine before the expiration of the agreement.

15 On animals and their role in the mining ecologies, see Andrews 2008, 129–135.

16 The Italians migrated to French-speaking countries, following the famous terms used by François Cavanna in his book *Les Ritals*. See Cavanna 1978.

17 Several studies touch on this theme, for instance: Luconi 2015; Gabaccia 2000.

18 The four UNESCO World Heritage Sites in Wallonia are Grand Hornu, near Mons; Bois-du-Cazier, Marcinelle, in the periphery of Charleroi; Bois-du-Luc, not far from La Louvière, and Blegny-Mine, in the Liège province.

References

Alaimo, S. 2010 *Bodily natures. Science, environment, and the material self,* Indiana University Press, Bloomington

Andrews, T.G. 2008 *Killing for coal: America's deadliest labor war,* Harvard University Press, Cambridge

Armiero, M. 2010 *From Garlic Gill to Goatsville. Italians in the American landscape,* Paper presented at 70th Anglo-American Conference of Historians, London

Bertucelli, L. Ed. 2012 *L'Emilia al centro dell'Europa. Emigrazione in Belgio: storia e memorie di molte partenze e di qualche ritorno,* Unicopli, Milano

Bourdieu, P. 1994 *Raisons pratiques: sur la théorie de l'action,* Seuil, Paris

Bourdieu, P. and Passeron, J.C. 1970 *La reproduction. Éléments pour une théorie du système d'enseignement*, Éditions Minuit, Paris

Canovi, A. 2011 L'immagine degli italiani in Belgio. Appunti geostorici, *Diacronie* 5 1 8

Cavanna, F. 1978 *Les Ritals*, Belfont, Paris

Cumoli, F. 2012 *Un tetto a chi lavora. Mondi operai e migrazioni italiane nell'Europa degli anni Cinquanta*, Guerini e associati, Milano

Ferretti, M. 2003 *Gueules Noires*, NonSoloParole, Pollena Trocchia, Napoli

Gabaccia, D. 2000 *Italy's many diasporas*, University of Washington Press, Seattle

Geerkens, E. 2009 Quand la silicose n'était pas une maladie professionnelle. Genèse de la réparation des pathologies respiratoires des mineurs en Belgique (1927–1940), *Revue d'histoire moderne et contemporaine* 56 1

Halbwachs, M. 1950 *La mémoire collective*, Presses Universitaires de France, Paris

Luconi, S. 2015 *Lontane da casa: Donne italiane e diaspora globale dall'inizio del Novecento a oggi*, Academy Press, Torino

Mayeur Le, J. 1830. La gloire belgique, Vanlinthout & Vandenzande, Louvain

Mitchell, D. 1996. The lie of the land. Migrant workers and the California Landscape, University of Minnesota Press, Minneapolis

Morelli, M. 1988 L'appel à la main d'oeuvre italienne pour les charbonnages et sa prise en charge à son arrivée en Belgique dans l'immédiat après-guerre, *Revue d'Histoire Belgique* 19 83–130

Mousscron, J. 1971 *Oeuvres Complètes*, Fayard, Paris

Noiriel, G. 2006 *Introduction à la socio-histoire*, La Découverte, Paris

Nora, P. 1984–1992 *Les lieux de mémoire*, III volumes, Gallimard, Paris

Rossetti, R. 1989 *Schiena di vetro. Memorie di unminatore*, Einaudi, Torino

Santocono, G. 1986 *Rue des Italiens*, Cérisier, Liège

Seiler, A.J. 1965 *"Siamo Italiani" Gespräche mit italienischen Arbeitern in der* Schweiz, Seismo, Zürich

Slongo, O. 1999 *Et elle a voulu sa part, cette roche obscure. . .*, Cérisier, Liège

Swyngedouw, E. 2003 Metabolic urbanization: the making of cyborg cities. In Heynen, N., Kaika, M., and Swyngedouw, E., eds *Urban political ecology and the politics of urban metabolism*, Routledge, London, 20–39

UNESCO 2012 Major mining sites of Wallonia, available online at http://whc.unesco.org/en/list/1344 (accessed 19 January 2017)

Verlaine, P. 1872 *Romans sans paroles*, Belin-Gallimard, Paris

Part II

Racializing natures

While it is not always easy to recognize how much the body is nature in the sense illustrated in Part I, the naturalization of the immigrant's body has been a popular exercise in the racialization of ethnic minorities. Nativist hatred against newcomers is not a new theme in the history of migration. New, instead, is the attempt made by these authors to connect the nativist discourses with the environment. Fei Sheng illustrates how Chinese in Australia were accused of jeopardizing local natural resources, especially water, or blamed for contaminating the agricultural products with their fertilizing practices. More broadly, Chinese were perceived as filthy, a vehicle of moral and epidemic contagion. The intersection between biology and morality is also at the center of the wave of rage against the Filipino agricultural workers in California accused of having sexual intercourse with white women. Linda Ivey, also, illustrates the role played by a specific crop, lettuce, in the racial arrangement of the California fields. David Naguib Pellow and Lisa Sun-Hee Park explore the contemporary version of the nativist discourse and its links to some kind of environmentalism. Instead of focusing on immigrants' communities, Pellow and Park address the issue of white privilege, employing as case study the elitist community of Aspen, Colorado.

By and large the chapters in Part II unearth the histories of environmental racism to which immigrants were and still are exposed. These authors demonstrate that an environmental history of migrations is not confined to traditional themes in the discipline but can actually contribute to some general research topics in the history of migration, including racism and nativism.

Part II

Racializing natures

6   Riotous environments

Filipino immigrants in the fields of California

Linda L. Ivey

Abstract

In 1930, anti-Filipino riots erupted in rural California. This analysis highlights community relationships with the environment in explaining the violence. Across agricultural California, commercial industrialized production was booming, and while some long-time growers profited, others struggled to stay afloat. Immigrants were caught in the crosshairs, as anti-immigrant voices accused Filipinos working as "cheap labor" of creating this economically precarious situation. Further, California nativists had repeatedly feared Asian immigrants "invading" agricultural land that in their minds should be reserved for white citizens. Recognizing the environment as a key element in this story provides deeper understanding of the context into which thousands of immigrants to the 20th century US arrived.

If iceberg lettuce could speak...

What can iceberg lettuce tell us about five days of race riots in the early 20th century United States?

This is the basic inquiry of the study that follows, odd as it may seem at first reading. This work investigates a racist act in an era, and a region, where anti-foreign sentiment was palpable. In approaching this story from the perspective of environmental history, however, we can focus on the economic, cultural and environmental context to understand why xenophobia exploded into physical attacks on a particular migrant population. This investigation demonstrates how a society's cultural relationship with the natural environment is an essential factor in understanding the experience of migrating/immigrating peoples in a new region. While historical studies of immigration to the United States in the early 20th century discuss at length the role of racism and nativism, this study looks at the impact of *environmental* nativism, a dynamic where the "protective" fearful responses of nativists are directly tied to natural resources and national cultural attachments to the natural environment. This chapter re-examines the anti-Filipino riots using this environmental lens, and in doing so deepens our understanding of why incidents of nativist violence flare up at certain times and places.[1]

The social dynamics in rural regions of early 20th century California were notoriously volatile. As industrialized agriculture took hold of an increasing amount of acreage in the state, it curtailed opportunity for smaller holdings, and threatened the last vestiges of an agrarian ideal held dear by independent growers and aspirational Anglo-American farmworkers. Simultaneously, labor became increasingly vocal in the years leading up to World War II, as the disparity in wealth grew and the rights of all workers to a living wage—including those in the fields supporting large industrial agricultural operations—flailed. Although the reality on the ground was quite complex, with diverse experiences across the state and across individual agricultural operations, social conflict was common. It was into this contentious space that immigrants and migrants entered as agricultural labor.

The nature of the conflict, however, has not been fully unpacked. Race, ethnicity, nationality, political affiliation and socio-economic class have been the starting points for explaining social turmoil in these rural settings. Incorporating a perspective on the cultural environmental relationships makes these traditional axes of social conflict become more meaningful for understanding the experience of foreign immigrants (and domestic migrants, as well).

In the 1920s, larger narratives converged to focus controversy on immigrants to the western United States from the Philippines. By 1924, nativist agitation had all but closed major streams of immigration to the United States (Daniels 2004).[2] The Philippines, however, was a US protectorate; Filipinos carried US passports, and were legally still allowed to enter the country. As previous pools of inexpensive labor began to dry up in the aftermath of immigration restriction, this group inadvertently inherited the labor conflicts and social tensions experienced by previous migrant groups (Ngai 2004).[3] In this same time period, lettuce—a most unsuspecting villain—began to take hold as a major crop in the fields of central California. The lucrative green at once re-cemented the need for seasonal and inexpensive labor and threatened the livelihood of smaller growers in the region. As a result, many locals in these communities perceived Filipino immigrants to California to be supporting a high stakes cash crop that was crippling some of the last remnants of agrarian idealism in a modernizing agricultural industry. It is within this matrix of industrial agriculture, cultural-environmental ideals and immigration that the Anti-Filipino Riots of 1930 occurred.

Riots in Watsonville, California, 1930

On January 22, 1930, a young Filipino lettuce picker named Fermin Tobera was shot to death in his bunk house on the John Murphy Ranch, in the Pajaro Valley on the coast of central California. By most reports, the fatality was caused by a shower of bullets indiscriminately sprayed into the barracks by a gang of youths from the nearby town of Watsonville. There had been a social gathering that night on nearby Palm Beach. The local Filipino club had hired a dozen or so professional female dancing partners from Santa Barbara county to work the event, and a group of local whites, purportedly furious at the thought of this racial intermixing, gathered to disrupt the dance. When their efforts were thwarted by the club's owners, anywhere from 200 to 400 reported "whites" formed "Filipino hunting parties," and roamed the county "in search of stray brown men." A local paper relayed the probable events surrounding the murder with drama: "The unfortunate men (or boys) trapped like rats were forced into a closet where they huddled and prayed." It wasn't until the next morning that "it was discovered that a heavy bullet, tearing through the walls and a door of the bunkhouse, had pierced Tobera's heart" (*Evening Pajaronian*, January 20–23, 1930).

According to the newspaper coverage and subsequent reports, the killing was the culmination of five days of rioting in the area, a slow-brewed violent eruption between members of the local white population and Filipino farm workers. Following on the heels of other anti-Filipino violence in California agricultural regions such as Stockton and Exeter, reported "packs" of angry local whites —mobs ranging in size from 200 to 700 people in some accounts— engaged in confrontational acts ranging from vocal harassment to outright physical attacks. A specific spark to the action in Watsonville is not evident. There are references to statewide reports on vice and crime in the Filipino community contributing to the mood, and the local *Evening Pajaronian* featured an inflammatory rant from Judge D.W. Rohrback, a notorious anti-Filipino voice in Pajaro Township. Even recent historical analysis notes that the reasons for the outburst of violence were not entirely clear (*Evening Pajaronian* 1930; DeWitt 1979; Mabalon 2003; Ngai 2004).

Following the Tobera murder, newspapers, academic studies and government reports scrambled to make sense of the senseless, and called upon the traditional scripts of anti-Asian agitation to discuss immigration issues in that era: Was the Filipino population causing otherwise avoidable social disruption? Were they a health risk, carrying disease sustained in their squalid living conditions? Were they lowering the standards of living in California, keeping down wages and taking work away from deserving white Americans? Were they mixing with white women and endangering the purity of American blood? These suppositions reflect the larger picture of nativism and anti-Asian prejudice of American-Californian history. The riots, and the murder of Tobera, dramatically chronicled in the local press, were illustrative of egregious hostility faced by Filipino laborers in California—and they serve as an entrée into the larger patterns of nativism experienced by migrants into rural California in this enviro-cultural context.

The party at Palm Beach on January 22 was a culminating moment of a long tradition of nativist fear and anger—anger against Asian immigrants in California, and against immigrant labor in general. In this context of a community struggling to maintain stability in the face of broad social and economic changes, traditional nativist attitudes erupted into violent and racist action.

Environmental nativism and the fields of California

The particular story of the migration of labor into, and through, the fields of California's nascent agricultural empire in the early 20th century is a well-trod tale of social conflict. The poverty and disillusionment of early-century displaced farmers and farmworkers were well documented by the likes of author John Steinbeck, economist Paul Taylor and photographer Dorothea Lange. It is a poignant historical chapter in the history of migrating peoples, and how specific environmental contexts have profound impacts on their experience. While Steinbeck and Lange are more known for their documentation of domestic migrants, the locale of rural California had long been a part of persistent global migration systems since the Gold Rush beginning in 1848. And from that time, access to natural resources for foreign immigrants, including agricultural land, was a topic of much debate. California had become US territory in 1848; in one sense, those resources, be they gold, timber or land, represented a chance for Americans once again to become self-made men. Any threat to this privilege, and the promise of becoming an independent, self-made man (a promise already in peril as industrialization and modernization swept through the US at the turn of the 20th century), tended to spark reactionary rhetoric and activism. Environmentally informed nativism emerged as political and community voices tapped into a fear of foreign settlers cornering access to those natural resources, access to which was presumed to be an American right. A broader conversation about American citizen entitlement to these resources emerged.

These issues morphed, in part, into concerns about labor competition during the late 19th century industrialization of the American West. The context of the natural environment remained entwined in early California anti-immigration rhetoric. This is in part evidenced in the racial tones of the early labor movement (Lee 2003). Specifically, this held true in California during the arrival of Chinese immigrants in the 1850s. Exaggerated fears of an "Asian invasion" germinated during the years following the Gold Rush that began in 1848, born initially out of proprietary claims on mineral resources. The degree to which the nativism expressed during the Gold Rush is rooted in environmental relationships rather than strictly competitive capitalist relationships is arguable. The language of the Foreign Miners Tax regulations, however, points to something more complex than economic competition and racism. It speaks to an American sense of entitlement to natural resources on what was now American land, and to the way in which those resources should be used —what I have herein termed environmental nativism, that is tied into aspects of American identity including agrarianism and capitalism. The Foreign Miners Tax targeted the Chinese in particular. In many cases, noncitizen miners who were generally white, northern European immigrants escaped enforcement of the tax. The argument eventually developed that the miners who *could* become citizens should be exempt from such a tax, as elucidated in the 1855 version of the law. For all white males, naturalization was possible. For Asian immigrants, there was no path to legitimate status; they were labeled "incompetent" to become citizens (Kanazawa 2005). They could never become American citizens and therefore should not have access to American ore.

The Foreign Miners Tax reflects an American cultural expectation about the natural resources of the US that is acutely evidenced in the agricultural regions of the growing country. A cultural affinity to the Jeffersonian ideal of individual landownership had survived through the great land rushes of the 19th century, and California was one of the last staging areas for this American drama—reclaiming the American wilderness and bringing it under cultivation. So in the context of arable land, xenophobic protectionism was not only about rights to American land, but also the preservation of an iconographic American vocation. Again, nativists drew upon the threat of the "Asian invasion," a warning to which struggling small landowners were particularly sensitive. In 1913, the Alien Land Act in California—a reaction to Japanese immigrants settling on land as independent growers —reserved in non-specific terms agricultural lands for those who were "eligible for citizenship" (Van Nuys 1994). Here, race and nationality are framed as an aspect of an idealized citizenry, allowing for exclusion in a more palatable discourse. Sometimes the rhetoric was less palatable, more overt. In the 1920 US Senate race, Senator James D. Phelan, intent on alarming Anglo-American voters, ran on the platform "Keep California White," and his posters included statistics on the numbers of foreign-born children specifically in agricultural regions of California. Other posters encouraged voters to help him "stop the silent invasion" (Cherny n.d.).[4]

Nativist voices also blamed immigrant populations for "supporting" the industrial complexes—such as large-scale industrialized agriculture—in the very act of supplying their labor. When California's agricultural empire emerged in the late 19th century, the promise for small farmers seemed specious. In the late 1870s, when California growers were still debating the benefits of growing fruit over wheat, anti-Asian activists in the state had tried to make a connection between environmental degradation and race and a racialized class of laborers. During the US Senate hearings on Chinese immigration in 1877, one anti-Asian senator pushed the counsel for the Chinese into acknowledging that the Chinese were in large part responsible for soil degradation because of their willingness to work in fields for low wages. In reference to the large tracts of wheat that dominated rural California at that time, the nativist argument contended that without this labor pool, white farmers would be forced to limit the size of their farms (closer to a small, individually-owned farm ideal) and cultivate less, easing up on soil abuse.

Benjamin S. Brooks, counsel for the Chinese, countered that the troubles of soil exhaustion were rooted in cultivation techniques, not the laborers. This was the era when wheat was beginning to fall out of favor; Brooks categorized the industry as "exhaustive," noting "we add nothing to the land [...] we take all from it." On the other hand, Senator Aaron A. Sargent of California, representing the Joint Special Committee to Investigate Chinese Immigration, insisted that the Chinese made the abuse of such land easier. He posed the question to Brooks: "Would it not be better to have more diversified farming, requiring less Chinese labor?" Though Brooks insisted that the Chinese had "no influence upon the mode of cultivation" and were "only used as auxiliaries," the Senator was not convinced. He concluded:

> You could not gather the grain if it were not for the Chinese labor [...] this Chinese labor is not helping us, but exhausting our lands, and thereby impoverishing the state [...] It makes it easier to carry on the present system. With a little high priced labor (the growers) would have to go to some other kind of farming.
>
> (Senate 1877)

Initially, as fruit replaced grain as the mainstay of agricultural pursuits in California, horticulture was cast as a possible savior for the land as it pried growers away from soil-exhausting wheat.[5] However, horticulture—and the perishability of certain crops—cemented the reliance on an inexpensive, migratory labor force. So as the growers of central California had made horticulture their raison d'etre, they were cultivating, alongside of their crops, social kudzu. The white people of the Pajaro Valley, the heart of this agricultural community where the riots occurred, wanted to recreate a preindustrial, small-town agricultural community; they simultaneously and aggressively pursued a capitalist endeavor dependent on foreign labor. Though many locals were aware that their agricultural success was the result of a multicultural effort, a troubling social rupture remained (Ivey 2007).

Lettuce

"Changes in the dietary habits of Americans have elevated the lowly lettuce from a bit of pleasant garnish to an important food product," (Lasker 1931, 358). A seemingly mundane detail of a 1931 study of this region introduces one of the most significant and potentially disruptive changes along the coast of California in the years leading up to the 1930 riots. Local growers remember the dramatic shift on the central coast when lettuce became a "glamour crop," characterized by high demand and quick money (Crosetti and Jarrell 1993). The crop appeared in the Pajaro Valley first, grown regularly for commercial profit by the early 1920s. The Salinas Valley growers caught on after that, eclipsing the Pajaro Valley's lettuce production, and earning the nickname "Valley of Green Gold." But the introduction of this crop had its price for the smaller farmer, as the lettuce industry introduced "outside capital and outside companies, which leased large acreages from the local landowners and, without the same direct interest that local growers have in the consequences of their operations" (Lasker 1931, 358).

Lettuce indeed brought in quick money, but also had the social repercussions of crowding out smaller growers while renewing a call for labor. In fact, lettuce brought a whole new production system to the area, requiring lots of hands: the modern-era product not only had to be grown, but the lettuce had to be trimmed, packed in wooden crates, iced by hand, guided by conveyor to railway cars and stacked onto those cars. Not only was lettuce packaged with strict, labor-intensive icing techniques, it was packaged on a tight timetable.[6] The perishability of this crop, illustrated by the intense harvest techniques, gave organized workers an edge, and heightened tensions between the workers and the community into which they arrived. When lettuce was ready to be harvested, it had to be harvested, iced and packed, right away. Otherwise, the entire crop could be lost. It follows that an available and skilled work force was essential to success, and although the crop was a financial boon, its vulnerability to spoilage made it a risky venture, and put profits at the mercy of potential strikers. This peculiarity of the crop and the labor dynamic brought more volatility into agricultural regions across the state.

So the economic impact of lettuce, together with the vulnerability of a labor-intensive perishable crop, created a specifically tense social climate for the Filipino immigrants working in lettuce. In this context, although the environment did not engender anti-Filipino sentiment in the 1920s, it is an essential factor in understanding cultural elements that shaped the agitation.

Labor competition?

When Filipinos began to arrive in California in significant numbers, those offended by a foreign influx into the US leaned on the same stereotypes and prejudicial exaggerations endured by the Chinese and Japanese populations that had preceded them. By 1928, Californians had been warned of the burgeoning "Filipino problem" and the impending invasion of the "brown horde," despite comparatively small numbers of immigrants (McWilliams 1964). In fact, though Filipino immigration did continue to increase during the 1920s, their overall numbers remained quite small. According to census figures, there were fewer than 2,700 Filipinos in the United States in 1920, and an average of 4,000 per year entered between 1923 and 1929. Although these numbers are relatively small, the concentration of Filipinos in agricultural regions hit a collective nerve. By 1930, approximately 82% of the Filipinos in the US were employed as farm labor; about 72% of Filipino farm labor was in California (DeWitt 1976). It was enough for the press and other nativist sources to draw statewide attention to another wave of "oriental invasion." As the 1920s drew to a close, nativist voices circulating in the little city of Watsonville began to home in on the increasing population of Filipinos, and reintroduce many of the same sentiments that had led to previous exclusionary measures. However, a telling report to come out of the Watsonville incident aptly summed up the danger by stating: "the most serious 'problem' of Filipino immigration is the state of feeling which it has aroused" (Lasker 1931, 328).

As the Filipinos arrived in California, the lettuce industry provided employment in the fields, and arguably the availability of this "more affordable" labor source allowed the lettuce industry to thrive. Several hundred acres of land in the Valley under large-scale lettuce cultivation "may have previously offered seasonally or even all–year–round employment to local white workers" (Lasker 1931, 359). A contemporary sociological study on the incident, written by prominent sociologist Emory S. Bogardus, suggested the psychological impact on the broader community: "The invasion charge is not canceled in the minds of Watsonville laborers by the fact that the lettuce industry, one of the largest in the Watsonville district, has been built there largely upon Filipino 'stoop labor'" (Bogardus 1930, 101).

Notably, the same report went on to detail the following:

> No one else seems to be available to do the 'stoop labor' at early hours in the morning as efficiently as do the Filipinos, even at higher wages. Itinerant white laborers, living from auto camp to auto camp, do not furnish the steady labor needed throughout the season. Many of them work a few days, but do not like the work and move on. The town boys, the unskilled hangers–about–town are even more unsatisfactory to the lettuce and asparagus farmers.
>
> (Bogardus 1930, 101)

The role of labor competition in this story is a tricky one to nail down. In labor conflicts throughout California's history, especially in agriculture, the notion of immigrant labor undercutting white workers has often competed with concurrent suppositions that whites were not willing to do the work involved. Reports from various contemporary social scientists examining the riots focus heavily on the impact on white workers as the key to understanding the antagonism. Contemporary social worker and defender of immigrant rights Bruno Lasker compared the labor situation to that of the old south, where African slave labor had "degraded" certain labor in the eyes of whites: "Here in California, the living and working conditions of the agricultural laborer created a social barrier between this job and the ordinary white laborer" (Lasker 1931, 101). While Filipinos may not have been directly displacing white workers, the lettuce industry had so destabilized the economy for smaller, presumably Anglo growers in the region that the presence of the Filipino triggered a sense of being invaded, replaced and crowded out.

The environmental aspect of this conflict is obscured in the historical record by the overt racism that was applied to this particular group of migrants. Local nativist voices like Judge Rohrback played on the fear of "invasion" by warning of the arrival of "thousands of little brown men, but ten years removed from bolo and breechclout (sic.)." Rohrback stoked resentment by adding that for every boatload of Filipinos:

> [...] a boat load of American men and women are thrown out of the labor markets to lives of crime, indolence and poverty because for a wage that a white man cannot exist on, the Filipinos will take the job

and, through the clannish low-standard mode of housing and feeding practiced among them, will soon be well-clothed and [...] strutting about like a peacock [...]

(*Evening Pajaronian*, January 1, 1930)

In some cases, those *not* in favor of excluding Filipinos-often, expressly, those who benefited from the lower cost of labor—acknowledged the potential for a problem in similarly angry words and argued their position as defenders of the Filipino. A leader in a California agricultural association publication averred:

It must be realized that the Filipino is just the same as the manure that we put on the land—just the same. He is not "our little brown brother." He is no brother at all! He is not our social equal, and we don't propose to make him that or pretend that he is. Why, the Filipino should be greatly appreciative of what we have given him [...] We have got to have the Filipino do this work. But that's his place in <u>this</u> society [...]

(Wood 2016)

Whether reliant on Filipino labor or not, the popular scripts of anti-Asian discrimination shaped the rhetoric swirling around this group of workers, and the lettuce industry seemed to evoke a particularly virulent strain. A final detail of the Lasker report further highlights how this evolution in land use brought on conflict. While confirming that Filipinos were not generally in direct competition with white laborers, the report claimed that the Filipino presence did have an impact upon the local population of smaller-scale farmers. By the sheer fact that the lettuce industry drew Filipinos to the area, it made it possible "for a few local fruit growers occasionally to employ Filipinos at fruit picking, peeling and coring (in other industries outside of lettuce) in competition with white American workers" (Lasker 1931, 359). The report added:

[...] for large numbers of local families, occupying exceedingly small holdings of their own—so small, in fact, as barely to deserve the name of farm or ranch—opportunities of occasional labor, whether for a few days or for a few weeks at a time, are essential to eke out a precarious livelihood. And it is these dud jobs and short seasonal employment of all sorts which the Filipino, easily found available in sufficient numbers, is likely to get.

(Lasker 1931, 359–360)

In the historical context of the Watsonville violence, the presence of Filipino labor was a potential threat to either 1) the elusive, pre-1930s white laborer, who would expect higher wages and therefore lose out to cheaper Filipinos, or, more likely, 2) the remaining, struggling family yeoman farmers, desperately trying to keep their head above water in the 1920s. Whether the threat to Anglo independent farmers was real or merely perceived, the tension created is the real story behind this episode of violence.

Did lettuce cause a race riot?

The historical analyses of the 1930 Watsonville Riots, and other contemporary incidents of anti-Filipino violence in California, focus exclusively on racism as the root of the conflict, anti-Asian sentiment in particular, and often discuss economic issues via job competition. References to the environmental cultural context are sparse, and not explicit. Discussions also include how inter-racial mingling generated widespread concern about morality in smaller farming communities. In this regard, analysis of the Watsonville Riot consistently puts sexual politics front and center, locating the impetus of violence as moral outrage at the dance hall parties. Upon second examination, however, even arguments on morality issues come back to the image of an agricultural community perhaps mourning a dissolving virtuous, small-town agrarian ideal. As one local white commented after the Watsonville incident,

> Taxi dance halls where white girls dance with orientals may be all right in San Francisco or Los Angeles, but not in our community. We are a small city and have had nothing of the kind before. We won't stand for anything of the kind.

> (Bogardus 1930, 101)

So while race, sex and work are central aspects of the Filipino migration experience, they do not fully describe the deeper national cultural contexts that may explain why racism erupts when it does. US Immigration history is replete with narratives concerning labor competition, and certainly this is true with Asian immigration to the American West. But the enviro-cultural context has not yet been given attention as a formative aspect of nativism and anti-immigration agitation. One may argue that the migration of foreign peoples into this region allowed for the growth of a successful industrial agriculture complex in California that continues to thrive on inexpensive, mobile foreign labor. I have previously argued that the agro-cultural baggage brought by migrants to this area allowed for local agricultural industry to develop in unique ways based on specific multicultural contributions. But the relationship between migration and the environment has a cultural element as well that speaks to a receiving society's relationship with the natural environment—both in terms of "native" entitlement, and nationalist aspirations for living in the land.

Only a handful of historical research has treated the Filipino Race Riot in Watsonville with any depth in the last 40 years. Historian Howard DeWitt is among the few scholars to directly examine anti-Filipino violence in the 20th century. In 1979, he argued that (p)rior to the Great Depression, the primary argument against the use of Filipino labor was a social-sexual one"(DeWitt 1979, 293). However, DeWitt does write at length about the status of "cheap labor,"specifically in terms of small grower anxiety about the encroachment of corporations in rural California:

A close study of the composition of the vigilante group indicates that the attacks on Filipino leaders represented a psychological outburst against the giant corporations controlling the lettuce fields. No longer were Watsonville citizens able to prevent the use of ethnic farm labor. The status of local merchants and labor contractors declined as disinterested corporations began to dominate the lettuce fields.

(DeWitt 1979, 298)

Like DeWitt, historian Michael Showalter organizes his 1989 explanation of the riots around racism, specifically in the failure to indict the murderers of Tobera. Showalter's research, too, discusses the intense economic concern underlying the break out of violence. But, he notes, "underlying the economic reasoning was severe racial stereotyping based on sexual, cultural, and public health myths" (Showalter 1989, 342). More recently, Mai M. Ngai's 2008 work notes how growers as well as Filipino farm labor were targeted in incidents of anti-Filipino violence in the late 1920s. The work focuses on the sense of labor competition primarily being "fueled by long-standing racial animus towards Asiatics." Ngai also briefly notes "the ideology of white entitlement to the resources of the West" as the "central element of the hostility" (Ngai 2004, 106–115). In 1974, historian Brett Melendy had suggested an additional facet to consider: the sheer numbers of Filipinos entering the area of Watsonville were the source of the eruption, noting that "the dependence upon nonwhite labor sowed the seeds for conflict, for Watsonville was a town not prepared to accommodate such an influx" (Melendy 1977, 54). Controversy over the real numbers of Filipino immigrants and the degree of labor competition aside, Watsonville had a long history of foreign immigrant labor, and in significant numbers. Rather, something else was afoot.

Something had shifted from previous years: the balance of agrarian culture in modern industrialized agriculture had been destabilized. None of the above expert analyses are in conflict with a nod to the environmental context— in each case, we find confirmation of the cultural environmental relationship playing a role, and considering this element adds another layer of understanding as to what set off this action. Certainly, there was racial hostility and discrimination: those workers were targeted because of their race. The tradition of anti-Asian rhetoric and activity provided a familiar script that triggered community response, and these migrants' nationality and socio-economic status as farm labor further explain this particular outbreak of violence in the context of rural California.

What lettuce *can* tell us about race riots is that the volatility of a particular relationship with the environment—in this case, local economic dependence on a high-stakes cash crop—will have an impact on migrants entering that space. It can tell us a great deal about violence and social conflict when a defined group is perceived as potentially destabilizing balance—not just in economic opportunity, but in specific access to a cherished, and no longer easily attainable lifestyle. In 1929, labor advocate Paul Scharrenberg wrote: "Californians [...]

were forced into unpleasant anti-Asiatic campaigns because successive waves of migrations from the Orient seriously menaced the very livelihood of industrial workers, farmers and small tradesmen" (Scharrenberg 1929). But in the end, the threat was not only about the race of the workers but what those workers symbolized: the undoing of an American environmental dream.

Notes

1 Nativism is most succinctly defined as a fear of foreigners, but is used historically to describe a set of behaviors of those who see themselves as "native" Americans (read white Anglo Protestant, as opposed to indigenous) and actively seek to curtail or eliminate the immigration of foreign groups into the United States. Historian John Higham popularized this phrase in the historical vernacular, and identified three major themes, including anti-Catholicism, anti-radicalism and racism. Nativists— those who openly espoused these ideas—were often journalists and politicians seeking to garner favor from a particular constituency, but could also be used to describe any person who believed American should be kept "safe" from a foreign influx. See Higham 1955.
2 After a slow progression towards what historian Roger Daniels calls the "Triumph of Nativism," with measures including literacy tests and labor restrictions, in 1921 the US Federal Government passed a restriction act introduced by Congressman Albert Johnson—for the first time putting a numerical limit on immigrants from specific regions, targeting immigrants from Southern and Eastern Europe and virtually eliminating immigration from Asia. In 1924, the National Quota Act introduced more strict regulations of numbers, supported by a nation "gripped by xenophobia." See Daniels 2004.
3 In the aftermath of the immigration restriction acts of 1924, immigrants from the Western Hemisphere were also largely exempt from quotas. In California agriculture, specifically, it was Filipinos and Mexicans who immigrated in in the largest numbers to fill the need for labor. See Ngai 2004.
4 According to the *Sausalito News*, the Phelan campaign changed the slogan before Election Day to "Keep California American," in response to opposition in Southern counties with larger populations of non-white voters. See *Sausalito News*, Volume 36, Number 42, October 16, 1920.
5 Although horticulture did generally lead to smaller holdings, smaller farm size did not necessarily bring kinder cultivation. Nor did stable land tenure, with locally-situated growers owning and caring for their land. The scientific innovations that accompanied this industry over time brought unforeseen consequences. The benefits of crop diversification were counteracted by chemical herbicides and pesticides, erosion-causing cultivation techniques, and inadequate rotations of a monocrop culture that drained the soil of nutrients. Indeed, after decades of intense, *small*-scale farming, the Pajaro Valley faced severe problems, such as soil degradation. See Ivey 2014.
6 Lettuce was in fact *expertly* packed with the most recent of cooling technology: customarily, workers would shave a 300 pound block of ice with ice picks, put the chips into a wheelbarrow, and wheel the wheelbarrow over to the packers who "would pack a layer of lettuce, get a scoop of ice, and put the scoop of ice in the crate ... the one layer of lettuce, a scoop of ice, another layer of lettuce, and another scoop of ice. The crates would then be fitted with a lid, and transported to a 'reefer car' where a 'loader' would use tongs to pick more blocks of ice and toss them on top of the crates. The iced lettuce was mostly shipped by railroad. In many cases the railroad cars were right alongside the packing shed; crates were put on rollers and rolled right into the car. In some cases the lettuce would be trucked." See Crosetti and Jarrell 1993, 18.

References

Bogardus, E.S. 1930 *Anti-Filipino race riots: a report made to the Ingram Institute of Social Science, of San Diego, May 15, 1930,* T.G. Dawson for Ingram Institute, San Diego

Cherny, R. n.d. "James D. Phelan," FoundSF.org, http://foundsf.org/index.php?title=Mayor_James_Phelan, accessed January 28, 2016

Crosetti J.J. and Jarrell R. 1993 *J.J. Crosetti: Pajaro Valley Agriculture, 1927–1977,* interviewed and edited by Randall Jarrell, 1993, transcript, University of California at Santa Cruz Regional History Office, Santa Cruz, California

Daniels, R. 2004 *Guarding the Golden Door,* Hill and Wang, New York

DeWitt, H.A. 1976 *Anti-Filipino movements In California,* R and E Research Associates, San Francisco

DeWitt, H.A. 1979 The Watsonville anti-Filipino riot of 1930: a case study of the Great Depression and ethnic conflict in California, *Southern California Quarterly* 61.3: 291–302

Evening Pajaronian (Watsonville, California). 1930 January1, 20–23: n.p.

Higham, J. 1955 *Strangers in the land: patterns of American nativism, 1860–1925,* Rutgers University Press, New Brunswick, New Jersey

Ivey, L. 2007 Ethnicity in the land: lost stories in California agriculture, *Agricultural History* 81.1: 98–124

Ivey, L. 2014 Apples and experts: evolving notions of sustainable agriculture, *Global Environment* 2: 102–129

Kanazawa, M. 2005 Immigration, exclusion, and taxation: anti-Chinese legislation in Gold Rush California, *The Journal of Economic History* 65.03: 779–805

Lasker, B. 1931 *Filipino immigration to continental United States and to Hawaii,* University of Chicago Press, Chicago

Lee, E. 2003 *At America's Gates,* University of North Carolina Press, Chapel Hill

Mabalon, D.B. 2003 *Little Manila is in the heart: the making of the Filipina/o American community in Stockton, California,* Duke University Press, Durham, North Carolina

McWilliams C. 1964 *Brothers under the skin,* Little, Brown, Boston

Melendy H.B. 1977 *Asians in America,* Twayne Publishers, Boston

Ngai, M.M. 2004 *Impossible subjects,* Princeton University Press, Princeton, New Jersey

Sausalito News (Sausalito, California) 1920 Volume 36, Number 42, October 16: no page

Scharrenberg, P. 1929 The Philippine problem: attitude of American labor toward Filipino immigration and Philippine independence, *Pacific Affairs* 2.2: 49

Showalter,M.P. 1989 The Watsonville Anti-Filipino riot of 1930: a reconsideration of Fermin Tobera's murder, *Southern California Quarterly* 71.4: 341–348

Senate. 1877 44th Congress. 2nd session. Report #689. Report of the Joint Special Committee to Investigate Chinese Immigration. Washington DC: Government Printing Office, 1877: 52–53

Van Nuys, F.W. 1994 A progressive confronts the race question: Chester Rowell, the California Alien Land Act of 1913, and the contradictions of early twentieth-century racial thought, *California History* 73.1: 2–13

Wood, J. 2016 Notes. James Earl Wood collection on Filipinos in California, circa 1929–1934, Berkeley, California

7 Creating the threatening "others"

Environment, Chinese immigrants and racist discourse in colonial Australia

Fei Sheng

Abstract

The migration of Chinese to Australia stimulated by the discovery of gold triggered a white racist discourse in the second half of the nineteenth century. The anti-Chinese propaganda was not only rooted in economic and cultural rationalities, but also used ecological factors to justify the view that Chinese immigrants constituted a harmful species for Australia. In the 1850s, "water grievances" of European miners towards Chinese caused violent racial conflicts and led to the earliest discriminatory legislation. The anti-Chinese discourse diminished over the next two decades because the growth of the Chinese population slowed and Chinese immigrants proved useful in the development of agricultural industries and making the Australian natural environment profitable. When a feeling of nationalism and imperialism quickly grew in the 1880s, Chinese bodies were again condemned as dirty, corrupted and disease-causing. The middle class, especially the politicians and media elites, preached the danger of Chinese emigration to Australia. By looking at the development of the white racist discourse from an environmental perspective, this chapter illustrates how environmental arguments were successfully used to support European domination in the developing Australian economy and society.

It has been widely proved that Chinese immigrants had a significant influence on modern Australian history. However, as late as the mid-1970s the Australian Chinese were still a group of "aliens" in the public mind. In this chapter, I will briefly discuss how this anti-Chinese discourse was developed by exploiting environmental and ecological anxieties, rather than simply an economic or cultural bias, against the specific activities of Chinese immigrants. The dispute in allocating natural resources, and the image of Chinese bodies as dirty, strengthened a racist ideology rooted in the view of Australia as a remote European colony surrounded by an Asian population.

Chinese immigrants in Australian Environmental History

Within the context of Australian history, the Anthropocene—that is, the age dominated by humans'agency—did not simply begin with European settlement in 1789, but refers to a much longer time period when the first generation of Aboriginal people arrived in this southern continent at least 55,000 years ago (Garden 2005, 12). While it is widely recognized that both the Australian environment and society had been greatly transformed since the time when the First Fleet arrived, Australian environmental history is essentially the product of different groups of immigrants who interacted with each other and with the local environment.

As in many other settler societies, the complicated and extensive interactions between the European immigrants and the Aboriginal people were the most arresting stories. Consequently, disputes around Western colonialism, capitalism and conservationists' response to these trends contributed greatly to the studies of Australian environmental history. Beyond this popular and well-known narrative, one should not forget that Australia is a multicultural society. That means that not only have the British and Aboriginal heritage had an impact on Australian society, but other ethnic groups including Chinese immigrants also had agency in Australian history. Nonetheless, in Australian environmental history studies one can hardly find any works on immigrants other than the British. In fact, with limited exceptions such as Heather Goodall, who has worked on various immigrant groups and their relationships with the environment, few environmental historians pay attention to non-European immigrants' experiences (Goodall 2012 and 2010).

The absent role of Chinese immigrants in Australian environmental history should be addressed because Chinese immigrants and their descendants have constituted the largest non-European ethnic group since the 1850s. The earliest recorded Chinese settled in Sydney in 1818. There were four more significant waves of Chinese emigrations to Australia from the mid-nineteenth century when global migration movements to the antipodes developed. The first wave, and the largest and the most significant one in the colonial period, brought at least 42,000 Chinese immigrants to Australia as gold diggers, starting in 1853 when the gold rush reached its peak. Later, these people spread all around the continent and engaged widely in various industries, especially in agriculture.[1] With the birth of the Australian Commonwealth and the White Australia Policy, which strictly banned Chinese emigration to Australia, the Australian Chinese population quickly dwindled. Chinese emigration to Australia was not resumed until 1950 when the Colombo Plan[2] opened a door to the Chinese living in the British Commonwealth to become educated and trained in Australia. Most of these immigrants were not given citizenship until the 1970s. The third wave was the "Boat People" or refugees, including many Chinese, from Indo-China after the Vietnam War. The fourth wave rose after the abolishment of the White Australia Policy and the launch of the Reform and Open-door Policy in China in the late 1970s. Since then, the number of Chinese immigrants has skyrocketed.

Obviously, the trajectory of the Chinese emigrations to Australia was influenced by Australian migration policy. As a racist discourse, the White Australia Policy was the key reason that explains why Australian historians practically ignored Chinese experiences. In the gold rush days, the anti-Chinese propaganda and violence, prevalent in the white miners' society, was largely based on the environmental influence of Chinese miners on the goldfields. This created a fear of Chinese immigrants as an environmental threat to Australia. As a basis for the future White Australia Policy, the racist propaganda drove the administration to impose a special poll-tax on Chinese immigrants. In the last two decades of the nineteenth century, the rise of Australian nationalism more frequently seized upon and used the stereotype of the Chinese as an environmentally threatening "other" to consolidate their ideal European society transplanted to the antipodes. The Chinese were considered both unclean and dangerous in their constructed environments and in their physical bodies. Since 1901 when the White Australia Policy forbade new Chinese emigration to Australia, Australian Chinese history was consequently neglected as Chinese immigrants never truly belonged to this land.

What do these Chinese experiences mean in Australian environmental history, especially during the foundational days of modern Australia? From an environmental perspective, this chapter aims to examine how the Australian anti-Chinese discourse was constructed and developed during the second half of the nineteenth century. Ann Curthoys, a leading historian of the Australian racial relations, writes, "people could get along, but only when the Chinese were seen as a declining force, only when the colonial Australians' sense of European and particularly British political, social and economic dominance was unthreatened" (Curthoys 2001, 118). In effect, no matter how the Chinese immigrants were assimilated into the Australian environment and society, the whites could use their cultural and political power to create a racist discourse.

"Water grievance" and the rise of anti-Chinese propaganda

From the time the New South Wales colony was established, Australia was divided into several penal colonies and did not receive massive waves of free migrants until the mid-nineteenth century. The decisive stimulus was newly-discovered gold in 1851. The Australian population tripled in the following ten years and Victoria, with the largest goldfield, absorbed most of these new immigrants (McCalman, Cook, and Reeves 2001, 19; Fahey 2010, 149). The Chinese were part of this huge migration, and they soon named Victoria the "New Gold Mountain," a reference to California—the "Old Gold Mountain". In some of the main goldfield areas, Chinese accounted for 25 percent and even up to 35 percent of the male population (Lovejoy 2007, 41). More significantly, "gold rush migration provided an unusual experience for Britons, many of whom had never mixed so freely with foreigners, especially the Chinese" (Fahey 2010, 149). As a consequence, conflicts quickly arose between Chinese and European immigrants around the distribution of major natural resources, in particular the use of water. Much evidence shows that the "water grievances" frequently gave rise to the bitterest confrontation between the Chinese and European miners.

Figure 7.1 Relic of alluvial field near a Chinese camp at Castlemaine, Australia
Source: Photograph by the author

In traditional Australian historical narrative, there has been a stereotype of Chinese miners as "fossickers" and "water wasters": they rarely opened new claims but simply focused on re-washing tailings on old claims. Compared to the European miners who worked as individuals or as a family, the Chinese always worked collectively, which meant they consumed additional water. These digging methods caused the water supply to deteriorate and led to the "water grievances" of white miners. Based on a miner's record of 1859, Geoffrey Serle, an authoritative Australian historian, wrote that

> Chinese quickly settled down [...] to work abandoned ground, reworking "tailings," and seeking and often finding pockets in creek-beds which had been overlooked [....] the Chinese had been causing widespread irritation through their mining methods and ignorance of the regulations and accepted conventions: waste of water, "muddying" water and ground, and use of and damage to carefully constructed water-holes were frequently mentioned.
>
> (Serle 1968, 321)

Another popular historical reader describes how "Chinese wash their dirt in one water hole and let the mud run into the next, thus spoiling two holes"

(Gittins 1981, 74). All these criticisms were proved by official records: after the Eureka Stockade Riot,[3] the only violent struggle between workers and the administration in Australian history, the Victorian legislative council installed a commission with the purpose of enquiring into the conditions of the gold fields in the state. In its report the commission stated that:

> The Chinese are content with very small earnings acquired under the rudest modes of mining. In rewashing the old grounds, which seems their chief mode, they use up and waste the water with a thoughtless profusion, disregarding often the reservoirs of drinking water, and they thus occasion many wrangling scenes by their inability or unwillingness to understand the representations of the authorities or the adjacent miners.[4]

This report was so historically influential that it promoted the earliest poll-tax imposed exclusively on Chinese in order to restrict Chinese influx.

Before this report was finalized, there was already evidence which illustrated clearly the general negative attitude regarding the Chinese's use of water. Questioned on the Chinese presence in the area, an American miner at Ballarat, Charles James Kenworthy, answered:

> They are the greatest nuisance on the diggings, and government ought to take some steps, if not for their removal, at all events to prevent their increase; they are [a] nuisance; they spoil all the water on the gold fields, and will merely work upon the surface.
>
> (McLaren 1985, 8)

For him, Chinese miners spoiled the water "by washing in it; they do nothing but surfacing" (McLaren 1985, 8). Henry Melville, a former storekeeper at Castlemaine, added: "they take the water out of one hole, and let their 'tailings' fall into another one, and so destroy the water of two holes" (McLaren 1985, 9). The key evidence was presented by Joseph Anderson Panton, Resident Commissioner at Sandhurst (Bendigo):

> At one time they were a nuisance in the back gullies; they destroyed the water, which the Europeans would not have done, from the fact of their washing whatever stuff they could lay hold of. They would not dig holes, and take the washing-stuff alone and wash it; but they went about the gullies, and scraped up whatever they thought would pay them. In that way they were perpetually washing while other men were digging.
>
> (McLaren 1985, 11)

From those three testimonies it would seem that the Chinese were undoubtedly destroying the water supply. However, the interview with Howqua, a Cantonese who could speak fluent English, offers, obviously, a different version of the story:

The Chinamen take away the water at the diggings, and make the diggers angry?—Yes; that is what I have been speaking about. Do the Chinaman understand now the injury they are doing by taking such a large quantity of water?—Yes, they understand it. In the winter time you go and take plenty of water, in the summer time you cannot take a drop of water.

(McLaren 1985, 12–13)

Among the people who were heard Howqua was the only Chinese witness and he proved that Chinese miners learned how to use water sustainably by respecting the change of seasons. Even though the Chinese miners constrained their activities, the fact of wasting water and jeopardizing European interests was not acceptable.

Other reasons may help us understand why Chinese were seen as water wasting fossickers. Firstly, the shortage of water existed widely in Australia and the water supply problem was a challenge to all immigrants whether they were miners or not. At the beginning of the gold rushes, some noticed that

[…] the streams of Victoria, like those of Australia generally, bear no resemblance to the fine river[s] of Europe or America. They were few in number; and the Hume, or the upper Murray, and a portion of the Yarra Yarra excepted, all insignificant, and quite useless for purposes of inland navigation.

(Lancelott 1852, 55)

Every new immigrant to Australia had to get used to the shortage of water.

Secondly, the arrival time of the Chinese immigrants also made them prone to work on second-hand claims. The earliest Chinese diggers came to Australia at the end of 1853 when the rush had lasted for two years and the average outcome of surface mining was declining, so a growing number of miners turned to shaft mining but abandoned surface claims. So it was not an accident that the Chinese chose to work on the surface claims, which required less investment and energy, and had been worked by the earlier miners.

Thirdly, the intelligence of Chinese was different from that of the Europeans. European miners usually lacked "steadiness"—they "repeatedly left payable claims, deceived by wild rumors of fabulous wealth at new fields. (…) Most lost heavily by rushing, but could not resist the gamble" (Curthoys and Markus 1978, 39–40). Chasing after gold nuggets but not grains, the European miners abandoned claims and tailings which sometimes contained enough gold for a lengthy washing. In turn, they scorned the Chinese who toiled for a meager income and "wasted" water, as they did not stop washing until the smallest grain was found. In fact, this process saved quantities of gold that might have been lost.

In fact, "water grievance" was largely a result rather than a cause of racist ideology against the Chinese. Using his archaeological research into main southern New South Wales goldfields, Barry McGowan established that the Chinese had often worked on first-hand claims and did not just wash tailings (McGowan 2005). Chinese miners sometimes had to work on old claims (and used more water) because they could hardly keep the new ones under the threat and attack of the European miners. As early as 1854 there had been a court record showing that European miners violently expelled the Chinese from a claim. In 1854 and 1855, the most important newspapers including the *Argus* and *Ballarat Star,* frequently reported that the Chinese miners were sometimes beaten and expelled from new goldfields. The most notorious case was in 1857, when 700 Chinese miners were traveling overland from the Port of Robe, South Australia, to the Central Goldfields of Victoria. Replenishing their water supplies at a spring some 400 kilometers due east of Robe, they discovered by chance the Canton Lead, the world's richest shallow alluvial goldfield that stretched five kilometers in length. In the following three months they harvested rich gold and established Ararat, a small town which still survives today. However at the end of 1857, most Chinese miners were ousted from residence and expelled from the site by the British miners who heard the news and came in.

"Water grievance" was increasingly used as an excuse for the racist propaganda against Chinese after 1855. In 1860 to 1861, the goldfields reported six riots against Chinese miners. Ironically, the first three happened during the winter when there was lots of water. The latter three occurred in drought season when the goldfield administration had already segregated the races on fields with separate water supplies. After having investigating the goldfields, even the New South Wales premier, Charles Cowper, was convinced that the miners' appeal about "water grievance" was absurd. He told the European miners that:

> [...] the Chinese have not really injured you. True, the supply of water is inadequate to your wants, but this has not arisen from the use of it by the Chinamen [....] Your grievances are not as great as you would try to make out.
>
> (Curthoys and Markus 1978, 40)

The racist propaganda avoided the fact that the European immigrants should take greater responsibility for the decline of the Australian goldfield environment. As Geoffrey Bolton states, "the impact of Europeans on the Australian environment before 1850 would seem puny compared with what came after gold" (Bolton 1981, 68).There were four particular environmental impacts of gold rushes: population influx and the establishment of numerous urban centers; localized damage from digging and the spread of subsoil as mullock or tailings; the clearing and consumption of timber; and the degradation of water systems (Garden 2005, 83). All four of these impacts could cause the reduction of water, while European miners merely blamed the Chinese miners.

In the mid-nineteenth century, new European immigrants to Australia, mainly from Britain, combined imperialism with racism when they created an anti-Chinese discourse. In 1856, a reader of the *Argus*, the most popular contemporary newspaper in Victoria, wrote to draw the attention of our fellow-colonists to the curse that we are allowing to be entailed on this fine colony, and its future inhabitants, by permitting the introduction of hordes of Mongolian pagans, whose present object in coming here is for the purpose of gutting this country of its wealth and returning elsewhere to spend it.[5]

Not coincidentally, in 1857, the Legislative Council of Victoria promoted a new bill "to control the flood of Chinese immigration setting in to this Colony, and effectually prevent the Gold Fields of Australia Felix from becoming the property of the Emperor of China and of the Mongolian and Tartar hordes of Asia". [6]

It is not hard to understand why the European racists, from both private and official corners, were eagerly utilizing "water grievance" to restrict Chinese emigration to Australia.

Chinese contribution to agricultural industries and the decline of racist discourse

Gold rushes began to subside starting in 1861 and Chinese emigration to Australia also slowed. However, gold rushes stimulated many other natural resource extraction industries that supported mining and the growing communities. For example, in Victoria "the presence of agricultural, pastoral and timber resources helped to keep down mining costs, just as mining provided hinterland settlers with ready markets" (Bate 1988, 5). It offered Chinese immigrants an opportunity to work in various industries other than solely the goldfields. As skillful agricultural workers, many Chinese fulfilled the need for expanding Australian agricultural industries. The racist propaganda against the Chinese community also lessened somewhat.

In fact, Chinese were very successful in helping establish a profitable new agricultural ecosystem in Australia. In evidence in the 1855 report, the Parliament Commission asked Howqua: "Would they be able to grow wheat and vegetables?" He replied: "Yes, all Chinamen like farming."[7] Especially after 1865, Chinese turned to market gardens and took advantage of Section 42 of the Amending Land Act which allowed people to reside on and cultivate Crown Land in and around the goldfields under annual licenses.

Among all the Chinese agricultural activities, market gardening was the most significant contribution to Australian society (Yong 1977, 49–54). It developed in close ties with mining activities. When shallow digging was popular in Victoria in the early 1850s, miners had to shift claims frequently, so they could seldom stay in one place long enough to establish a vegetable garden or market system. By the early 1860s with the rise of quartz mining on large Victorian goldfields such as Bendigo, the more settled miners provided a stable market for vegetables. Many Chinese migrants found it difficult to gain opportunities in the quartz mining gangs, so the migrants who wanted to stay turned to agricultural work around the goldfields (Stanin 2004, 23). Northeastern Victoria experienced a very similar process. In the 1860s, vegetables from the Chinese gardens quickly dominated the Beechworth market (Frost 2002, 116–117). In Queensland and New South Wales, although Chinese market gardening was not always developed by miners, the planting skills were connected with those in Victoria, mainly because the gardeners came from similar backgrounds.

The locations of vegetable gardens were varied, but cultivators generally preferred fertile soil and flat fields. For example, in the Loddon River district in Castlemaine, a planting site usually required "a rich alluvial soil, a nearby water source and a reasonably flat aspect" (Stanin 2004, 14). Chinese could also grow vegetables more successfully in poorer soils than European market gardeners. In Bendigo, an "editor particularly admired the facility with which the Chinese could take infertile land situated in the midst of old gold workings, all 'stiff clay' and 'quartz pebbles,' and make it fertile."[8] It is notable that many of the Chinese market gardens were scattered on abandoned alluvial diggings, showing that Chinese migrants did create wastelands as miners, but were also sometimes able to restore these wastelands and make them fruitful.

Traditional Chinese irrigation and planting skills were used to improve the condition of a field. Before the Chinese gardens were equipped with tap water, the water needed for planting was shouldered to gardens by laborers. Considering the low rainfall of the Australian goldfields, this work could be considerable, especially in the hot, dry summers. Chinese usually watered the fields before sunrise in order to avoid the burning sunshine and undue evaporation. A Chinese agricultural worker remembered that he and his fellows had to carry hundreds of barrels of water early every morning (Zheng 1992, 75). In a typical Chinese garden, all the crops were planted in straight, parallel rows and furrows, arranged to the very edge of the property. The fields demonstrated very painstaking farming customs.

Although the Chinese successfully developed market gardening by bringing their own traditional experience to the Australian environment, they also adapted to local conditions and borrowed European traditions at times. At first, Chinese miners grew favorite vegetables and fruits for their own use (Moore and Tully 2000). However, when market gardening boomed, they grew European products for the expanding market. The potato was not an important food in the Cantonese diet, but it was widely planted on the goldfields substituting for sweet potatoes. Lettuce and cabbage from Chinese gardens were very popular among European societies, although they were not traditional Chinese vegetables. In the Bendigo area, Chinese started the tomato industry that flourished in the nineteenth century before it moved north to better irrigated districts (Lovejoy 2007, 31). Moreover, Chinese learned from Europeans to inter-plant other crops between rows of maize so they would be protected by the faster growing maize (Frost 2002, 122). In 1877, J. Dundas Crawford, commenting on the impact of Chinese immigration to Australia, said that Chinese gardeners had "reduced vegetables from an expensive luxury [...] to a cheap and universal article of diet" (Lovejoy 2007, 31). All this evidence shows that Chinese were capable of quickly learning to grow plants that had not been familiar to them before arriving in Australia.

Although market gardening was the most influential farming activity of Chinese migrants in the gold rushes, it was just one dimension of their broader participation in Australian agriculture. European farmers employed Chinese in a variety of jobs. William Young's report on Chinese miners showed they had also been employed as seasonal workers for harvesting (McLaren, 1985). A lot of Chinese miners were also active in vineyards, tobacco plantations, and were even precursors to the hop industry in Victoria. As early as 1855, the *Argus* praised the Chinese for their orchard skills:

> Chinese gardeners are not unskillful in this branch of gardening, as they often wrench or cut a strip of the bark off for some time previous to their detaching the cutting, in order to get it into a proper state for emitting roots when put into the soil.[9]

Some of their activities had an aesthetic aim. A noteworthy case was that Chinese miners widely transplanted plum trees into Victorian diggings in order to beautify the local landscape because there was no other flower blooming during the Spring Festival in the local goldfields (Stanin 2004, 39). In fact, many Chinese shifted their jobs between mining and agriculture. Farming was a convenient way for Chinese migrants to settle down as new Australians.

In Queensland, where heat, humidity and pests stopped the advance of the European colonists, many Chinese became tropical fruit growers, especially in banana plantations. Since the late 1870s, Queensland became the main supplier of bananas in Australia. Chinese immigrants introduced the first banana plant to Northern Queensland, where conditions were particularly suited to banana growing. Much of the land in these areas was cleared by Chinese banana growers under the practice of clearing new land to plant new crops rather than replanting areas that had been already cleared. The early prosperity and survival of the Cairns and Innisfail area has been directly attributed to the success of the Chinese in the banana industry. Both Chinese and non-Chinese businesses in these towns provided goods and services to Chinese banana growers. Chinese merchants in particular played an important role as commission agents and by assisting growers with finance.

In the wake of gold rushes, with the expansion of the capitalist market and accumulation of wealth, all Australian colonies, particularly the tropical Queensland and the hinterlands of Victoria and New South Wales, experienced an ecological transformation as a result of the exploitation of natural resources. Although a European-dominated agriculture and grazing system was established, the Chinese immigrants contributed their toil and moil. More significantly, the Chinese immigrants brought unique techniques and skills to Australia and supplemented the limited local labor market. When Australian were exploring and exploiting the tough hinterland before the early 1880s, anti-Chinese racism was rarely rampant.

The only dispute on Chinese agricultural activity was over the methods to fertilize poor land. There were two traditional ways. The first way was using so-called "green fertilizer" (*Lv Fei*) or herbaceous fertilizer. See Yap people had a long tradition of reaping fresh wild grass and burying it into the fields to prepare them for growing plants. When the grass decayed, it became an "essential fertilizer" (*Ji Fei*) that improved fields. The second method was to bury fermented manure, especially urine (mixed with water), in a field after planting. Although there was no direct evidence that "green fertilizer" was used on the Australian goldfields, the latter method was well known to locals. For example, Angus Mackay, an instructor of Agriculture for the Board of Technical Education in New South Wales, openly criticized the Chinese gardens for being smelly because of the use of "ammonia" from the manure.[10] In fact, Chinese immigrants strictly piled night soil and organic rubbish onto specific sites where gardeners could transfer and use them later for fertilizer (Cronin 1982, 92).

The Chinese were able to offer their contribution to the shaping of the Australian environments, adapting their skills and techniques to it and participating with the other European immigrants in the making of modern Australia. However, the situation changed again in the late nineteenth century.

Environmentally threatening "others" in urban areas

In the 1880s, with urbanization and the establishment of a mature economic system in Australia, Chinese immigrants gradually moved to large cities and suburban areas. Consequently, Chinese communities expanded steadily in downtown Sydney and Melbourne. Over time, as in California, Australian society also developed a connection between disease and environment, especially in urban areas where people lived more closely together and engaged in various social activities (Nash 2006; Mitman 2007). This gave anti-Chinese sectors the excuse for the second rise of anti-Chinese propaganda with the urgent assertion that urban diseases had a Chinese connection. Fundamentally, it finally shaped the White Australia Policy to protect the purity and dominance of whiteness.

This revival of racist discourse was based on a more scientific belief, Social Darwinism, which was widely accepted and cited by the European imperialists. Middle class elites took advantage of an anti-Chinese sentiment coming from the European working class in the 1850s who worried that the Chinese immigrants would bring down the cost of labor. Given that according to the colonial discourse Australia had already become one of the most civilized places, and was no longer an Aboriginal wild of the British Empire, the axiom "survival of the fittest" offered European immigrants a ready and simple defense of the status quo of conquest, a rationale of white expansion. However, Social Darwinism gave no guarantee that the white race would always win out when they faced Chinese immigrants.

In late 1870s and early 1880s, a concern about the expected growth of Chinese immigrants created new anti-Chinese propaganda. One of the reasons was that the United States of America, especially California, which had been a popular destination for Chinese overseas emigrants, now became more unfriendly to Chinese immigrants. Therefore some Chinese turned to Australia to make new lives. For example in Victoria, during the five years between 1877 and 1881, annual Chinese immigration increased from 449 to 1348 (Cronin 1982, 125). Although the number declined quickly in the following years, these new Chinese immigrants, mainly competitive physical laborers, aroused an uneasy atmosphere in the Australian working class in large cities with a strong press market.

As early as in 1856, Edward Wilson, editor of the *Argus*, queried:

> We take the country from the blacks because we can put it to better uses than they would do. But [...] if a race were to present themselves who would take measures to apply the country to still better purposes, are we prepare to resign it to them?[11]

The renewed emigration of Chinese miners made this an important issue, for many workers witnessed that the Chinese succeeded in many industries, other than gold mining, particularly agriculture, and might prove "too numerous and sturdy to be extirpated" (Cronin 1982, 72).

However, the European publicists, scientists, and popular writers were too preoccupied with the idea of progress and evolution. As compared to the circumstances in 1850s and 1860s, European immigrants and their descendants were more responsive to Social Darwinism as it was not only a belief easily understood by the less educated white men but also a theoretical weapon for many elites to consolidate a white Australian identity. Many politicians and opinion leaders promoted an image of the arriving Chinese people as an invading species. Since they found the Chinese could not be repressed as the Aboriginal people were, they emphasized that the Chinese were polluting the Australian environment and spreading disease. In fact, the Chinese communities were accused of creating a dirty and dangerous environment as early as in 1857 when some European miners complained about the Chinese camps on the goldfields:

> The serious risks that the whole community run where these people are located, from the indiscriminate huddling together of their tents, so extremely small in size that their very construction prevents a free circulation of air, which is strongly impregnated all around with the effluvia aris-
> ing from the various refuse scattered about, added to personal uncleanness, which should an epidemic attack the spot they have settled down upon, it is fearful to contemplate the results to the surrounding district.[12]

However, this unclean environment was not simply a result of the Chinese miners habit of neglecting public sanitation, but a consequence of racist discrimination. From September of 1855, to avoid a further conflict between Chinese and

European immigrants, all Chinese on the goldfields were compelled to live collectively in so-called protected areas separated from the European community by the goldfield administration. This order was not abolished until 1863 and during this period, all Chinese residents had to pay a special duty to the government for maintaining public sanitation. However, the Chinese immigrant population increased but the protected areas were not expanded. Moreover, the government only took a small portion of the duty to sustain sanitary affairs (Ngai 2010). Therefore it was very hard for a Chinese village to keep clean. When the Chinese residents could freely settle down again, the public sanitary problem quickly disappeared. Moreover, a report from 1867 showed how they initiated a law to self-administration in Ballarat:

> Europeans pay strict regard to cleanliness. No heaps of fetid filthy stuff must be allowed to accumulate by the sides of tents, nor must such places be used as water-closets. If any act of impropriety of this kind be witnessed by any individual, he is authorized to mention the name of the person so offending to the manager of the club-house, and the offender shall be punished with twenty stripes.
>
> (McLaren 1985, 30)

Even though the Chinese were aware that they should take care of the sanitation problem to reduce the potential criticism from the whites, the unclean image had already become a stereotype of the Chinese settlers.

In the 1880s, although the Chinese communities were not always dirty and unhealthy in the cities, the elites still asserted that Chinese were a species with terrible, corrupted customs and were threatening the Australian social ecology. They produced a figure called "Ah Sin" who was supposedly corrupt, opium smoking, whoring and "leprosy-sodden" in urban areas.[13] To a great extent, this was not fully calumniating, but the Chinese "dirty" activities had a complicated background.[14]

The opium smoking, gambling and whoring did not happen by accident. Most Chinese emigrants to Australia did not bring families when they first went abroad. As a consequence, the female Chinese population was too small to support a heterosexual-family-based Chinese immigrant society. For example, a statistic showed that in 1881 there were 11,871 male but only 261 female Chinese in Victoria (Cronin 1982, 136). After a tough, physical day's work, there were no other choices but opium smoking and gambling to fulfill the need for entertainment and to fight homesickness in a primarily male population (Booth 1999, 200). It was also not surprising that prostitution was popular in the Chinese communities. Ironically, anti-Chinese activists attacked those behaviors while the European merchants and local administration earned a large sum of money through selling opium to Chinese and levying tax on these entertainments: "The tax on the opium business was the highest in New South Wales. For every box you should paid for 48 pounds, and cigarette from Philippine had to pay 6 shillings for every 500 grams" (Xue 2001, 129).

The criticism was also ridiculous because the opium smoking problem existed widely in the white communities, too. In April 1891, the Victorian administration found there were 700 white people smoking opium in one detection (Booth 1999, 201). By deliberately neglecting the Europeans' problem, the anti-Chinese propaganda simply stressed that the Chinese were harmful bodies to a healthy modern Australian society.

The most arbitrary and horrible condemnation was that the Chinese immigrants would cause epidemics. Many middle class elites believed that certain races had aptitudes or immunities to particular diseases and that Chinese would infect Europeans with the "darker maladies" of cholera, typhoid, small-pox and leprosy (Cronin 1982, 69). This unfounded idea could also be traced back to Chinese communities on the goldfields. In 1857, three lepers were found residing in a Ballarat Chinese camp and the Ballarat and Catstlemaine protectors ordered all camps to be relocated and the old villages cleared and burnt. It warned that every precaution should be taken to prevent Chinese staying amongst the diggers. When another European person in Melbourne was found to have small-pox, all Chinese were ordered to be compulsorily vaccinated (Cronin 1982, 92).

The Chinese community was much larger in Sydney and Melbourne in the 1880s than those in the 1850s. Therefore when an unexpected epidemic came, the Chinese were at once blamed for causing it. From May, 1881 to February, 1882, Sydney experienced the most severe small-pox epidemic since the Europeans' arrival. However, when a large group of 450 Chinese immigrants, carried by the SS *Ocean*, a steamboat from Hong Kong, coincidentally arrived in Sydney harbor, they drew great attention and irritation from the white communities. Many press and political elites believed that the Chinese were introducing and spreading the plague, although they had only very ambiguous evidence: the first patient was a half-Chinese descendant living in a European community. The colonial government led by Sir Henry Parkes, a well-known anti-Chinese politician, ardently encouraged this belief to distract the public attention away from the truth of his government's lack of preparation for dealing with this epidemic. The Sydney small-pox epidemic in May most probably came from London, where they had already suffered from the same disease. In contrast, Hong Kong, the main port for transporting Chinese to Australia, was free of it. Medical officers checked at least 3500 Chinese entering Australia in 1880 and found no case of the disease at all. During the epidemic only three Chinese, including a child, were found infected amongst the 163 reported victims. However, Henry Parkes still forbade the landing of the SS *Ocean*. Parkes insisted that the boat should be quarantined indefinitely and was reluctant to supply any food, water and fuel. Therefore, the *Ocean* had to turn to Melbourne to disembark 222 Chinese there. When it transported the remaining passengers who were supposed to land in Sydney two weeks later, the boat was quarantined again for 21 days. When these Chinese passengers were finally allowed to enter Sydney they were required to burn all their belongings including clothes (Watters 2002, 333–335).

Figure 7.2 Sydney Chinatown. These days it is a famous tourist site, whereas in the 1890s it became a symbol of the dirt and disease of the Chinese community. The narrow street has retained its original width.

Source: Used under Creative Commons license

This small-pox epidemic successfully incited hatred toward the Chinese immigrants and gave the finest excuse for influential politicians to promote stricter legislation against further Chinese immigration. During the peak of the epidemic, Parkes introduced an anti-Chinese bill, which applied a poll tax of ten pounds on Chinese immigrants and a limit of one Chinese immigrant for every 100 tons of a ship's registered capacity. In an earlier inter-colonial conference in January 1881 in which Chinese issues were also discussed, these measures had been generally agreed upon by the Australasian colonies. However, Parkes insisted on two special sections: the first denied key civil rights to Chinese migrating to New South Wales, and the second, also the most controversial section, required that any further Chinese arriving in Sydney would undergo the same quarantine measures that the passengers on the *Ocean* had suffered. It presumed the Chinese ports and Chinese immigrants were always infected.[15] The image of Chinese as an environmental hazard was thus institutionally established. The image was frequently quoted by politicians who endeavored to build a pure, white Australian society and environment, not limited to New South Wales. For example, Richard Vale, a parliamentarian in Victoria, counseled: "not only was there a risk of leprosy from the presence of Chinese, but there was also danger of the spread of typhoid fever and germ diseases."[16] If the Chinese "were degraded and corrupt, carriers of leprosy and vice, what could we expect from such people but contamination?" (Palmer 1980, 67). At the end of nineteenth century, all Australian colonies agreed to forbid Chinese emigration to Australia and when the Australian Commonwealth was established, the White Australian Policy, which denied a Chinese immigrant the right to become an Australian, became a doctrine to strengthen a modern nationalist identity.

Conclusion

To every immigrant in the nineteenth century, including Europeans and Chinese, the Australian environment was strange and challenging. Wherever they came from, the immigrant competed for a better life through exploiting Australian natural resources and inevitably transformed the Aboriginal environment and ecosystem. As the white colonists treated the Aboriginal people and the environment of the antipodes terribly, they also condemned Chinese immigrants, a minority group, as environmentally harmful and threatening. Through a mixed sentiment of exclusionism, imperialism, and Social Darwinism, the European immigrants and their descendants finally established white hegemony in the Antipodes by obliterating the influence of Chinese immigrants.

As Ann Curthoys wrote:

> British colonists, by and large, firstly used racist criteria to judge which peoples could assimilate and which could not, secondly made assimilation possible, or at least easy only for those judged able to assimilate, and thirdly saw assimilation or lack of it as proof of the validity of those racist criteria.
>
> (Curthoys 1973, 595)

One should note that when the white immigrants created an anti-Chinese discourse, they did not only preach for an economic or cultural rationality, but also utilized environmental factors to justify their claim against Chinese.

The gold rushes initiated competition between the Chinese and European immigrants in Australia. Although there was also great cooperation between the whites and the Chinese, their relationship was exacerbated by conflicts revolving around many issues, including an environmental dispute. At the very beginning, the European workers criticized the Chinese for wasting water and destroying the soil. This created a stereotype that the Chinese could ruin the Australian land and steal its wealth. When the Chinese immigrants proved capable or even successful in agricultural industries, they were somewhat accepted and helped the white colonists conquer and transform the tougher hinterland of Australia into a profitable setting. However, when the Chinese population became overly compatible and was expected to increase, they were blamed for causing diseases and threatening public health. By making the Chinese who lived in and contributed to Australia for decades into the threatening "others," middle class elites joined with the workers to create a more homogenous society through strict legislation to stop Chinese emigration to Australia at the end of nineteenth century. The ecological concern of Australian society was not only a direct reaction to the challenging physical environment, but was also rooted in a metaphor of the environmentally threatening "others."

Notes

1 "Legislative Council on the Subject of Chinese Immigration," *Votes and Proceedings of the Legislative Council,*Victoria (hereafter *VPLC*), 1856–57, D.19.
2 The Colombo Plan is a regional organization that was sponsored by the U.S. and Britain to offer training programs to British Commonwealth citizens in the Asia-Pacific region. Australia accepted a few Chinese immigrants who lived in British Colonies.
3 The Eureka Riot of the year 1854 was a historically significant rebellion of Australian gold miners who revolted against the colonial authority. This riot has been considered the founding event on which the Australian democracy was built.
4 "Commission Appointed to Enquire into the Conditions of the Gold Fields of Victoria" (March, 1855), A.76, *VPLC,* 1854–55.
5 *Argus*, November 15, 1856
6 "The subject of Chinese Immigration (November 17, 1857)", *VPLC*, 1856–57, D.19.
7 "Evidence Presented to the Commission on the Chinese, including those of J.A. Panton and the Chinese Howqua," in *VPLC*, 1855, p. 336.
8 *Bendigo Advertiser,* July 22, 1862.
9 *Argus*, June 23, 1855.
10 *Bendigo Advertiser,* May 4, 1887.
11 *Argus*, March 17, 1856.
12 "Petition of Castlemaine Local Court Members" (July 17, 1857) E.18, *VPLC*, 1856–57.
13 "Ah Sin" was a popular nickname in Guang Dong Province in China from where most Australian Chinese originated who came to Australia before 1900.
14 "Report and Minutes of Evidence of the Select committee of the Victorian Legislative Council on Chinese Immigration," *Victorian Council Records*, 1856.
15 *Sydney Morning Herald,* July 9, 1881.
16 "Richard Vale Papers," *Parliament Documents of Victoria*, October 18, 1882, vol. 58, p. 1612.

References

Bate, W. 1988 *Victorian Gold Rushes*, McPhee Gribble, Fitzroy
Bolton, G. 1981 *Spoils and spoilers: Australians make their environment 1788–1980*, George Allen and Unwin, Sydney
Booth, M. 1999 *Opium: a history* (Chinese edition), Hai Nan Press, Haikou

Cronin, K. 1982 *Colonial Casualties: Chinese in Early Victoria*, Melbourne University Press, Carlton

Curthoys, A. 1973 Race and ethnicity: a study of the response of British colonists to Aboriginals, Chinese and non-British Europeans in New South Wales, 1856–1881, Unpublished PhD thesis, Department of History, Macquarie University, Sydney

Curthoys, A. 2001 "Men of all nations, except Chinamen: Europeans and Chinese on the goldfields of New South Wales" in McCalman, I., Cook, A., Reeves, K. (eds) *Gold: forgotten histories and lost objects of Australia*, Cambridge University Press, Cambridge

Curthoys, A. and Markus, A. 1978 (eds) *Who are our enemies? Racism and the Australian working class*, Hale and Iremonger, Neutral Bay

Fahey, C. 2010 Peopling the Victorian Goldfields: From Boom to Bust, 1851–1901, *Australian Economic History Review* 2 148–161

Frost, W. 2002 Migrants and Technological Transfer: Chinese Farming in Australia, 1850–1920, *Australian Economic History Review* 2 113–131

Garden, D. 2005 *Australia, New Zealand, and the Pacific: an environmental history*, ABC-Clio, Santa Barbara, California

Gittins, J. 1981 *The diggers from China: the story of the Chinese on the goldfield*, Quartet Books, Melbourne

Goodall, H. 2012 Remaking the places of belonging. Arabic immigrants and the urban environment along Sydney's Georges river, *Miradas en Movimiento* 1

Goodall, H. 2010 "Nets, backyards and the bush: the clashing cultures of nature on the Georges River" in Lunney, D., Hutchings, P. Hochuli, D. (eds) The Natural History of Sydney, Royal Zoological Society of New South Wales, Mosman

Lancelott, F. 1852 *Australia as it is: its settlements, farms, and gold fields* (Vol. 2), Colburn and Co., London

Lovejoy, V. 2007 The things that unite: inquests into Chinese deaths on the Bendigo Goldfields 1854–65, *The Journal of Public Record Office Victoria* 6

McCalman, I., Cook, A., Reeves, K. 2001 (eds) *Gold: forgotten histories and lost objects of Australia*, Cambridge University Press, Cambridge

McGowan, B. 2005 The economics and organization of Chinese mining in colonial Australia, *Australian Economic History Review* 2 119–138

McLaren, I.F. (ed.) 1985 *The Chinese in Victoria: official reports and documents*, Red Rooster Press, Ascot Vale

Mitman, G. 2005 In search of health: landscape and disease in American Environmental History, *Environmental History* 2 184–210

Moore, R., Tully, J. 2000 *A difficult case: an autobiography of a Chinese miner on the Central Victorian goldfields*, Jim Crow Press, Daylesford

Nash, L. 2006 *Inescapable ecologies: a history of environment, disease, and knowledge*, University of California Press, Berkeley and Los Angeles

Ngai, M.M. 2010 Chinese miners, headmen, and protectors on the Victorian goldfields, 1853–1863, *Australian Historical Studies* 1 10–24

Palmer, W. 1980 *The legend of the nineties*, Melbourne University Press, Carlton

Serle, G. 1968 *The Gold Age: a history of the Colony of Victoria, 1851–1861*, Melbourne University Press, Melbourne

Stanin, Z. 2004 From Li Chun to Yong Kit: A Market Garden on the Loddon, 1851–1912, *Journal of Australian Colonial History* 6 14–34

Watters, G. 2002 The S.S. Ocean: dealing with Boat People in the 1880s, *Australia Historical Study* 1 331–343

Xue, F.C. 2001 *Diaries of a diplomat to four countries*, reprinted by Social Sciences Academic Press, Beijing (Chu Shi Si Guo Ri Ji, Beijing: She Hui Ke Xue Wen Xian Chu Ban She)

Yong, C.F. 1977 *The New Gold Mountain: the Chinese in Australia, 1901–1921*, Raphael Arts, Richmond

Zheng, J.R. 1992 "The Way of Zheng Ri to the (New) Gold Mountain" in Zhong Shan People's Political Consultative Conference (ed.) *The Local Historical Studies of Zhong Shan City*, Zhong Shan Press, Zhong Shan

8 Nativist politics and environmental privilege

Ecological and cultural conflicts concerning Latin American migration to the United States

David Naguib Pellow and Lisa Sun-Hee Park

Abstract

For more than three decades, studies in environmental justice have demonstrated that poor, working class, indigenous, and people of color communities face greater threats from pollution and industrial hazards than other groups. Fewer studies consider the flipside of that reality: *environmental privilege*. Environmental privilege results from the exercise of economic, political, and cultural power that some groups enjoy. This chapter examines how environmental privilege is manifest and maintained through immigration politics, specifically the ideology and application of nativism (or immigration control practices and discourses) through state actions aimed at reducing the flow of immigrants into the United States. We focus on a case study of a wealthy, politically liberal enclave in the United States where the city council unanimously approved a resolution that declared (1) that the city should continue to be a model sustainable, green municipality and (2) in order to achieve and maintain that status, immigration from Latin America would have to be severely curtailed. We explore the historical driving forces behind environmental privilege and consider its implications for ongoing debates and policy making over race, immigration/citizenship, globalization, and environment.

Introduction

Scholars working in the field of environmental justice studies have, for at least four decades, presented evidence that poor, working class, indigenous, and people of color communities face greater threats from pollution and industrial hazards than other groups. While these studies reveal the hardships and crimes associated with environmental inequality, fewer studies consider the flipside of that reality: *environmental privilege*. Environmental privilege results from the exercise of economic, political, and cultural power that some groups enjoy, which enables them near exclusive access to coveted environmental amenities such as forests, parks, mountains, rivers, coastal property, open lands, and elite neighborhoods. Environmental privilege is embodied in the fact that some groups can access spaces and resources that are protected from the kinds of ecological harm that other groups are forced to contend with every day. These advantages include organic and pesticide-free foods, neighborhoods with healthier air quality, and energy and other products siphoned from the living environments of other peoples. In this chapter, we explore how environmental privileges accrue to the few while environmental burdens confront the many, including lack of access to clean air, land, water, and open spaces. If environmental racism and injustice are abundant and we can readily observe them around the world, then surely the same can be said for environmental privilege. We cannot have one without the other; they are two sides of the same coin.

This research is based on fieldwork we conducted from 2000 to 2009 in the town of Aspen, Colorado (U.S.), during which we examined the troubling intersections of citizenship, race, economics, and environmental politics in the area. We began by conducting archival research of the local history, followed by a series of interviews with key actors in the local debate concerning immigration, labor, and environmental policy. With respect to archival materials, we examined a wide range of sources—government documents, scholarly books, personal letters, newspapers, and nongovernmental organizational reports—at the Aspen Historical Society, the Pitkin County Public Library, the Colorado Historical Society (Denver), the Denver Public Library, and the library at the University of Colorado–Boulder. With respect to the interviews, we spoke with city council members, county commissioners, service industry employers, social service providers, housing advocates, local immigration attorneys, local and federal law enforcement and immigration control officials, school teachers, nonprofit immigrant advocacy organizations, ethnic media personnel, and, most importantly, Latino immigrant residents, workers, and their families. In face-to-face meetings and focus groups, we interviewed seventy people. In addition, we analyzed the contents of several local newspapers, including the *Aspen Times*, *Aspen Daily News*, *Glenwood Springs Post Independent*, *Valley Journal*, *Mountain Gazette*, *Carbondale Echo*, and the recently established Spanish-language paper, *La Misión* (now *La Unión*). We also scoured the pages of historical periodicals, including the *Rocky Mountain Sun* and the *Aspen Democratic-Times* and the more contemporary *Aspen Magazine*. This range of research methods allowed us to approach this study from multiple vantage points, exploring differing points of view on the key themes examined herein. This research culminated in the publication of our book *The Slums of Aspen* (Park and Pellow 2011). In this chapter, we focus on the anti-immigrant and pro-environmental discourse and policy-making in Aspen as well as the response to this nativist environmentalism by Latin American immigrants themselves.

Immigrants in the U.S. environment

The call of immigrants to America's shores is one of the nation's most foundational stories. This narrative has served as a comforting cover for the realities of conquest, slavery, and imperialism that are also fundamental to that nation's founding. Since at least the 18th century, every wave of people immigrating to the United States has confronted the antagonism of those who immigrated before. The result has been a cycle of nativism, perpetrated by the white Anglo Saxon Protestant community in particular and by successive groups of European Americans in general (Feagin 1997). Citing historian John Higham, legal scholar Juan F. Perea writes that nativism is an "intense opposition to an internal minority on the grounds of its foreign (i.e. 'un-American') connections" (Perea 1997, 1, 167). Perea writes that, during periods of nativism, "democratic processes are turned against internal minorities deemed foreign or 'un-American,' resulting in discriminatory legislation and immigration restrictions" (Perea 1997, 1). These legislative maneuvers function to demarcate particular communities as marginal to the nation and undeserving of the privileges normally associated with citizenship. Nativist movements today are not fundamentally different from those of yesterday. The claims of threats to "quality of life," "American culture," and the anxiety over "limited resources" continue to animate and motivate these groups (Gottlieb 1993, 256). In this chapter, we focus on how environmentalism is intertwined within this nativist history.

We argue that U.S. environmentalist history does not just harbor strains of nativism here and there; rather nativism is embedded throughout U.S. environmental history. Intrinsic to the triumphant immigration saga are the images of American landscapes, with their majestic mountains, valleys, and great natural riches, "from sea to shining sea." But that glory is not without its problems. While many people who support the goals of ecological sustainability and an awareness of our ecological impacts are motivated by genuine concern for our planet, there is also a troubling dimension to such efforts. Many efforts aimed at protecting the earth's finite resources are also deeply connected to the idea of controlling the world's population for the benefit of a powerful minority.

In the early 20th century, many European American elites turned their sights on newcomers and identified immigrants as a primary cause of ecological woes in the cities. Specifically, immigrants were blamed for the rise in urban pollution, when in fact, these populations were associated with polluted spaces because they were forced to live and work in smoke-choked neighborhoods and occupationally hazardous factories and sweatshops (Gottlieb 1993). Many leaders of environmental preservationist groups at the time—including William Hornaday, Madison Grant, and Henry Fairfield Osborn—decried the influx of Jewish immigrants and other newcomers from Italy, China, and Japan as a threat to American values concerning the sanctity of wild places. In some locations, tensions arose between members of the upper classes who hunted for sport and trophies, while many European immigrants hunted for food sources (Jacoby 2003).

In addition, prominent environmentalists in the early 1900s worked with the eugenics movement in the U.S., viewing immigrants and people of color as naturally inferior to Anglos, and voicing approval of reproductive restrictions on these groups (Gottlieb and Dreier 1998). In fact, noted preservationist and eugenicist Madison Grant collaborated with Margaret Sanger, the early U.S. women's movement leader and supporter of birth control technologies, on parallel agendas, revealing how gender and women's reproductive capacity underpin ideological battles over immigration and population growth.

Despite significant advances at the beginning of the 21st century, the power of racism continually presents itself in both environmentalist and nativist movements. At the 1987 Round River Rendezvous gathering of environmentalists, Earth First! founder Dave Foreman and fellow EF! activist and author Edward Abbey insulted the peoples of Latin America and the Caribbean by describing them as backward and primitive (Panagioti 2006). Abbey's 1988 book, *One Life at a Time, Please*, featured his favorite essay—"Immigration and Liberal Taboos." Abbey, who has inspired innumerable radical ecologists the world over, wrote in that essay, "it might be wise for us as American citizens to consider calling a halt to the mass influx of even more millions of hungry, ignorant, unskilled and culturally-morally-genetically impoverished people" (*ibid.* 8).

There are many possible explanations for the persistence of nativist environmentalism. Historically, nativist scholars, politicians, and activists in the U.S. have often harbored concerns about the prospect of "race suicide" that might result from either a lack of white population growth or from being "overrun" and outpaced reproductively by non-whites (Roediger 2005). More recently, since the 2000 and 2010 censuses revealed several U.S. states as having "majority minority" populations, predictions that the United States will one day constitute a white minority have generated considerable anxiety. For the first time, almost half of the one hundred largest cities in the U.S. are "majority minority" cities (Schmitt 2001). Reports of these demographic shifts have produced fear among many native-born whites concerned that it is not just "their jobs," but now "their *country*" that is in danger of being taken over by foreigners. This apprehension is directed toward immigrants as whites and other citizens try to restrict access to education, health and social services, decent jobs, housing, and a broad range of environmental amenities.

These longstanding concerns are now tinged with even greater consequences. The dangerous coupling of nativist *and* environmental movements— what we term "nativist environmentalism" —is today all the more potent because of what we now know. It is common knowledge that the planet's ecological systems are in peril and that the U.S. has contributed as much or more than any other nation to that crisis through its economic and military policies, and through its consumption and production practices—independent of immigration flows into its borders. Despite that fact, many nativist environmentalists see the vast interior spaces in the U.S. as relatively pristine and capable of being "saved" from humankind's ravages, including, in their view, continued immigration. The urgency of today's nativist environmentalism is punctuated by pressing global environmental crises such as climate disruption, which has heightened the sense of preciousness of particular places and their populations.

Aspen, Colorado, and the Roaring Fork Valley

Aspen, Colorado sits high in the Rocky Mountains and is a mecca for wealthy skiers, hikers, nature enthusiasts, environmentalists, European concert music lovers, and economic, political, and cultural elites from around the world. The average price of a home there was around $6 million in 2015. Even the homes in the trailer parks sell for $300,000 and up, and professionals like doctors, architects, and lawyers are among the residents there. Above all, Aspen is a place for relaxation, rejuvenation, and the enjoyment of nature's beauty. That is, unless you happen to be an immigrant laborer whose very purpose is to make possible and facilitate that rendezvous with Mother Earth for the rest of Aspen's visitors. Located within Colorado's Roaring Fork River Valley, more than 600 miles from the U.S.-Mexico border, Aspen is an exclusive resort town with an international reputation for high-end service and a stunning landscape of pristine mountains, all configured to welcome wealthy skiers in the winter and well-heeled nature lovers in the summer. And, like many communities in the U.S., Aspen depends upon low wage immigrant labor to fuel its service economy.

In recent years, the traditional fusion of environmentalism and nativism has reared its head in this Colorado town—where white ecologists seek to expel Latin American migrant workers—and we consider both the roots and implications of this development. We explore the social and ecological impact of what we call *the Aspen logic*—which is a way of seeing and shaping the world that preserves systems of inequality and injustice in a self-justifying manner. The Aspen logic appears to be a form of neoliberal discourse with a green facelift. However, it is more than just a green wash; in fact, it is a *white* wash because it embraces social, environmental, and economic claims to pureness and goodness, to *whiteness*. That is, Aspenites link environmental sustainability to whiteness by excluding people of color and immigrants from the town via formal and informal mechanisms.

We first visited this exclusive town in 2000 to investigate the recent passage of an anti-immigration resolution by the city council. On December 13, 1999, the City Council of Aspen unanimously passed a resolution petitioning the U.S. Congress and the President to do more to restrict the number of immigrants entering the United States. One of their primary reasons for encouraging tougher immigration laws was the purported negative impact of immigrants on the ecosystems. Concerns about immigration's environmental impacts nationally generally include issues such as urban/suburban sprawl, the loss of urban green space, and overdevelopment of wilderness and agricultural lands. In Aspen, more specific complaints include everything from car exhaust pollution associated with older model vehicles many immigrants drive (since workers drive anywhere from a 30 to 140 mile round trip to work in Aspen's tourist industry), littering, and population growth.

The City Council of Aspen's resolution petitioned the U.S. Congress and the President to enact legislation that would stabilize the nation's population.

The language of the resolution suggests that this goal could be achieved by enforcing existing laws regulating undocumented immigration and reducing authorized immigration. City Council member Terry Paulson, a long-time immigration critic and self-avowed environmentalist, led this effort. He received guidance from nationally prominent immigration control organizations such as the Carrying Capacity Network and the Center for Immigration Studies, who reportedly told him, "other communities haven't had the courage to do so [....] Because many current immigrants are members of minority groups in the U.S., attempts to limit immigration may be seen as racist" (Heiman 1999).

One of the resolution's goals is to make Aspen a "City beautiful," a beacon of sustainability and social responsibility. Unfortunately, underpinning this goal is nativist ideology. Aspen Councilman Terry Paulson sponsored the resolution with the following opening statement:

> Fellow Council Members, this resolution we will be considering for adoption tonight could be the most important consideration we will ever make as representatives of our constituents and their children [....] 'We have agitated, confused and deluded ourselves with the illusion that we are being overwhelmed by many, many problems—when in fact we have primarily only one. But it is the one that terrifies us the most, and we handle that terror by chattering endlessly about everything else. Denying [...] and minimizing population growth in the 1990s is a *hate crime against future generations*, and it must end.' Please, join me [...], by passing this resolution as written, and thereby insuring a sustainable future for America and her children.
>
> (Paulson 1999)

Almost immediately afterward, the County passed a similar resolution. The countywide resolution contained the following statement: "Immigration is the leading cause of population growth in the Unites States. Population is the leading cause of environmental degradation" (Pitkin County 2000). Thus, by implication, immigration must be the leading cause of ecological degradation. Both the Aspen and Pitkin County resolutions underscore the longstanding link between nativism and environmentalism in the U.S. and elsewhere.

These narratives that define immigration (particularly from Latin America) as a leading ecological threat stand in stark contrast to the everyday reality of Aspen, which is, in many ways, a playground for the rich that depends upon low wage immigrant labor to provide the kinds of luxury goods and services that make Aspen function. In some respects, this is a bizarre story of an environmentally conscious town whose City Council can regularly approve the construction of yet another 10,000 square foot vacation home with a heated outdoor driveway, and simultaneously decry the trailer homes where low-income immigrants live as an eyesore and threat to the integrity of local ecosystems. In other respects, this is a familiar story of increasingly brutal inequality and the accompanying uneasy racial and class demarcations that become more pronounced as cities across the nation negotiate the fast-paced global economy and its flows of money, ideas, and people. Most elite jetsetters with second or third homes in the Aspen area actually spend very little time there, but often want their multi-million dollar domiciles ready for them whenever they arrive. One property manager stated that his job was to look after absentee homes while their owners were out of town. Most of the properties he managed were empty forty-five or more weeks of the year, yet they wanted to have their homes heated the entire year, including their swimming pools, so they would be ready whenever the owners arrived.

The visual images that gloss magazine covers in Aspen feature stretch Range Rover limousines, toy poodles with diamond encrusted collars, world-class ski slopes, and film celebrities who live part of the year in multi-million dollar single-family homes. At the same time, Aspen is also a place where foreign-born workers drive long daily commutes to work in low-status jobs for low wages with few benefits. Many of these workers live in deplorable housing conditions, including cars and campers. When we asked an immigrant resident/worker what he thought about the natural beauty of Aspen's mountains, he replied, "Mountain? What mountain?" There are two Aspens: one marked by environmental privilege and exclusion and the other marked by poverty and marginalization.

Nativist environmental organizing in Aspen

In June 1999, an organization calling itself the Valley Alliance for Social and Environmental Responsibility formed in Aspen. Mike McGarry is an outspoken local activist who, along with Aspen City Council member Terry Paulson, founded the Alliance. The same week the Alliance was launched, former Colorado Governor Dick Lamm spoke at a men's club luncheon in Aspen, where he warned his audience about the social and environmental degradation—such as urban sprawl—that he declared results from continuing immigration into the U.S. Lamm has a second home in Aspen and is adamant about protecting Colorado's ecosystems from population growth and other threats. He publicly supports the Alliance and is on the board of directors of the Federation for American Immigration Reform (FAIR). The Alliance is one of many nativist groups in the state of Colorado and in the Rocky Mountain Region that is well networked, a group that includes the Colorado Alliance for Immigration Reform (CAIR), a state affiliate of FAIR. The Alliance has friends and supporters in Congress, at FAIR, NumbersUSA, and other nationally active and highly visible nativist groups.

Alliance founders McGarry and Paulson spoke to us about the strength of ecological ethics and policies in the Aspen area. They both embraced the Aspen Wilderness Workshop—a local environmental group—because, as Paulson claimed,

> They're one of the few environmental organizations that I admire that really goes out and does something [....] They've taken the Aspen ski company on for various issues, making them be responsible. As a result, the ski company has been getting a lot of these green awards for recycling, they even started using a kind of diesel fuel that's more ecological. As a corporation I think that they're ahead of most. You know the sundeck at the top of Aspen Mountain: it's made of all recycled and biodegradable materials. It's made out of plastic, basically. They didn't have to do that, you know, but they decided that this is what they want to do and it's costing them a lot more to do it.
>
> (Author interviews)

McGarry proudly chimed in, "I have a lot of respect for them, as far as corporations go. I think that if we look at the big picture, Aspen is as environmentally conscious and as conservation oriented and as aware as any town." Like other towns, Aspen requires positive "mitigations" to offset development that might be ecologically harmful. In other words, projects that are intended to improve local ecosystems when other efforts cause harm. However, in Aspen, these development practices have a distinctive flair. As Terry Paulson explained, "For instance if someone wants to put in a heated driveway [...] so you don't have to shovel snow [...] he has to mitigate that somehow, he has to make small changes in his other plans." We queried, "Did you just say a heated driveway?" McGarry stepped in, "They're all over the place up here."

McGarry and Paulson's views reflect what we call the Aspen logic—an idea that hinges on the marriage of capitalism and environmentalism and has been a hallmark of Aspen's institutional history for years, far ahead of current initiatives by large corporations such as Walmart. Auden Schendler, director of environmental affairs at the Aspen Skiing Company—known to Aspenites as 'SkiCo'—is a staunch believer and practitioner of the Aspen logic. He boasts,

> We don't just have one green building; we have a green development policy and many green buildings. We don't just buy renewable energy; we're currently exploring a new goal of 25 percent renewable power, and now we're making clean power on the hill with our hydroelectric station on Snowmass.
>
> (McGovern 2004)

Schendler makes these claims despite studies that reveal the ski industry is one of the most highly polluting sectors in the U.S. economy, contributing massively to soil erosion, deforestation, river pollution, air pollution, and climate change. But the Aspen logic is alluring for "green consumers" who wish to maintain their high status lifestyle while supporting environmental causes. *Aspen Magazine* published a story about locals who love their scooters:

[...] how green our town is extends beyond organic produce to the trend of environmentally friendly scooters [....] Not only are they the most stylish way to get around in the summer, they also make parking in our congested downtown considerably easier. In the summertime, Aspen proves that Rome isn't the only place where scooters rule. "My Italjet gets a kabillion miles to the gallon. I never fill it up," says Maria DeGraeve, manager of the Aspen Bulgari store and avid scooter rider. "And it's a lot more ecologically friendly than my SUV." Valerie Alexander, who works for Bluegreen (a planning/design firm), says riding the vintage Vespa takes her to another place. "I feel like I should be in Europe, heading to lunch with the girls, scarf blowing in the wind, and a baguette in my backpack— except I'm in Aspen."

(O'Grady 2004)

The references to Rome and Europe are consistent with a long and conscious history of constructing U.S. ski towns as Bavarian or Alpine Villages of the Rockies, as exclusive European spaces. The father of modern Aspen, Walter Paepcke, lovingly referred to the town as an American Salzburg. After World War II, ski resort promoters deliberately marketed these developments as European ski resorts within the U.S. West, thus securing environmental privileges by excluding, making invisible, or exoticizing people of color who worked or lived in these places.

In present day Aspen, elected officials are no less aggressive about desiring exclusion and cultural purity. For example, Aspen Council member Tom McCabe cautioned, "The planet's a finite resource [....] We can't indefinitely welcome people and expect to maintain our quality of life." And that's precisely the point: Aspenites and others in similarly privileged places across the U.S. want to protect *their* "quality of life," which includes resources and wealth derived from the ecosystems that only they have access to, and from the hard work of others. The innocent claim that environmentalists in the Roaring Fork Valley only want to "preserve our way of life" is belied by the fact that such a lifestyle requires the domination of the environment and of certain groups of people (e.g., people of color, immigrants, and workers who make such privileges possible for the wealthy and mostly white elite). It also underscores an enduring belief that there are essential differences between people of different ethnic, racial, and national backgrounds. A number of scholars have recently described this kind of language as a core part of the "new racism," a racism that no longer relies on outdated and abhorrent biological notions of superior versus inferior peoples. Instead, the new racism is based on the idea that there are insurmountable and incompatible cultural distinctions between peoples. However, while we agree with scholars writing about the "new racism" that many biological notions of racial difference have given way to other frameworks (Winant 2001), our focus on the immigration-environment nexus reveals that such ideas are unfortunately not entirely outdated. In fact, in the case of the Roaring Fork Valley and the general immigration-environment debate, we observe both cultural and biological arguments at work, because nativist environmentalists claim that nations must obey the laws of nature in order to achieve (and not threaten) a "natural" biological balance of population and environment. This is implied in terms like "carrying capacity" and "population-environment balance." These are cultural ideas masked as scientific "facts," and are therefore not open to debate in the minds of advocates.

This is perhaps the greatest challenge for the environmental movement in the United States: the underlying cultural, racial, and economic elitism of environmentalism, which is rooted in biological and natural scientific ideas of how the world should be. Consider the fact that the creation of many U.S. national parks was made possible through the explicit removal or containment of Native American tribes. This is what Betsy Hartmann (2003) calls "coercive conservation," the violent expulsion of local people from wilderness preserves. What we term *nativist environmentalism* seeks to extend this practice beyond indigenous populations by expelling immigrants and preventing future new-comers from gaining entry.

Aspen and the surrounding Roaring Fork Valley of Colorado is just one of many sites on the planet built as a refuge from undesirable people and where nature can be manipulated for the convenience and enjoyment of a handful of elites. Moreover, in the case of the nativist environmental-ists of Aspen, these environmentally privileged communities are claiming victim status. A Roaring Fork Valley area progressive activist and educator told us:

> Environmental racism is when people of color are dumped on. But here, especially in Aspen, we have rich white folks who are saying *we're* getting dumped on! So it's like the idea has been totally turned around and upside down.
>
> (Author interviews)

In other words, Aspenites are essentially crying "reverse environmental racism" because they view immigrants not only as a cause of environmental harm, but as a kind of social contamination, a form of pollution. This strongly parallels much of the discourse on population control within the U.S. environmental movement historically.

Aspen is a new kind of "ghost town" where many homeowners live there just two weeks each year and the immigrant workers who service the town are present but socially invisible and are targeted for exclusion. Even nature is an illusion. Like many ski resorts they even have fake snow made by machines on the mountain. At the same time, the mountains are unreal for most immigrant workers because they have little or no access to them. Through the privatiza-tion of nature—which is what a ski resort is, after all—the mountain becomes a product to consume, a replicable commodity.

Challenging environmental privilege

Immigrant residents of the Roaring Fork Valley primarily come from Mexico, with smaller populations from Argentina, El Salvador, Guatemala, Paraguay, Peru, and Uruguay. They may not always be visible and public with their politics, but this does not mean they do not have strong feelings about the way they are treated. We asked local resident, worker, and activist José Cordova what he thought about the claim that immigrants harm local ecosystems. He stated, "I think that's a misperception because I've been working with construction companies and [...] there's no ecological preservation. They just throw away everything. I don't think it's the Latinos affecting the environment." He also reframed the social problem as one of privilege:

> My position is that that the concept of overpopulation is not that accurate. That's one of the arguments of groups to justify policies, to say there is poverty because of overpopulation. But if we go into details about wealth and the lands that are available, we see that maybe we may all fit in the world. I don't think the problem is overpopulation; the problem is redistribution of the wealth and the redistribution of knowledge.
>
> (Author interviews)

Cordova's analysis and assessment of U.S. environmental politics coincides with what progressive scholars, policy makers, business leaders, and activists here and in other nations have been arguing for years (Agyeman, Bullard, and Evans 2003). His appraisal of the population-environment debate speaks directly to the overarching quest for environmental privilege in the Roaring Fork Valley and elsewhere. Environmental privilege is not just about maintaining exclusive access to ecological amenities (mountains, rivers, lakes, beaches, parks, trails, etc.); it is also about maintaining access and belonging to the broader reality of social place, of which both ecological and non-ecological amenities are a part. Environmental privilege is ultimately an exertion of power that employs nativism and its racist logic to demarcate where particular people belong. In other words, environmental privilege is part and parcel of the larger problem of social privilege.

Carlos Loya works as a laborer throughout the Valley and has had plenty of experience with racism. Sometimes when native-born whites yell epithets at him he responds in one of two ways. He might tell Anglos, "My ancestors were here in Aspen long before you got here. This land used to be our land." Or he poses a question: "You call me wetback because I crossed a river, so what can I call you? You crossed an ocean." Loya stated, "Without knowing it, they are making us tough and giving us patience and strength when they do this. We have a strong shell" (Aguilera 2004).

Loya's response to nativists questions environmental privilege by evoking a new narrative of national origins. He asks, what demarcates belonging?

Who arrived here first? And, if my migration makes me inferior, what does your migration across the Atlantic mean? How are you not an immigrant? Loya exerts his power by interrogating history and questioning the Anglo American taken for granted entitlement of place. Finally, a local activist named Felicia Trevor told us, "[we reject] the whole idea of only the wealthy can have beautiful [mountain] views and things like that, so that's part of what we deal with."

Conclusion: making sense of Aspen

We see the turmoil in Colorado's Roaring Fork Valley as part of the larger problem of immigration and environmental politics in the U.S. Our interviews with city council members, environmentalists, and immigrant workers exposed a familiar paradox that underlies the presence of immigrants in the United States—the simultaneous economic dependence upon and social contempt for low-wage immigrant labor. That social contempt frequently reinforces the invisibility and political disempowerment of immigrant labor. We found that many people in the Valley use the environment as a way to promote a particular romantic image of the area as a post-industrial refuge. The paradoxical necessity and invisibility of "unskilled" immigrants is central to this environmental image, which forms the foundation of what makes Aspen, according to its wealthy residents, "heaven on earth." Efforts to ensure immigrants' invisibility are particularly strident given the stark and ever-present realities of inequality in Aspen.

The environmental movement's indifference (at best or antagonism at worst) to social issues like immigration is unfortunate and tragic. Environmentalism could become a transformative force that embraces justice for all, given our shared global ecosystem. Instead, we have constructed political, economic, and social borders to protect only certain people's ecosystems and human communities. These borders are not only artificial; they are also the *source* of environmental devastation. The exclusive "protection" of the backyard of the privileged is absolutely dependent upon the impoverishment of someone else's common space. The volume of resources—both human and non-human—required to maintain the heavenly experience of the very few in Aspen is profound. If environmentalists are truly committed to ecological sustainability, they must find ways of reducing ecological damage through an acknowledgment and alleviation of social inequality rather than fixating on immigrants and population control.

The case of Aspen, Colorado illustrates the importance of understanding environmental racism, poverty and inequality by getting out of the "ghetto" and "*el barrio*" and into places where racial and economic and environmental privilege are produced. The fact that communities of color and working class populations face greater environmental harm is indeed a social problem, but we must frame the existence of environmental privilege as a social problem as well. This is important because the recent calls for moving beyond the distributive paradigm in Environmental Justice (EJ) studies miss the fact that the distribution of *power*—not just the distribution of environmental harm— is and has always been the fundamental focus of critical EJ studies. Early EJ scholars actually went to great pains to point out that they were not simply advocating a more democratic and even distribution of industrial pollution and other hazards—they wanted to see the entire system that produced these hazards transformed. Social inequality is at the root of the problem and this is inherently a distributional question.

Moreover, we would contend that the dynamic nature of distributional politics and impacts has still yet to be fully explored. For example, environmental inequality has almost entirely been defined through the lens of environmental "bads" while *environmental privilege* goes largely unexamined. In our view, environmental privilege is the flipside *and source* of environmental injustice/inequality. Thus, while we agree that earlier studies that only sought to document the distribution of environmental harm are limited, the deeper distributional questions around where power resides and how privilege drives environmental injustice are only beginning to be explored. So we indeed have a distributional problem that we can only "move beyond" when we have addressed the vast disparities in power within and across societies that produce environmental injustice and its partner, environmental privilege.

References

Aguilera, E. 2004 A wealth of diversity in a valley of riches, The *Denver Post*, July 20

Agyeman, J., R. Bullard, and B. Evans (eds) 2003 *Just sustainabilities: development in an unequal world*, The MIT Press, Cambridge

Author interviews (D. Pellow and L. Park), Aspen, Colorado, 2000–2004

Feagin, J. 1997 "Old poison in new bottles: the deep roots of modern nativism," in Juan F. Perea (ed.) *Immigrants Out!: the new nativism and the anti-immigrant impulse in the United States*, New York University Press, New York, pp. 13–40

Gottlieb, R. 1993 *Forcing the spring: the transformation of the American environmental movement*, Island Press, Washington, D.C.

Gottlieb, R. and P. Dreier 1998 Sierra Club wrestles with the nativism in environmentalism, *The Los Angeles Times*, March 1

Hartmann, B. 2003 Conserving racism: the greening of hate at home and abroad, *Znet*, December 10. www.zmag.org

Heiman, J. 1999. City Council Passes Resolution Requesting Immigration Limits, *Aspen Times*, December 20

Jacoby, K. 2003 *Crimes against nature: squatters, poachers, thieves, and the hidden history of American conservation*, University of California Press, Berkeley and Los Angeles

McGovern, J. 2004 Modern-day movers and shakers, *Aspen Times Weekly*, vol. 125, no 29, July 17 and 18, A21

O'Grady, J. 2004 Editor's Letter, *Aspen Magazine*, Summer, 16

Panagioti 2006 Down with borders, up with spring! *Earth First!* July–August, pp. 8–11

Park, L. Sun-Hee and D.N. Pellow 2011 *The slums of Aspen: immigrants vs. the environment in America's Eden*, New York University Press, New York

156   *David Naguib Pellow and Lisa Sun-Hee Park*

Paulson, T. 1999 Opening statement, Aspen City Council meeting, December 13

Perea, J. 1997 *Immigrants Out! The new nativism and the anti-immigrant impulse in the United States*, New York University Press, New York

Pitkin County 2000 A Resolution of the Board of County Commissioners of Pitkin County, Colorado, Supporting Population Stabilization in the United States, March 22

Roediger, D. 2005 *Working toward whiteness: how America's immigrants became white*, Basic Books, New York

Schmitt, E. 2001 Whites in minority in largest cities, the census shows, *New York Times*, April 30

Winant, H. 2001 *The world is a ghetto: race and democracy since World War II*, Basic Books, New York

Part III

Naturalizing causes

In which ways do the causes of migration intertwine with the environment? In the last few years there has been a growing debate about the possibility that environmental changes, mainly climate change, will cause, or perhaps have already originated, dramatic migrations. In the following part, Angus Wright and Giovanni Bettini tackle this controversial issue, arriving, although with different approaches and methodologies, at almost the same conclusions. Both caution the reader against what they see as a naturalization of the causes of migrations. Building on his expertise on Latin American environmental history, Wright employs an empirical case study in order to demonstrate his thesis. He explains how in Brazilian history the construction of drought's migrants from the Northeast hides the fact that not only a natural phenomenon but actually a social organization of nature and people—the plantation economy—was the push factor for those who left. Bettini, instead, proposes a genealogy of climate change's refugee discourse, going back to Malthus and then to the population bomb literature of the 1960s and 1970s. Bettini argues that there is a centrality of the demographic discourse which connects the more contemporary debates on climate change refugees with the classical discourse on overpopulation, especially among the poor, and overexploitation of nature. Bettini, like Wright, suggests not ignoring nature but being aware of the risks of naturalizing the social. Ying Xing offers a case study of forced migrations caused by development projects, and in particular by the construction of large dams. The case of the Three Gorges Dam in China is exemplar of this phenomenon. In this case, not nature per se but the human arrangement of nature is the cause of the resettlement of more than one million people. In Xing's chapter, however, it is interesting to notice the combination between the technolandscape created by the dam and the ecology of the areas people have been relocated to, with the shift from project resettlers to ecological resettlers.

Part III

Naturalizing causes

9 Environmental degradation as a cause of migration

Cautionary tales from Brazil

Angus Wright

Abstract

The history of periodic droughts in the Brazilian Northeast provides a cautionary tale for those concerned with the design and implementation of policies and programs meant to address the problems of climate-induced human suffering and migration. Beginning at least as early as 1877, periodic severe droughts in the Brazilian Northeast gave birth to national, state, and local policies and programs that purported to mitigate the effects of drought and provide economic alternatives to those forced to migrate out of the region. These policies and programs were based on supposedly "scientific" explanations for the recurrence and severity of droughts as the cause for the endemic poverty of the region. The climate interpretation for poverty offered a perspective that tended to displace a variety of other theories, ranging from those based on blatantly racist pseudo-science to more credible analyses of social structure and institutions. Particularly as the climate explanation shifted blame away from regional and national elites and onto nature, it was often eagerly embraced by elite-controlled media, universities, and governments. The drought relief programs and policies were revealed over time to have been far more beneficial to the wealthy and powerful than they were to the poor who suffered in place or were forced to migrate. This was so much the case that by the mid-20th century, drought relief as a whole began to be referred to sarcastically as "The Drought Industry," that is, a whole complex of enduring programs and institutions that exploited the plight of the rural poor rather than addressed their needs. Brazil's "drought industry" warns us of a variety of definitional, theoretical, and practical problems in successfully addressing the problems of climate-induced migration now and in the future.

The importance of definitions

The way we define such terms as "environmental migrant" or "environmental refugee" will be a significant factor in how people affected by environmental change understand and organize themselves, how emergency and long-term national and international aid is allocated, how refugee and immigration categories are legally defined and administered, how development projects are designed, how legal claims for compensation are adjudicated, and how national and international policies directed to longer term solutions are formulated (cf. Vag 2009; Rubin 2010).

When we define migrants in terms of environmental causes, there is a danger that we thereby obfuscate the actions of society that are fundamental in creating the need for migration. This may lead not only to an analytical error, but to measures that fail to address the most important aspects of the problem and that may even facilitate the exploitation of crises in ways that will perpetuate and deepen the distress of affected people and the natural environment.

Here I briefly explore a historical case study that has long ignited controversies that are similar to those involved in defining and understanding the concept of future environmental migrants or refugees. The case examines the historical development and use of explanations applied to the long history of migration out of the Brazilian Northeast to the industrial heartland of Brazil to the south and to the Amazon Basin in the west. One of the advantages of considering this history is the existence of a centuries-old discourse about the Brazilian Northeast that constitutes a detailed argument about the relative roles of human beings and nature in the creation of human misery in general and human migration in particular.

The cautionary tale of the Brazilian Northeast and the creation of "the drought industry"

The Brazilian Northeast is a region that roughly corresponds to what is often called "the hump" in the South American continent. By most definitions, it occupies a little less than a third of national territory and in most of the 20th century accounted for very roughly a third of Brazil's population. It is the region of most of the early European settlement of the Atlantic coastline of South America. The Portuguese began their settlement of what would become Brazil in the middle decades of the 16th century, founding the formal government of their American territories in Salvador da Bahia de Todos os Santos, near the southern edge of what eventually would come to be called "The Northeast." The Northeast region became a source of fabulous riches exported to Europe, beginning with valuable dye-woods and timber and continuing with sugar and other tropical export commodities grown primarily in the deforested humid regions near the coast. Diamonds from the southern interior of the Northeast would become a source of immense wealth in the 18th century. Gold mining in an area a bit to the south of what is known as the Northeast —but politically, culturally, and socially linked to the Northeast—would also be a source of prodigious wealth in the colonial era.

Beginning in the 18th century and well consolidated by the mid-19th, the more dynamic sectors of the Brazilian economy had shifted southward to "the South East" or "the South Central" in the states of Rio de Janeiro, São Paulo, and Minas Gerais. (The state of Minas Gerais includes areas considered as South Central and areas usually considered part of the Northeast.) In the late 19th century, the far southern states of Paraná, Santa Catarina, and Rio Grande do Sul also would become prosperous centers of economic development. During the 19th century, the Northeast fell into economic decline even as many of its powerful families still played highly influential roles in national politics and in the economic growth of the southern regions. As in the rest of Brazil, slavery was not abolished until 1888. By the mid-19th century, the population of the Northeast was predominantly miserably poor, uneducated, and disease-ridden. The Northeast began to be seen as the great national problem—the center of economic backwardness.

Beginning in the late 19th century, periodic flows of hundreds of thousands and eventually many millions of migrants left the Northeast to work in the more rapidly growing regions to the south. The *"retirante,"* a migrant leaving the Northeast, became and remains one of the fabled figures central to the mythology of the Brazilian national sense of identity. As early as 1879, the Afro-Brazilian abolitionist and republican author, Jose do Patricinio, published the novel *Os retirantes*, giving the migrants a lasting place in Brazilian literature (Patricinio 1973 [1879]). One *retirante*, Luis Inacio da Silva (Lula), was elected in 2002 to become a two-term and immensely popular President of Brazil.

Many factors had contributed to the endemic poverty of the Northeast. The most obvious was the nature of the plantation economy. Plantations in the Brazilian Northeast derived from a colonial scheme of land ownership that rewarded a small class of people who were given extensive legal and quasi-legal powers of civil administration. Central authorities in regional capitals and Lisbon were mainly concerned about the productivity of the colony as a mercantile enterprise rather than in the welfare of their subjects. Powered by slave labor, the plantations formed the foundation for a society that was and still is rigidly stratified and grossly inequitable. It was profoundly racist and in many ways remains so today. The use of violence against labor and the poor was an endemic feature of Northeastern culture and remains a strong element in regional life.

Most of those who controlled this deeply divided realm were opposed on principle to the education of the majority of the populace, fearing it would make people less dependent on the plantation. Owners also often forbade slaves and free laborers to produce their own food or local market crops, making the region dependent on expensive imported food. The extreme export dependence of the Northeastern plantation complex made the regional economy subject to severe boom and bust cycles. International competition from tropical colonies around the world had by the 1830s created a more or less constant economic crisis in the Brazilian sugar economy, intensified by growing soil degradation (cf. Prado Junior 1969; Eisenberg 1974; Rogers 2010).

Though entrepreneurs and even some plantation owners sought to diversify economic activities, most politically powerful people were profoundly skeptical and often overtly hostile to anything that would create competition for labor or undermine the plantation owners' monopoly over political power.

Technological advance within the plantation economy and its potential spin-offs into skills and diversified economic activities came slowly because land and labor were so cheap. Investments by plantation owners in the 18th century gold and diamond mines of the interior produced great wealth, but the wealth was seldom invested in more diverse enterprises in Brazil itself and depletion of the mineral resources set in within decades. Many Brazilians, including prominent intellectuals and politicians (often embodied in the same individuals in a society in which education was available only to a narrow elite), had concluded that the plantation complex and its associated class and political structure was the fundamental cause of the lagging economic performance of the Northeast, and, in a larger sense, of all of Brazil, in comparison to the United States and other nations.

For some, slavery and the plantation economy were part of the same problem and as such would surely bring eventual ruin to the burgeoning coffee and cacao plantation regions further south as they had brought it to the sugar regions of the Northeastern coast. For others, slavery itself was the primary culprit, because it was slavery that maintained the monopoly of power and encouraged the wasteful use of land and labor that characterized plantation society. Free labor, it was argued, would intensify competition for land and therefore promote recognition of the need to conserve the soil's productive capability. The competitive and presumably higher price of free labor would force technological innovation that in turn would require a more educated work force. A class of free laborers and the emergence of a middle class would democratize education and political institutions. Abolition alone would be capable of undermining the egregious failings of the plantation economy. European liberalism and the Comtian positivism popular among much of Brazil's elite provided theoretical explanations for this perspective (cf. Schwarz 1962; Cruz Costa 1967; Wright 1995; Padua 2002).

For others, the malaise of the Northeast might have been created by slavery and the plantation economy but once they had become rooted in Brazilian soil a new and more pernicious problem had appeared that went beyond economic organization and deeper than slavery itself. The survival of significant populations of Indians, the mass importation of Africans, and the presence of poor Europeans, all subordinated to the plantation economy, had led to generalized mixing of races. In this view, racial diversity and mixed race populations were responsible for a populace that was intellectually and physically inferior to any of the pure racial stocks, but particularly inferior to Europeans. This view was popular within the Brazilian elite in the 19th and early 20th centuries (and not difficult to find in candid conversations or coded public discourse in the 21st century). It was encouraged by pseudo-scientific Brazilian interpretations of Charles Darwin, Auguste Comte, and Herbert Spencer, among others. Such interpretations flattered self-styled Euro-Brazilian elites and relieved them of blame for anything but the actions of their ancestors. They received encouragement from eugenicists in the United States and Europe. The problem was to be solved by massive European immigration and the associated advance of "civilization." "Civilization" was understood as some combination of urbanization, industrialization, and education, all to be ushered in under the patriarchal predominance of racially pure Euro-Brazilians enlightened by the sciences of evolution, sociology, and economics.

From the racist perspective, the problem of the Northeast had been greatly exacerbated by events that had filled the interior of the Northeast—often referred to as "*o sertão*"—with a poverty stricken population, who were either subsistence farmers or ignorant dependents of the ranching and commodity-producing (cotton, tobacco, sisal) economy of the region and who were of mixed racial descent. Through most of the colonial period and until abolition, slaves and free laborers escaped the conditions of the plantation economy by fleeing into remote areas of the Northeast. Sometimes migrants from the coast were following the opening of ranches or cotton plantations further inland. The highly diverse motivations and conditions that led to migration away from the coast also led, in the racist view, to the generalized mixing of European, Indian, and African racial stock. (These ideas are explored in an exhaustive and self-conflicted way by one of the most influential authors of Brazilian literature, Euclides da Cunha, in his 1902 *Os Sertões*.)

The "*cabôclo*" (an imprecise and flexible term which in most uses referred at least partly to mixed racial heritage) became the archetypical representative of the *sertanejo* population of the interior. The *sertanejo* was sometimes admired for his tough and ingenious adaptation to the difficult conditions of the Northeast, but he was seen explicitly or implicitly as representing "barbarism" or "atavism." The culture of violence and religious mysticism attributed to Northeasterners was held to be a result and proof of the deleterious effects of racial mixing. The interminable informal wars among powerful landowners and between landowners and the government were defined as part of this culture of violence among a mixed race people rather than as part of the political economy of the region. The endemic banditry of the region could similarly be diagnosed as symptomatic of the mixed-race population rather than as a consequence of inequality or corrupt and weak institutions. The violent and religiously obsessed *cabôclo* was the principal barrier to the Comtian positivist ideal of "*ordem e progresso*"enshrined on the Brazilian flag in 1889. This view was consistent with the self-satisfied way that racists used their supposedly objective and "scientific" perspective, part of the Comtian and/or Social Darwinist ideological structure that was envisioned as the midwife of Brazilian modernity. Elite perspectives on the problems of the Northeast, whether they were based on the failings of the plantation, on the evils of slavery, on the destruction of land and resources, or on the atavism that resulted from racial mixing in regions remote from urban civilization, were used in an overlapping and shifting hybrid discourse.

In the late 19th century, another perspective began to gain popularity. This view held that the problems of the Northeast were mostly the consequence of severe and periodic droughts that had plagued the region for centuries. Like the racist perspective, the climate explanation for the Northeast's problems also sometimes borrowed from the other explanations. It could also be bolstered by supposedly "scientific" authority, an authority that would prove more resilient than pseudo-scientific racism.

There is no question that the Northeast is periodically subjected to intense droughts that can last for many years. Native plant communities of the *sertão* are well adapted to take advantage of high average rainfall while also being able to survive prolonged drought with high evapotranspiration rates under the tropical sun. Droughts are particularly severe in the interior as opposed to the humid coastal regions. It is also clear that droughts complicate and sometimes defeat attempts to maintain stable agricultural economies based on large-scale commodity production or ranches. Major droughts of the Northeast that were severe enough to attract the attention of colonial or national officials occurred three or four times in both the 18th and 19th centuries, and again, periodically through the 20th century. For example, the severe drought of 1877–1879 was said by contemporaries to have killed half a million people, though later more sober estimates put the death toll at 150,000–200,000. A careful scholarly observer also noted that approximately 55,000 people migrated from the two most severely affected states to the Amazon region, then beginning to experience a boom in rubber production (Moura and Shukla 1981).

Each drought sent *retirantes* looking for food and work to humid coastal areas of the Northeast and to the more prosperous southern regions. In contrast to the weak response of previous colonial and national governments, in the

Table 9.1 Years of major droughts in Northeast Brazil to 1980

Years of major droughts in Northeast Brazil to 1980			
1603	1760	1824–1825★	1907
1614★	1772	1827	1915★
1691	1776–1777★	1830–1833	1919★
1711	1784	1845	1932–1933
1721	1790–1794★	1877–1879★	1936
1723–1724★	1804	1888–1889	1941–1944★
1736–1737	1809	1891	1951
1744–1746	1810	1898	1953
1754	1816–1817	1900★	1958★
		1902–1903	1980

Source: From Antonio D. Moura and Jagadesh Shukla, "On the Dynamics of Droughts in Northeast Brazil: Observations, Theory and Numerical Experiments with a General Circulation Model" *Journal of the Atmospheric Sciences*, Dec. 1981, 2653 ff.

Notes
1 Asterisks indicate years of extreme droughts.
2 Because populations were light in the interior during much of the colonial era, it is assumed that some droughts were not reported as such. These years are selected mostly on rainfall amounts while both the actual impacts of drought and the perception of impacts are subject to a variety of other factors such that this list does not entirely correspond to what Brazilians thought was happening in any given year. The table mainly serves to indicate the persistence of droughts through the history of the region.

severe drought that reached its extremes in 1877–1879 the federal and some state governments launched significant relief efforts said to reduce the scandalous levels of suffering, maintain a resident work force in the Northeastern interior, and avoid the problems created by the migrant waves in the cities of the Northeast and southern regions of Brazil. Historical memory of the 1877–1879 drought is best preserved by the photographs of desperate people congregated in what would become known as "concentration camps," camps that scandalized a nation while at the same time providing labor to regional ranches and plantations and railroads at rock-bottom prices. Other photographs of the era captured malnourished and desperate people apparently moving along roads and trails—more extreme versions of Dorothea Lange's photographs of Dust Bowl refugees, noting that in contrast to the "exo-dusters" of the US, *retirantes* of any era can hardly be imagined in their own cars, no matter how dilapidated. The severe drought culminating in 1944 corresponds to the "work front" established by the Brazilian government as the "rubber army" sent to the Amazon for rubber harvesting in response to the Japanese control of rubber plantations in Southeast Asia. That of 1958 corresponded to the enlistment of tens of thousands of workers to build Brasilia (Anais da Biblioteca Nacional 1994).

Drought as an explanation for "backwardness" and migration had several advantages over the competing explanations. It did not require a confrontation with the entrenched political economy of the plantation complex and those powerful families and politicians who controlled it. In the same vein, it did not require adherence to a belief in the abolition of slavery, and as an explanation it survived long beyond the time that the abolition of slavery failed to solve the problems of poverty and economic stagnation characteristic of the Northeast. The chronic abuse of the land and natural resources of the region could be blamed more on nature than on human action, since droughts could be and were advanced as explanations for environmental degradation, whether through the direct effects of periodic aridity, or through the effects of understandable human response to drought conditions. Particularly as racism and its pseudo-scientific trappings went out of polite fashion, and as other regions that shared the racially-mixed characteristics of the Northeast enjoyed relative economic prosperity, droughts offered an alternative explanation that seemed more scientific.

Some observers in the 18th and 19th century suggested that droughts and/ or their effects were exacerbated by the rampant deforestation of the coastal areas for sugar and the effects in the interior of deforestation due to ranching, cotton, and other agricultural enterprises, and fuel gathering for sugar mills, and, later, steel mills. This viewpoint, still under debate by climate scientists and geographers, had the advantage of explaining with the apparent authority of science why the problem just seemed to keep getting worse in spite of some efforts to mitigate it.

Perhaps the greatest advantage of all for the drought explanation as opposed to its rivals was the degree to which it gradually created a variety of economic and political opportunities that powerful people in the Northeast and beyond were able to exploit with great success. Beginning with sales of relief supplies to the federal and state governments, there were profits to be made from droughts. The Northeast in particular was governed, and to a considerable extent still is, by complex familial relationships that taken together constitute a system of rule called *"parentela."*[1] *Parentela* controlled virtually all initiatives of the state in which economic interests were at stake. These ensured the ability of a few families and their allies to monopolize government procurement. Relief supplies were a small opportunity, however, in comparison to the larger opportunities to monopolize water and the bounty that water could bring to agricultural land. The construction of dams initiated in the name of drought relief—and themselves opportunities for lucrative contracts and payoffs—were useful in providing water storage for lands in the *sertão* that were attractive for the opening of new frontiers in ranching, cotton and other commodity production. Dam and road construction to strengthen and extend the frontiers of commercial agriculture could be built at public expense by using the labor of "drought victims" working for mere subsistence in "work fronts" that were supposed to be a main feature of immediate drought relief (Otamar de Carvalho 1988). Greenfield observes that within the Northeast, *retirantes* were seen by elites as commodities much like slaves or livestock (Greenfield 2001).

Beginning with the founding of a federal government agency in 1909 and continuing with various reorganizations and reconceptualizations up to the present, the agricultural development projects for the rural Northeast focused first on simple water storage and, after 1959, on irrigation systems as the solution to chronic vulnerability to drought. Dams and irrigation works were systematically placed and designed to favor the wealthy and politically powerful. The creation by President Kubitschek in 1959 of SUDENE *(A Superintendência do Desenvolvimento do Nordeste*, or Superintendency for the Development of the Northeast)*, an agency charged with the overall economic development of the Northeast, led to a more aggressive overall strategy of development that used water storage and distribution to favor broader economic development. SUDENE's first director, economist Celso Furtado, proved willing to challenge many of the political structures and alliances that had prevailed in the Northeast, and he was able to pursue this work more aggressively as Minister of Planning in the government of João Goulart. Furtado also began to promote major industrialization and tourism projects in the cities of the Northeast, projects that in the long run have done more than anything else to provide some measure of economic stability to the Northeastern economy as a whole, but with scant benefits to the rural poor. Furtado's work was cut short by the military coup of 1964 against Goulart's government, sending Furtado into exile until 1979.

Under the military regime, the conservative national and international political alliances reasserted themselves through anti-drought measures that would be captured for the wealthy and do more harm than good for the majority of the rural poor. For decade after decade, independent observers interested in relief of poverty and building Brazil's economic prosperity watched in frustration as drought relief water projects were controlled by regional elites in cooperation with foreign export and engineering firms. These projects were increasingly financed by US foreign assistance programs that often required contracts to be given to construction and engineering project firms headquartered in the United States. Multi-lateral development banks (the World Bank and Inter-American Development Bank) were governed by Cold War strategies that often explicitly favored strengthening existing power structures. While the projects did sometimes provide a degree of economic growth, they offered relatively little relief to the rural poor of the region, who found that new chances for poorly paid seasonal work were not sufficient compensation for the way they were increasingly squeezed out of access to water and land.

Anthony Hall concluded that rural irrigation projects undertaken in the Northeast in the 1960s and early 1970s had on average displaced five times as many people among the rural poor as they provided with improved livelihoods. This reflected the underlying socio-political structures of the Northeastern elites, their international alliances, and the specific way in which people who were well placed to do so were able to seize the benefits of drought relief projects (Hall 1978).

Federal and state investment in alleviating problems caused by drought led critics at least as early as the 1950s to coin the term *"a industria da seca,"* or, "the drought industry." *"A industria da seca"* is best defined, according to Otamar de Carvalho (in a book whose publication was underwritten by the Brazilian National Association for Irrigation and Drainage), by those analysts who have shown that "the policies of combating drought [are] an instrument of reinforcement for the most conservative political and economic groups in the region [...]" (De Carvalho 1988, 2–3). Carvalho writes that the drought industry can be summed up as the complex of relationships, firms, policies, and projects that together make up a systematic political machine for the promotion and exploitation of the drought explanation for the troubles of the Northeast. The term also expressed the anger and frustration with the fact that the large amounts of money spent to solve the drought problem had not only failed to solve it but had actually made the consequences of the problem more severe in many respects. "Drought" in this sense is not simply a natural or human-induced climatic phenomenon—instead, it has become a politically and economically effective concept used to divert state resources to support the inequitable and anti-democratic political and economic arrangements that are the underlying problem of the Northeast. This produces new cycles of poverty, stagnation, and bursts of highly unequal growth that will in turn will be explained by the problem of drought.

My colleague, Wendy Wolford, and I uncovered a classic example of the enduring and pernicious character of the drought industry while researching a book on Brazil's agrarian reform movement (Wright and Wolford 2003, 166–173). We were urged by some leaders of the movement—the MST, or *Movimento dos Trabalhadores Rurais Sem-Terra*—to visit a large agrarian reform project called *Fazenda Catalunha* located along the São Francisco River in the state of Pernambuco. One of the MST leaders spoke of the project as "an example of what agrarian reform can accomplish." What we found was a project that featured a huge pumping complex meant to draw water directly from the river primarily for use by center pivot irrigation operations. The farm had been owned by a large construction firm centered in the capital of the state of Bahia, some hundreds of miles away. The firm was partially owned by the son-in-law of Antonio Carlos Magalhães, one of the Northeast's and Brazil's most powerful political bosses (and before driven out by a scandal, President of the Brazilian National Senate). At least $US10 million of public money loaned at low interest had been invested in the project, and water rights had been reinforced by Magalhães's informal control over the subsidiary of the publicly-owned electric company that has the heaviest interest in and control over the São Francisco's flow. MST organizers had been attracted to the project because it had been out of production for two years and therefore was subject to expropriation under Brazilian agrarian reform laws, although they were somewhat skeptical of their ability to obtain what they understood as a farm controlled by the fabled Magalhães. The Brazilian agrarian reform agency (INCRA—Instituto Nacional de Colonização e Reforma Agraria) investigators warned against expropriation because of soil and other technical problems they had discovered. Against the recommendations of INCRA's technical officials, an MST occupation of Fazenda Catalunha resulted in payment of $US16 million to the owners for expropriation and subsequent deeding of the property to the MST.

It turned out that there were good reasons for the warnings by the INCRA officials. Not only were many of the pumps and other irrigation facilities already broken or shortly to become so, but the irrigated soils had become highly saline. Much of the soil had become "perched," that is, a nearly impermeable layer only a couple of feet below the surface trapped water that became increasingly saline with evaporation through the topsoil. The MST farm was limping along, producing low yields with deteriorating land and equipment. The MST had no capacity to repair or maintain the equipment, and in any event the soils were quite likely beyond restoration at any reasonable cost. Fazenda Catalunha's status as a model only worked for those who gave the project a cursory glance, as many admirers have done. When questioned about this, the most prominent leader of the national MST in São Paulo admitted that Fazenda Catalunha came under MST control as a result of outmoded ideas of "modernity" that dazzled many of the technical people who worked for the movement.

Here was a project that summarized the latest shiny new model of "the drought industry." A single family, through its political machine based on classic *parentela* relationships, captured substantial state resources intended for relief of the drought-plagued region in the building of the project. They were then able to maneuver other state agencies into purchasing the failed project at a handsome price. This is the old part of the model, built into the frame.

The new part of the model is that the Magalhães machine—a politically conservative one—was able to show a cooperative attitude to Brazil's most radical rural social movement in the furtherance of the agrarian reform. The MST could declare a victory and settle a few thousand people on land, but it was left holding an asset that in the long run would do little good for poor people and almost certainly in the end create a great deal of disappointment and bitterness. Perhaps more than anything, the episode of Fazenda Catalunha demonstrates the enormous adaptability of Northeastern elites and the reach of their power. This is a characteristic that has underlain the success of the drought industry and the failure to seriously mitigate the poverty of rural Northeasterners.

As Hall concluded in his study of the relationship of economic stagnation to drought and irrigation schemes in the Northeast:

> To say that the "drought problem" is a total myth would be a gross exaggeration. However, it is true that many people have had, and continue to have, a vested interest in perpetuating the popular conception that the drought is the central cause of underdevelopment in the interior. Landowners and government planners anxious to promote water storage at the expense of every other development strategy use the drought as a convenient mask with which to obscure the basic causes of poverty.
>
> (Hall 1978, 125)

It is also worth noting that as the drought explanation has become broadly disseminated, the natural, occasional occurrence of drought has come to be seen as the chronic condition. The periodic event comes to be understood as the continual condition. As such, it becomes a more universal explanation for poverty than it would be otherwise—an explanation for all seasons, even when those seasons may be ones of abundant rain for many years in succession. It becomes an explanation, however inappropriate, that serves for every year, whether too dry, too wet, or ideal. The key is that *nature*—whether understood as nature itself or as a persistent, altered condition of natural forces shaped by human actions—is the problem. Therefore, contemporary individual human beings and human institutions are blameless. Their innocence frees them to pursue supposed solutions to the problem that exploit rather than resolve the problem.

The nearly ubiquitous image of the *retirante* in Brazilian culture bears many interpretations and meanings. Inevitably, any attempt to portray migrants of the Northeast risks falling into stereotype and invalid generalization, precisely because there are so many circumstances that lead to migration. Also, migrating populations are diverse in terms of the significantly distinct sub-regions from which they come and in terms of degree of desperation, ethnicity, dialect, occupation, gender, age, dress, and affect. However, for good or ill, a set of rather limited stereotypes have captured much of the discourse on the subject of migration, and have become stock items of popular representation. The stereotypes tend to strongly reinforce the idea that drought is the great cause of Northeastern poverty and migration.

The ghastly photographs of the malnourished and raggedy 19th century migrants were reborn with one of the most famous series of paintings by one of Brazil's most revered painters, Candido Portinari. The paintings, created in a year of intense Northeastern drought during World War II, feature nearly skeletal shadowy figures, usually a family with a starving dog or goat and a few pitiful possessions from which individuality is largely removed. Portinari, himself an unlettered child of poverty and a member of the Communist Party, was exiled a few years after completing the paintings. His paintings emphasize the condition and the horror of starving migrants in a drought-ravaged landscape rather than personalities or the diversity of the Northeastern geography.

Graciliano Ramos's novel *Vidas Sêcas* (Dry Lives), 1938, is routinely assigned to Brazilian high school and college students as an iconic and disturbing picture of Brazilian reality—as it was assigned to my beginning Portuguese class, where we were forced to struggle with strong regional dialects and odd expressions. Highly experimental in form and politically controversial in content, Ramos's novel inspired many imitators and a still-lively critical polemic. In the 20th century, numerous protest novels, plays, and songs posed many angry interpretations of the lives of retirantes—a movie of *Vidas Sêcas* released in 1963 is often considered the beginning of a whole new school of Brazilian cinema, simply called Cinema Novo. The *retirante* was a central figure in the songs and plays protesting the rise of Brazil's military dictatorship beginning in 1964 because the migrants seemed best to epitomize the many injustices of Brazil. Into the early 19th century, *retirantes* were portrayed as straggling along rough roads and trails. Later, *retirantes* would sometimes be described as "parrot-perches" because they often balanced for days or weeks on narrow little benches, packed into the beds of old trucks offering cheap transportation, usually along rough rural roads. While generalized rural poverty rather than drought migration was more responsible for packing Brazilian urban slums, the *retirante* was often portrayed as the central figure in the great migration to the cities in the mid-20th century, and sometimes still is.

One of the most popular forms of Brazilian folk art offered to urban folk and tourists are clay figurines that portray versions of the *retirante*. A single figure may be carrying a young goat, a water jug made from a dried gourd, and a backpack. Often families are pictured in clay walking in single file, with some assortment of dogs, goats, sheep, or pet birds. When the former Northeastern migrant, Luis Inacio da Silva, Lula, then President of Brazil, visited the Vatican in 2008, he presented a particularly well-made and cheerfully colored clay sculpture of a family of *retirantes* to a smiling Pope Benedict XVI (Globo.com 2008). (It should be noted that Lula was taken by his mother to Brazil's south for reasons faintly, if at all, related to drought.)

While all these art forms represent, to a degree, a sympathy with the *retirantes*, in their stereotypical and often brightly colored and humorous presentation they also represent a kind of softening and even exploitation of the dark realities. Perhaps the ultimate in this sense was the portrayal of the central figure of Jorge Amado's best-selling novel, *Gabriela, Cravo e Canela* (also a bestseller in English as *Gabriela, Clove and Cinnamon,* and an internationally successful movie starring Sonia Braga) in a very popular *telenovela* produced by the Globo TV network. (Like Portinari, Amado spent time in the Communist Party and an extended time in exile, in Amado's case in Czechoslovakia.) Gabriela, played by the former Playboy model and actress, Juliana Paes, is first encountered along the road covered in mud and revealing rags, but, true to her character in Amado's novel, she soon emerges as an incredibly erotic cook who charms the Syrian-Lebanese owner of a bar and its plantation-owner clientele in the then-booming cacao port of Ilheus. In the novel, as in the *telenovela,* the bar owner, Nacib, will have to learn that he can only enjoy Gabriela's love if he is willing to share her attentions with others—a turn of events which allows various interpretations of how we are to see the victims of Brazil's most scandalous poverty, and its women. If nothing else, the novel, book, films, and *telenovelas* of *Gabriela* remind of us the centrality of the figure of the *retirante* in Brazilian cultural discourse and popular imagination.

"Drought victims" into the Amazon: a new frontier of obfuscation

The drought theory of human suffering has had effects that range beyond the Brazilian Northeast and that give new life to natural deficiency as an explanation for poverty. The main migration of Northeasterners has been out of the countryside and into cities, including the coastal cities of the Northeast, but more importantly to the major industrial complexes of the South Central and Southeast. This has had the effect of keeping the industrial and urban cheap and of creating vast urban slums.

However, beginning as early as the 18th century there has been a trickle of migration from the Northeast into the Amazon that at times grew to a substantial stream and which since 1970 has become something of a flood. Beginning in the colonial era and continuing until abolition in 1888, slaves escaping plantations, some of them organized into *quilombos* (communities of escaped slaves), sought the relatively secure refuge of the Amazon, as did many Indians and *cabóclos*. This slow resettling of the Amazon, after the collapse of the populations native to the region, produced a great diversity of livelihood and cultures. Some dramatic migrations, such as the one that brought more than 50,000 people to the Amazon from Ceará and Piauí in 1877 to 1879, corresponded to Northeastern drought years (De Carvalho 1988). More continuous migration out of the Northeast during the decades before 1912 was driven by the Amazonian rubber boom and included those eager for opportunity and those recruited by force and intimidation. Other relatively large influxes included the "rubber army" of people persuaded and conscripted in the Northeast into national service as rubber gatherers during World War II (Garfield 2013). Railroad and harbor construction and mining and timber operations also brought small numbers of migrants from the Northeast to the Amazon through the late 19th and early 20th centuries. Some migration into the Amazon was almost completely divorced from the influence of migrations from the rest of Brazil—for example, largely successful Japanese colonization along the lower stretches of the Amazon supported by the Japanese government before World War II.

The size of the steady trickle of most years was governed by a variety of factors that varied significantly over time: labor markets; epidemic and endemic diseases; the intensity of battles over land and the river trade in the Amazon; the intensity of private wars over land in the Northeast; access to land that was reliably productive; and, of course, the weather in both the Northeast and the Amazon. Against this was balanced the relative ease—relative, that is, to the privation that Northeasterners tended to take for granted—of building a simple shed along a branch of the river to make a living from the river and forest as did what are called river people, or *ribeirinhos*. The continual intermarriage between migrants into the Amazon and Amer-Indian groups also facilitated migration for many, providing the relative security of group membership and the all-important knowledge of how to exploit the resources of the many regional and sub-regional environments.

Until the second half of the 20th century, the balance was usually on the side of the many hardships of the Amazon that kept migration to a minimum. It is now clear that until recent decades, and perhaps still, the human population of the Amazon has been substantially below pre-Conquest levels. One factor alone—the extremely favorable environment offered to major Old World diseases such as malaria and yellow fever—kept human numbers low. The construction of Brasilia in the late 1950s and early 1960s brought tens of thousands of laborers from the Northeast, partially motivated by the severe drought of 1958, to the relatively dry edge of the Amazon watershed, but few ventured into the humid forests nearby. Construction of the first major roads into the Amazon in the late 1960s encouraged settlement at a slow pace. Migration was driven more by opportunities for labor in cities, mines, and sawmills than by the quest for land.

Mass migration into the Amazon that began in 1970 was linked to the drought explanation of Brazil's troubles. The highly publicized government policy of Amazon colonization began in 1970, supposedly partly in response to that year's drought in portions of the Northeast. Few doubted at the time, however, that drought was not a significant and genuine motivation but rather part of a smokescreen for the military's real motives. The military government, supported by Cold Warriors in the US government, had seized power in 1964 partly because of conservative fear of the increasingly strong demands for nation-wide redistributive land reform. The military was quick to repress or exile those politicians who had become prominent in the demands for agrarian reform. The military also emasculated or destroyed rural unions, peasant leagues, and other organizations that had militated for land reform. The military officially recognized the need for land reform, passing its own reform measure called the *Estatuto da Terra*, but in fact, agrarian reform was a dead letter. Severe and often violent repression of any militancy for land reform became an ongoing task (Wright and Wolford 2003, Chapters 2, 3).

President Medicí announced the program for agricultural colonization with the famous phrase that the "Amazon was a land without people for a people without land," tying it specifically to the idea of giving land to the rural poor in a drought year in which *retirantes* where streaming out of the Northeast to cities of the Northeast and the industrial South Central region. While the poor were to receive land, the route into the Amazon through agricultural colonization need not disturb the older structures of the agrarian economy in the Northeast. Nor need it stand in the way of the drive for "conservative modernization" of the agricultural economy through large-scale corporate investment, displacing smallholders throughout Brazil, including family farmers producing wheat, corn, and soy in Brazil's relatively prosperous extreme south. "Conservative modernization" within the Northeast took the form of such corporate farming projects as the large-scale irrigation scheme fed from the new Sobradinho reservoir on the São Francisco River. The military government, in an attempt to quiet militant movements of disgruntled displaced farmers and rural workers, aggressively encouraged Northeasterners and Southern smallholders toward colonization projects.

The government used a carrot and stick policy to deal with demands for land reform. The stick was wielded by the army, police and private gunmen. The carrot consisted of offers of land in the Amazon. In some cases, potential settlers were taken by plane to view the colonization projects on offer. Lavish promises of land, hospitals, schools, and social services were made to contrast strongly with the conditions that rural people, especially those from the Northeast, knew at home. For reasons inherent in their own vision and organizational necessities, the significant land reform movements that would coalesce into the MST in 1984 opposed Amazon colonization.

However, the very simple formulation that had been built over decades now had significant popular appeal: those landless folk who languished where it was too dry would be sent to where it was wet and land was abundant. Social reform was unnecessary. In the early 1970s, those who opposed Amazon colonization saw the notion that the Amazon could provide agricultural livelihoods as a combination of cynical manipulation of legitimate demands for agrarian reform and misunderstanding of the agricultural potential of Amazon soils. What became more obvious as time went on was that the military had additional motives in mind. Land was the bait to lure a population into the Amazon to provide labor for massive extraction of timber and mineral resources and hydroelectric projects. When settlers failed as farmers, so much the better—they were more available as cheap labor, and once again it was nature in the form of nutrient-poor and erodible soils that could be blamed. The military was also deeply worried about national security in a thinly populated region bordering sometimes hostile neighboring countries, and saw populating the region as part of the solution (Hecht and Cockburn 1989; Wright and Wolford 2003, ch. 3).

The most thorough study done of the fate of settlers in the Amazon in the 1970s and 1980s shows that for the minority of those who actually received the institutional, technical, and financial support of the official colonization effort, Amazon settlement provided a substantial and relatively sustainable improvement in welfare (Ozorio de Almeida 1992). Proper site selection was of course essential in a complex and poorly understood environment in which, as in most regions of the world, most of the land is not suited for long-term crop production. Where site selection was competently accomplished with the help of well-trained agronomists, provision of the other kinds of support made sustainable farmsteads possible. For this minority of settlers who were privileged by deliberate institutional effort and/or by the rarer occurrence of fortunate circumstance, there was much less incentive to leave the initially colonized site. This avoided or substantially reduced the severity of the otherwise widespread problem of an advancing frontier of devastated land and low-yield extensive ranching operations from which few benefited. Where settlers enjoyed full-fledged support, the settlement of a small, carefully selected portion of the Amazon could be envisioned as a reasonable way to improve human life consistent with national development and the preservation of everything but a small fraction of the forest.

Unfortunately, those settlers whose fate was favorable because of the support they enjoyed from government found that the support tended to erode away over time. The pressure of chronic budget problems, institutional corruption and decay, and outright legal and violent attacks on the integrity of these settlements by private logging, cattle, and mining interests left most of the favored minority facing the problems of the majority of settlers who had never enjoyed institutional support. The legal impunity enjoyed by the powerful and the aggressive made it difficult or impossible to hold on to land or savings.

In spite of this, many environmentalists and champions of the rural poor in the Amazon join the rest of the ill-informed in over-emphasizing the difficulties imposed by nature rather than the failure of human institutions, just as the poverty of the rural Northeast continues to be understood by many as the failure of rain. One explanation based on the inadequacy of nature to support human settlement chases another, from dry country to wet, across an increasingly devastated landscape and a continuously victimized human population. Wet or dry, the interpretations are not only partial and inaccurate, but they both mask and reproduce new version of the problems they fail to explain.

The danger of categorization: the precarious fate of environmental refugees

The creation of categories is necessary, but it is dangerous. In identifying environmental migrants or environmental refugees, we must be careful not to repeat the Brazilian experience by which complex causation is reduced to oversimplified explanations to serve exploitive purposes. We surely do not want to create a self-serving international industry that exploits environmental migration and in the process deepens underlying problems. There are only a few cases of clear-cut "environmental migration" that do not involve complicated questions regarding the interaction of environmental change with human institutions and culture, and these cases involve relatively small numbers of people. The cases involving millions of migrants are socially complex in the extreme.

Proposals for remediation of the problems of climate-induced migrations proliferate, but we must not mistake apparently good intentions for adequate analysis. Such proposals can go badly wrong if:

a   They begin to create a body of bureaucratic personnel and expertise working in association with exploitive vested interests that produce environmental explanations for crises whether they are appropriate or not—the creation of an industry of environmental crisis that exploits and reproduces crisis;

b   They result in ignoring or masking other socio-economic factors and vested interests that play a strong role in the crises and that need to be clearly identified and addressed to properly resolve the problems;

c   They result in over-emphasizing adaption or mere response to local crisis rather than taking the sometimes more painful and divisive measures that would to some degree avoid the occurrence of crisis—clearly a major issue in the climate change debate;

d   They help to create a new pseudo-science of biologically and physically-based environmental explanations when more energetic and better-informed social science, politics, and social response is what is needed.

The understandable need for international unity to deal with the climate crisis increases the temptation to gloss over responsibility for problems. Once nature is held responsible, even a nature that has changed as result of human actions, it easily becomes the excuse that lets off the hook all those people, businesses, and institutions that share responsibility with natural forces. It is essential to avoid this mistake whenever possible. With climate change, as with so many other problems, the longer we wait to effectively identify the real problems and respond accordingly, the more difficult it will be to avoid the trap.

Note

1 For a superb discussion of *parentela* for one of the Northeast's most important political families, and a family deeply involved in what would become known as "the drought industry," see Lewin 1987.

References

Anais da Biblioteca Nacional 1994 Imagens da seca de 1877–78 no Ceará: uma contribuição para o conhecimento das origens de fotojornalismo na imprensa brasileira, *Rio* 114, 77–83

de Carvalho O. 1988 *A economia política do Nordeste: seca, irrigação e desenvolvimento*, Editora Campus, Rio de Janeiro

Cruz Costa J. 1967 *Contribuição a história das idéias no Brasil*, ed. Civilização Brasileira, Rio de Janeiro da Cunha E. 1962 *Rebellion in the backlands*, 9th ed., translated by Samuel Putnam, University of Chicago Press, Chicago (originally published as *Os Sertões*, 1902, Civilização Brasileira)

Eisenberg P.L. 1974 *The sugar industry in Pernambuco 1840–1910: modernization without change*, University of California Press, Berkeley and Los Angeles

Garfield S. 2013 *In search of the Amazon: Brazil, the United States, and the nature of a region*, Duke University Press, Durham

Globo.com 2008 Lula presentou Papa Bento XVI com uma escultura de barro que representa família de retirantes nordestinos, illustration for "Lula diz que Papa Bento XVI poderia dar conselho contra crise" 13 November, available at: http://g1.globo.com/Noticias/Politica/0,,MUL860937-5601,00-LULA+DIZ+QUE+PAPA+BENTO+XVI+PODERIA+DAR+CONSELHOZINHO+CONTRA+CRISE.html (accessed 19 January 2017)

Greenfield G. 2001 *The realities of images: imperial Brazil and the Great Drought*, Transaction of the American Philosphical Society, v 91, part 1

Hall A. 1978 *Drought and irrigation in North-East Brazil*, Cambridge University Press, Cambridge

Hecht S. and A. Cockburn 1989 *The fate of the forest: developers, destroyers and defenders of the Amazon*, Verso, London/New York

Lewin L. 1987 *Politics and parentela in Paraíba: a case study of family-based oligarchy in Brazil*, Princeton University Press, Princeton

Moura A.D. and J. Shukla 1981 On the dynamics of droughts in Northeast Brazil: observations, theory and numerical experiments with a general circulation model, *Journal of the Atmospheric Sciences*, December, 2653–2675

Ozorio de Almeida A.L. 1992 *The colonization of the Amazon*, University of Texas Press, Austin

Padua J.A. 2002 *Um sopro de destruicao: Pensamento politico e critica ambiental no Brasil escravista (1786–1888)*, Jorge Zahar, Rio De Janeiro

Patricinio J. do 1973 *Os Retirantes*, 2nd edition, Ed. Tres, São Paulo [1st edition 1879]

Prado J.C. 1969 *The colonial background of modern Brazil*, translated by Suzette Macedo, University of California Press, Berkeley and Los Angeles

Ramos G. 1938 *Vidas Sêcas*, Editoria Jose Olympio, Rio de Janeiro

Rogers T. 2010 *The deepest wounds: a labor and environmental history of sugar in Northeast Brazil*, University of North Carolina Press, Chapel Hill

Rubin J.S. 2010 *International law and the victims of climate change: creating a framework for managing impacts and displaced people*, Perspectives, American Security Project

Schwarz R. 1962 *Misplaced ideas: essays on Brazilian culture*, Verso, London/New York

Vag A. et al. 2009 *Environmental change and forced migration scenarios synthesis report*, European Commission, May 14 2009

Wright A. 1995 Nineteenth-century economic thought on Brazilian peasantry and twentieth-century consequences in Evelyn L. Forget and Richard Lobdell, eds, *The peasant in economic thought: the perfect republic*, Edward Elgar, Aldershot, UK; Brookfield, US

Wright A. and W. Wolford 2003 *To inherit the earth: the landless movement in the struggle for a new Brazil*, Food First! Books, Oakland, California, 166–175

10 The ecological and social vulnerability of the Three Gorges resettlement area, 1992–2012

Ying Xing

Abstract

The Three Gorges Project on the Yangtze River in Hubei province has produced the world's largest dam-displaced population. The forced resettlement of millions of people to an area which was already ecologically vulnerable intensified that process, inevitably. This brought social vulnerability, endangering the social order and social resilience in the resettlement area. The mutual reinforcement of ecological and social vulnerability has caused an unprecedented environmental crisis. As a result, dam resettlers became ecological resettlers and have since become a homeless population. The Three Gorges area has become a focal point for social instability.

Introduction

Dam resettlers, who constitute a unique type of resettler, have two distinct characteristics which differentiate them from other displaced populations. Firstly, government hydropower projects force them to resettle, causing greater stress than that faced by other resettlers (Cernea 1988, 3–8). Secondly, dam resettlers are relocated simultaneously within a short period of time, rather than successively in smaller numbers. This forced relocation of an entire group therefore creates environmental and social conflict. Indeed, dam resettlers are often associated with problems of impoverishment, environmental crisis and social instability (World Commission on Dams 2000, 102–108).

Dam resettlement is a worldwide phenomenon and especially common in developing countries. China has a large number of dam resettlers. Karl Wittfogel (1957) used the concept of *hydraulic empire* to analyze imperial China. Wittfogel's theory, which is based on Max Weber's theory of oriental despotism, pointed out the distinctive relationship between the hydraulic system and the political system in "oriental" society. Wittfogel analyzed how traditional state power, which had emerged from a society based on large-scale irrigated agriculture, which he calls hydraulic agriculture, had held back the development of a social autonomy able to resist the power of the central government. However, Wittfogel's analysis neglected the fact that though Weber stated that imperial China had enormous power, he also emphasized the fragility of this power (Weber 1951, 47–50). In fact, the state power of imperial China had been both too powerful and too fragile for thousands of years.

In the latter half of the 20th century, the *hydraulic empire* grew into a new phase. The massive construction of irrigation and hydro-electric projects became not only a key component of the nation's industrialization, but also an important means of political mobilization and penetration into rural society. The hydro projects were important to the communist state-building plan.

By the end of 1999, China had built over 86,000 reservoirs and hydro-electric plants. Today there are 17 million people displaced by dams in China (Tang Chuanli 2002, 1). The quantity of reservoirs and the quantity of reset-tlers are the largest in the world. However, these tremendous numbers are associated with an emerging unintended consequence. Specialists believe that one-third of this population has been relatively well resettled, one-third has been resettled with difficulty and the remaining one-third has not been well resettled (Li Boning 1996, 317). The reason why there are so many problems remaining in China's dam relocation is closely related to the char-acteristics of China's political system and the government's awareness of the resettlement issue.

Since 1949, the political system of modern China has been a typical party-state mobilization system, and the state has adopted the modernization strat-egy of "catch up and surpass." This political feature has, on the one hand, greatly exacerbated the original resistance of dam resettlers, and, on the other hand, has considered modernization, with dam building projects as a key fea-ture, as a far more important goal than environmental protection. The key problem is that the state approaches the relocation issue as merely a ques-tion of economic compensation. In their view this is supplementary to dam projects, an issue of how to educate the resettlers to sacrifice their own inter-ests for the sake of the national interest. In fact, the relocation issue is first and foremost a complicated social issue. Therefore, the attitude that treats reloca-tion as a simple matter makes relocation a breeding ground for constant social unrest, including petitions and collective actions (Jing 1996; Mou Mo and Cai Wenmei 1998; Ying Xing 2001).

The Three Gorges Project has the greatest scale among all dam projects in the world, and the Three Gorges resettlers have become the world's largest resettlement population. From 1992 to 2012, the total population of Three Gorges resettlers reached 1.2964 million, including 557,700 rural resettlers. The problem of ecological vulnerability in the Three Gorges resettlement area is very serious. In this area, the population is large but the land area is insuf-ficient; arable land is only 0.8 mu per capita (one mu equals 0.06 hectare). Fertile land is rare, and the majority of available land is on hillsides. The soil erosion is severe and the economic base is very weak, causing this to be one of the most well-known poor areas in China. There are 11 officially "poverty-stricken" counties among 20 counties in the area, making the resilience of the area very weak. Just as in R.H. Tawney's saying, the peasants here are "standing permanently up to [their] neck[s] in water, so that even a ripple is sufficient to drown [them]" (Tawney 1966, 77).

The Chinese government has also carried out ecological relocation projects. The so-called *ecological resettler* refers to the displaced population which resettled because of the deterioration of the environment or to protect the environment from destruction. For example, in Xihaigu region in Ningxia Autonomous Region, the population is in extreme poverty due to the acutely dry desert steppe environment paired with rapid population growth. In Ningxia, the historically prevalent style of farming was itinerant: the plots of land that are farmed are spread out, so that in some places land is tens of kilometers away from the village. In planting and harvesting season, farmers build caves and sheds as temporary local residences. After the planting and harvesting, they move back to their homes in villages. Some farmers even have several huts or shelters so they can rotate among them in planting and harvesting seasons. The ecological relocation carried out by local government in Ningxia in the 1980s took advantage of this farming practice. It was carried out by the government and became a formal and complete population displacement. The population moved from southern Ningxia, which was extremely arid, to the Hetao irrigation district in the north. Hetao is close to their irrigation area of the Yellow River and has more than 2 million mu (133,333 hectares) of arable land, which is suitable for agriculture and herding. Since 1983, the government has reclaimed 830,000 mu (55,333 ha) of land in the Hetao area in Ningxia, established 25 resettlement bases and relocated 412,000 poor people. This greatly eased the high tension caused by the land scarcity and population demand in the Xihaigu area. In some places, cultivated land is converted into forests and vegetation is recovered, and the vicious cycle of ecological destruction in the region is broken (Li Ning 2003).

However, there is a difference between the Three Gorges resettlement and the ecological relocation in Ningxia: the Three Gorges resettlers were not displaced to defuse the ecological dilemma, but in order to meet the economic development needs of the country. This has led to a unique process of ecological and social vulnerability and environmental crisis and left a large number of resettlers homeless. This chapter is a summary analysis of this historical process.

The plan of the Three Gorges resettlement and the law of unintended consequences

In 1970, Mao Zedong gave the following instruction in the report on the Gezhouba Dam project. "Approve the construction of the dam. The current plan [...] is one aspect, but the unexpected difficulty that will be encountered in the construction process is another aspect" (Mao 1998, 197). The Gezhouba Dam project was pushed ahead by the Ministry of Water

Resources when the launch of the Three Gorges project was delayed in the 1950s. Under the guiding ideology of simultaneous "launch, design and modify," the Gezhouba Dam project had produced many problems including sediment deposition and geological hazards among others, so was forced to shut down for two years. The law of unintended consequences, and indeed their emergence, is neither characteristic of one particular reservoir, nor of dam project construction. In fact, unintended consequences have appeared universally and repeatedly in various government construction projects in China since 1949. In Tocqueville's study of the political effects of administrative decentralization of the United States, he pointed out that "a central power, however enlightened, however learned one imagines it, cannot gather to itself alone all the details of the life of a great people. It cannot do [so] because such a [task] exceeds human strength" (Tocqueville 2000, 86). And Martin Whyte pointed out that the problem in bureaucratization of contemporary China was the distinction between "structural" bureaucratization and "functioning" bureaucratization (Whyte 1989, 239–241). *Structural bureaucratization* refers to the process in which all traditional forms of organization are abandoned or replaced by formal bureaucratic organization, and China becomes a society in which various resources and social life are almost entirely dominated by new, large-scale organizations. *Functioning bureaucratization* is the process in which various rational formal rules and standardized procedures of formal bureaucratic organizations are consciously rejected or unintentionally neglected. The reason why "unintended consequences" are continually generated in Chinese dam projects is that China is powerful in promoting government construction projects through social mobilization under the party-state system, but is weak in solving specific problems in the process of state-building. In Michael Mann's concept, the state's *despotic power* is very strong, but the *infrastructural power* is very weak (Mann 1984).

The Three Gorges Project was launched forcibly when its critics were silenced after the "Tiananmen incident" in 1989 (Barber and Ryder 1993, xx; Dai Qing 1994). Officials from the Ministry of Water Resources directed the feasibility study of the Three Gorges project, and focused only on the Three Gorges project separately, but avoided talking about the overall plan of the Yangtze River basin and the possibility of an alternative plan. In so doing, the difficulty of resettlement and environmental problems were largely underestimated. For example, in 1992, when the Three Gorges project was approved by the Chinese National People's Congress, the resettlement plan of "local relocation" for rural resettlers and "resettlement with development" was proposed. However, facts later proved that such a plan was almost impracticable in the Three Gorges reservoir area where there were serious environmental problems. Moreover, the resolution stated that the geological condition in the Three Gorges reservoir area was stable, so there was no need for large investments. Later experience showed that this rash assertion had brought serious consequences.

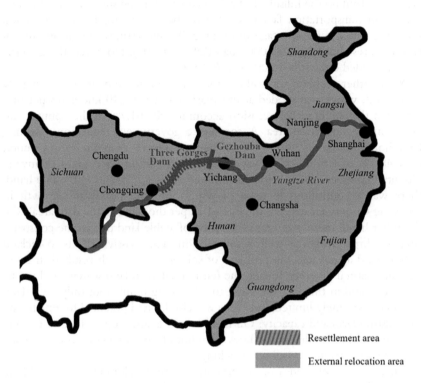

Figure 10.1 Three Gorges Dam resettlement areas
Source: Created by the author

Ecological and social vulnerability in the Three Gorges relocation area

Ecological vulnerability in local relocation

The difficulty in the Three Gorges relocation was the relocation of rural resettlers. According to the plan in 1992, the policy of rural resettler relocation was mainly local agricultural resettlement relocation in reservoir areas. The key problem in the Three Gorges relocation was that the area had insufficient land resources for local relocation. For example, in Yunyang County, Chongqing Municipality, there were 66,000 mu (4,400 ha) of land to be submerged, making the problem of land scarcity even more serious. The per capita arable land was only 0.879 mu (0.05 ha) in the county and one-fourth of farmers had only 0.5 mu (0.03 ha) of land per person. Although the submerged land accounted for only 4.8% of the county's total arable land, it was the most fertile land in the Yangtze Valley. The land designated for new settlement was on barren hillsides with impoverished soil and little water. The government had invested 17.36 million yuan (US$2.6 million) from 1985 to 1992 to reclaim 17,600 mu

(1,173 ha) land on the hillside, but achieved very limited success since it lacked water and transportation facilities. One of the reasons for the failure in soil improvement was the shortage of funding. To successfully enrich one mu of land requires about 2,000–4,000 yuan (US$300–600). However, the government provided only 400–1,200 yuan (US$60–180).

Yet another problem was soil erosion. The soil in the dam site was mainly purple soil, which was eroded at the yearly rate of 10,240 kilograms per mu. The area that suffered land erosion accounted for 61.7% in the county, and 66.2% in the relocation area. According to government regulations, farming land should not be on a slope over 25 degrees. However in Yunyang County, over 48.1% of farming land was on slopes exceeding 25 degrees (Yunyang County Gazetteer Compilation Committee 1999, 97; 207). On the one hand, there was a continuous increase of population (the population growth in Yunyang County far exceeds the rate of 12 per thousand in the dam area). On the other hand, there was a rapid decrease of arable land due to the construction of Three Gorges as well as soil erosion. The massive efforts to reclaim hillside land aggravated the problem of soil erosion, which resulted in more frequent natural disasters. In fact, the tension between land scarcity and population demand in the area was close to a breaking point. Not only were land resources extremely limited, but there was also limited potential for enhancing the existing farmland capacity. On these barren lands, crop yields and income were low and the hydraulic facilities were not fit, meaning conditions to guarantee people's basic survival were lacking.

There was another idea of "resettlement with development" in the Three Gorges relocation plan. At that time, some people within the government proposed the idea of developing high-yielding ecological agriculture in the area. But the dam region did not have the base conditions for this sort of development plan. First, most hillside land was impoverished, barren land requiring many years to become arable, even after soil improvement. Second, the natural climate was very severe in the area. There were frequent floods, droughts, storms and frosts. For instance, Yunyang County suffered minor droughts almost every year, and severe droughts once every two years. In the spring season there were frequent cold air currents, and in the early summer and fall there were often rain storms (Yunyang County Gazetteer Compilation Committee 1999, 114–122.) Third, the area did not have a strong technical team, which was necessary for developing a high-yield ecological agriculture. Lastly and most importantly, the area did not have the necessary financial resources. The development of high-yielding agriculture required massive funding, but the dam region was known for its weak economic base, and state funds for relocation were very limited.

We might point to several experimental pieces of high-yielding eco-farming in the area, but these were basically "planted" by money. Some specialists described it as a situation in which "the state gives out money, and farmers cultivate land." But how much money could the state provide for a majority of the local people to conduct eco-farming in the area? Even if all relocated farmers were able to grow vegetables under plastic shields as promoted by eco-farming advocators, there was also a problem of finding a market. Another attempted solution for the limited space for land development was a government effort to adjust the agricultural structure of the reservoir area to develop citrus, forestry, animal husbandry and aquaculture. This was also unsuccessful for effective relocation.

High hopes were pinned on citrus, for example. In the Three Gorges reservoir area, the winter is warm, the spring is early, the autumn is short and the summer is long. Rain and hot weather come in the same season, so it is very suitable for growing citrus. However, the breed of citrus in the reservoir area was not good, and there was a lack of processing plants, so the economic value of citrus was very low. The phenomenon of citrus decay was frequent, and many farmers even peeled the citrus to sell only the rind. The economic value of citrus could be improved by genetic improvements to the varieties, technology enhancements and increased processing capacity. Nevertheless, the funding and technology required for these improvements were lacking

Other industries also faced problems. In forestry, for example, in many places in the reservoir area, the quantity of saplings was small, cultivation technology was insufficient, and management was poor. The survival rate of saplings planted in areas which once were farmland was quite low, and some of the trees which had been planted for years were no thicker than chopsticks. In animal husbandry, as another example, the prolonged influence of traditional farming methods, transportation, cultural communication, dietary habit and so on, meant that the production of herbivorous livestock in the reservoir area was low. In addition, the quality of species was poor, the per capita consumption of herbivorous livestock and their products was low, the breeding technology and production efficiency was limited, and the degree of industrialization of forage and herbivorous livestock negligible. Furthermore, the storage of the Three Gorges reservoir brought negative impacts on aquaculture. While the Three Gorges reservoir formed, the original eight spawning grounds in the reservoir area all disappeared due to river water pollution and sedimentation. Many species, including those endemic to the upper reaches of the Yangtze River (coreius guichenoti, rock carp, etc.) became rare or disappeared completely.

Therefore, the three major factors which restrict the development of China's rural areas—a large population, the shortage of resources per capita (especially land resource per capita), and a fragile ecological environment—had been very prominent in the Three Gorges reservoir rural area. Moreover, the relocation of rural resettlers principally through local relocation intensified the tension between land scarcity and population demand. Among the 557,700 Three Gorges rural resettlers, there are 196,000 people who were forcibly relocated into such an environment (The Three Gorges Resettlement Project 2015).

Social vulnerability in external relocation

Due to the pressure of environmental vulnerability, especially after the flood in the Yangtze in 1998, the Chinese government had to adjust the policy of the Three Gorges rural resettlers starting in 1999. The initially planned external relocation of 83,000 people soared to 361,700 people in 2009. This is 64.86% of the total population of rural resettlers. Most of the areas of external relocation are in China's more developed coastal areas, such as Shanghai, Guangdong, and Zhejiang, and Shandong Province.

The external relocation of the Three Gorges resettlers on the one hand affects the life of the original residents in the relocation area, and on the other hand affects the living standard of the externally relocated resettlers. First, the amount of arable land is greatly insufficient. Both the original residents and the externally relocated resettlers live mainly from traditional agricultural production. The amount of arable land in relocation areas is vastly insufficient due to the land occupation of urbanization and relocation. The arable land per capita is only 0.02 ha in some places; thus, both resettlers and original residents face the problem of seeking *other ways of household production*. Second, the incomes of externally relocated resettlers and original residents *are both declining* in this scenario. Since the amount of arable land is reduced, the revenue of traditional agriculture has dropped significantly. The industrial basis of many relocation areas is weak, and the business and service market has limited capacity and intense competition. Therefore, externally relocated resettlers and original residents, except the families who work in construction, suffer from various degrees of income decline. Third, the lack of employment is another significant problem for resettlers and original residents. According to an internal survey from a research group of the Chinese Academy of Sciences, the employment rate of the Three Gorges resettlers in their original homes was 75.80%, but is only 55.23% after the relocation; the employment rate of the original inhabitants was 85.97% before the relocation, but dropped to 65.33% after the relocation. The existence of large numbers of surplus labor directly affects the economic development and social stability of both the resettlers and original residents.

Moreover, when compared with the original residents, the externally relocated resettlers have some particular difficulties, such as adapting to the language, natural environment, means of production, lifestyle, and culture (World Commission on Dams 2000, 102–103). One of the most prominent problems was relative deprivation, which was triggered when externally relocated resettlers compared themselves to some frame of reference. Relative deprivation is the negative disparity between reality and expectation, and is the source of feelings of dissatisfaction (Merton 1968, 281–289).When people find they are far worse off than the reference group, they will feel they are being deprived; and when their endurance exceeds its limit, these people are likely to take various kinds of actions (petitions, mass disturbance, etc.) to fight for their rights. Specifically, the following were the sources of relative deprivation of externally relocated resettlers.

The difference when compared with local farmers in relocation areas

Local farmers were able to provide land to the Three Gorges resettlers because great change in the local economic structure had taken place in the economically developed relocation area. There were many opportunities for non-agricultural employment, and the locals' high standard of living came mainly from non-agricultural industries such as township and village enterprises. Due to factors such as language, skills, relationships, culture and others, the Three Gorges resettlers' opportunities to get non-agricultural jobs in the relocation area were much lower than that of local farmers. Therefore, the relocation methods of the Three Gorges resettlers had to be based on agriculture and land, and there was a noticeable contrast between the Three Gorges resettlers' employment in traditional agriculture and the local residents' opportunities for non-agricultural employment, as well as a huge gap in income between the two groups. Since the compensation funds and personal savings of resettlers were mainly spent on housing, the economic pressures on resettlers were particularly prominent in confronting the high consumption level in relocation areas. Research on the resettlers of Chongming County in Shanghai reveals that, among the respondents of 149 families of the Three Gorges resettlers, there were 135 families who considered the economic pressure high, and 121 families of resettlers, 81.2% of the respondents, listed the economic pressure as the greatest difficulty after relocation (Sun Yang and Sun Xiangming 2002, 40).

The difference when compared with exaggerated propaganda

In order to successfully complete the external relocation task, many county governments in the Three Gorges reservoir area had propagandized the advantage of relocation area, exaggerating in varying degrees to encourage resettlers to participate energetically. Therefore, resettlers came to the relocation area with very high expectations. However, the more relocation conditions were promoted, the greater the demands the resettlers would have. When these demands could not be achieved in reality, resettlers had more intense feelings of dissatisfaction. Although the general level of development of external relocation areas was high, this did not mean that the conditions offered to the Three Gorges resettlers were better. In fact, the land provided for resettlers in many relocation areas was spread out, fragmented and low yield, and thus did not meet the basic needs of resettlers.

The difference when compared with other relocation areas

Due to various factors, the conditions of each relocation area were very different. Chinese farmers, because of the profound traditional value of dividing equally, always used to make comparisons among themselves. Although the distance between relocation areas is hundreds and thousands of kilometers, in today's information society external resettlers are aware of the general situation of other relocation areas. Generally, the place with the best relocation situation was also the place which was most energetically advertised by television, newspapers and other media. This always made the resettlers from other relocated areas feel disappointed.

The imbalance of the relocation compensation standard

One of the principles in the relocation compensation plan was that the payment was calculated based on the original values, standards and scales. However, did the compensation coincide with the principle of fairness? How to view the underdeveloped situation in the dam area? The poor natural environment, weak economic base, low education level and a lack of transportation and communication facilities were the characteristic elements of the region. But we have to recognize that the region had received almost no development investment in the previous four decades due to the Three Gorges project. This is the pain of "waiting for the dam" described by Patrick McCully:

> as soon as a dam is proposed, people in the reservoir area begin to suffer the withdrawal of government and private investment. Property prices fall, banks refuse to give loans, no new schools or health centers are built. Existing facilities may be closed long before people move out of the area. By the time resettlement starts, the oustees are often already much worse off than people in neighbouring areas.
>
> (McCully 1996, 72)

For instance, in Yunyang County, the state investment was merely 98.81 yuan (US$14) per capita between 1950 and 1985. The figure was only 9.6% of the national average per capita of 1,028 yuan (us$150). There were also policies that streets below the submergence level should not be widened or updated, no new housing projects should be undertaken and factories should not be allotted new equipment. Residents of the reservoir area had made great sacrifices due to the decades-long postponement of the Three Gorges Project. However, this historical debt was not considered in compensation for resettlement. The reservoir area lost opportunities for development prior to the dam, made great sacrifices for relocation, and the little benefit it gained from the Three Gorges project (electricity, shipping, etc.) was far less than the losses due to the further deterioration of its ecological environment.

The issue of fair compensation was especially prominent in rural reservoir areas. For example, with regard to housing compensation, there was a huge difference between the compensation of urban residents and rural resettlers. According to the government's compensation standards, the same brick and wood structured house was calculated to cost 189 yuan (US$28) for city residents, 179 yuan (US$27) for township residents, and 134 yuan (US$19) for rural residents. Due to the poor transportation conditions in rural areas, the transportation costs of local relocation there were higher than in the towns, especially as those who had to be externally relocated were mainly landless farmers, whose costs for housing were higher. This kind of standard of "compensation for original values" neglected an important fact, that the accumulation of capital and the affordability for resettlement of rural residents could hardly be compared to those of urban residents. While the relocation compensation seemed to cover the resettlers' houses, it not only strengthened the inherent differences between urban and rural populations and left resettlers in debt, but also directly threatened the minimum standard of peasant life because recovery was virtually impossible to achieve.

The impoundment of the Three Gorges dam: from project resettlers to ecological resettlers and homeless people

The Three Gorges Project impounded to 135 meters in 2003, completed the construction in 2009, and reached the maximum water level of 175 meters for the first time in 2010. With the continual increase of the water level of the Three Gorges dam, the originally hidden "unintended consequences" of resettlement were gradually exposed.

From project resettlers to ecological resettlers

As mentioned earlier, the Three Gorges resettlers were originally project resettlers rather than ecological resettlers. However, after the Three Gorges dam was impounded to the high water level, the living conditions of resettlers who were locally relocated continued to deteriorate, the geological hazards on the reservoir grew, geological disasters occurred frequently, and the ecological environment in the reservoir directly threatened the lives of some resettlers. As a result, the Chinese government had to arrange so-called "risk avoidance relocation." Therefore, some of the Three Gorges resettlers became ecological resettlers.

In the feasibility studies of the Three Gorges project, it was claimed that there were only 16 kilometers in the reservoir bank slope, which had a total length of 1300 kilometers, that were poor in stability. After the impoundment of the Three Gorges reservoir, the reservoir landslides began to expose the characteristics of high quantity, high density, large-scale, heavy damage. The protection of the reservoir banks had to be increased from 16 kilometers to 172.7 kilometers. Previously, China had only used 600 million of 40 billion yuan (US$87 million of US$5.7 billion) in resettlement funds for geological prevention and treatment. Since 2000, geological disasters had become the chief problem in the unintended consequences of the reservoir area. China's government had spent a total of 11 billion yuan (US$1.5 billion) on *511 treatment projects*. In the reservoir area in Chongqing Municipality, the confirmed number of geological disasters including collapses, landslides, collapsed rock and collapsed bank was more than 5000, of which 1150 were landslides concentrated in the low mountainous area outside the canyon. This low mountainous area was the major area of relocation and reconstruction of urban resettlers. Moreover, the geological control projects completed before 2008 were mostly aimed at geological disaster sites identified before the impoundment of the Three Gorges Project. After the Three Gorges Project impounded, especially to the high water level, it generated many new landslides and bank collapses, which were not repaired (Fan Xiao 2014,165–169). Therefore, the treatment project alone was not enough to solve the landslide problem.

From 2008, the government had begun to organize resettlers to carry out "risk-avoidance relocation." In Chongqing, the risk-avoidance relocation resettlers reached 37,051 people in 2008, and 21,000 of these ecological resettlers were generated in 2009 (Three Gorges Resettlement Project 2015). In the "follow-up work plan of the Three Gorges" formulated by the State Council in 2011, geological disaster prevention and treatment was listed as one of the main problems to be solved in the Three Gorges reservoir area. From then on, the numbers of ecological resettlers of the Three Gorges would grow continuously and on a large scale.

From resettlers to homeless people

Starting in 2002, a considerable segment of externally relocated resettlers began to return to their original residence in the reservoir area. There were many causes for the resettlers' return. Among the causes, the most important one was dissatisfaction with the production or living conditions provided by the external relocation area. For example, nearly 100 resettlers from Baidi Town in Fengjie County, Chongqing Municipality, were externally relocated to Tanqiao Town in Jiangling County, Hubei Province. Unexpectedly, it was found that the relocation area was a schistosomiasis infected area. In the following year, most resettlers moved back to their home in Fengjie County. In addition, a lot of resettlers were "blank registered residence," a term which referred to resettlers who completed the resettlement procedures but neither had land nor built houses in the relocation areas. They merely moved their official residence into the relocation areas, but still lived in the reservoir area. Some local governments cheated in the external relocation task by creating a large number of "blank registered residences." For example, the town which had the largest number of resettlers in the reservoir rural area, Gaoyang Townin Yunyang County, claimed in 2002 that 3,800 people were relocated to Jiangjin City and Tongliang County, Chongqing Municipality. However, thousands of people were "blank registered residences"; Jiangjin City and Tongliang County did not distribute land to them.

Those who moved back to their home towns and those with "blank registered residence" have become homeless people or shed dwellers. The returning resettlers left the relocation areas arranged for them by the government, but their old houses in the reservoir area were demolished and their land submerged. Where do they reside and how do they survive now? Their solution is to temporarily build very simple shanties beside the river and struggle to survive on their compensation fund from the government. Once their shanties are submerged due to the rise of the water level of the Three Gorges, they become completely homeless people. When the compensation money is gone, they will habitually ask the government for solutions; the "shed people" have often been the source of local riots (Averill 1983, 84–126). The homeless people and shed people from the Three Gorges resettlement have brought tremendous unintended consequences for the social order of the reservoir area.

Conclusions

In 2009, the Chinese government announced that the Three Gorges resettlement task had been largely completed. However, the "unintended consequences" of the Three Gorges resettlement are far from being fully resolved. After 2008, nearly 100,000 ecological resettlers were generated as a result of serious geological disasters alone. In the future, when more ecological problems (such as soil erosion, silting, water pollution and climate issues) and social problems emerge, more ecological resettlers and homeless people will be created. In this sense, perhaps the resettlement of 1.29 million is just the beginning of the large-scale resettlement of the Three Gorges project.

The phenomenon of "unintended consequences" which are "finished but unsolved" in the Three Gorges resettlement area is closely related to the contradictions in the operation of the Chinese socialist authoritarian regime. Large dam critics and the range of tactics they employ are likely to be much more effective in democratic institutional contexts (Khagram 2004, 3). It can also be concluded that the convergence of the social and ecological conflicts in the Three Gorges resettlement is a clear reflection of the disadvantage of the Chinese party–state political system.

References

Averill S. 1983 The Shed people and the opening of the Yangzi Highlands, *Modern China* 9.1 84–126

Barber M. and Ryder G. (eds) 1993 *Damming the Three Gorges: what dam builders don't want you to know*, Earthscan Publications, Toronto

Cernea M. 1988 *Involuntary resettlement in development projects: policy guidelines in World Bank-financed projects* World Bank, Washington

Dai Qing 1994 *Yangtze! Yangtze!* Earthscan Publications, London

Fan Xiao 2014 The striking change of environment in post-Three Gorges Era, *China National Geography* 1 165–172

Jing J. 1996 *The temple of memories: history, power, and morality in a Chinese village*, Stanford University Press, Stanford

Khagram S. 2004 *Dams and development: transnational struggles for water and power*, Cornell University Press, New York

Li Boning 1996 *My dream of water conservancy*, Three Gorges Press, Beijing

Li Ning (ed.) 2003 *Ningxia Diaozhuang Resettlement*, China Film Press, Beijing

Mann M. 1984 The autonomous power of the state: its origins, mechanisms and results, *European Journal of Sociology* 25.2 185–213

Mao Zedong 1998 *Mao Zedong's articles after the founding of PRC*, XIII Central Literature Press, Beijing

McCully P. 1996 *Silenced rivers: the ecology and politics of large dams*, Zed Books, London

Merton R. 1968 *Social theory and social structure*, The Free Press, NewYork

Mou Mo and Cai Wenmei 1998 Resettlement in the Xin'an River Power Station Project, in Dai Qing (ed.) *The River Dragon Has Come!* M.E. Sharpe, New York, 104–123

Sun Yang and Sun Xiangming 2002 Characteristics and problems of the external relocation of Three Gorges Reservoir Area, *Journal of Economics of Water Resources* 3: 38–41

Tang Chuanli 2002 The policy and practice of China reservoir resettlement, in Tang Chuanli (ed.) *Resettlement and Social Development*, Hehai University Press, Nanjing, 1–8

Tawney R.H. 1966 *Land and labor in China*, Beacon Press, Boston

Tocqueville A. 2000 *Democracy in America*, The University of Chicago, Chicago.

Three Gorges Resettlement Project 2015 (www.3g.gov.cn/3Gxxxq.ycs?GUID=4507), accessed 1 October 2015

Weber M. 1951 *The religion of China*, The Free Press, Glencoe

Whyte M. 1989 Who hates bureaucracy? in Stark D. and Needs V. *Remaking the socialist economic institutions*, Stanford University Press, Stanford, 233–254

Wittfogel K. 1957 *Oriental despotism: a comparative study of total power*, Yale University Press, New Haven

World Commission on Dams 2000 *Dams and development: a new framework for decision-making—the report of the World Commission on Dams*, Earthscan Publications, London

Ying Xing 2001 *The story of the Dahe Dam*, Joint Publishing, Beijing

Yunyang County Gazetteer Compilation Committee 1999 *Gazetteer of Yunyang County*, Sichuan People's Publishing House, Chengdu

11 Archaeologies of the future

Tracing the lineage of contemporary
discourses on the climate–migration nexus

Giovanni Bettini

Abstract

This chapter traces the historical lineage of today's concerns over climate migration, a topic of increasing salience in international (climate) policy arenas. The starting point is the idea that the widespread emphasis on the novelty of climate migration obfuscates the 'old' ideological roots on which contemporary discourses build. By producing a lineage of contemporary debates, the chapter highlights their ideal continuity with 'ancient' debates on populations and resources in classical political economy, as well as with the spectre of the unruly and swelling population in the 'global South' that has haunted Northern environmental discourses since the late 1960s. The historical vista offered by the chapter also contributes to clearly detecting the emergence of new articulations of the link migration-environment-development, with aspects of radical discontinuity from the past. In the light of these specific continuities and ruptures, the debates on climate migration fall under a shadow – they appear not only as the response to the new set of challenges posed by climate change, but as a (re)emergence of the fear of/fixation with populations in the global South (seen as a dangerous threat to socio-economic and/or ecological stability), rearticulated via neoliberal discourses that aim at ruling through the production of resilient subjects.

Moving climates – growing concerns

The question of how climate change will influence human migration has become a source of great concern, in academia, policy and advocacy domains. Both in the natural and social sciences, there is almost unanimous consensus on the importance of addressing the climate change–mobility nexus (Baldwin and Gemenne 2013; IPCC 2014). Even migration scholars and advocacy organizations, once alienated by the environmental determinism of the early debates on environmentally induced displacement (cfr. Black 2001; Castles 2002), are now engaging with the nexus. The 'success' of climate-related migration (hereafter, CM) could be witnessed at the latest Conference of Parties (COP) to the United Nations Framework Convention on Climate Change

(UNFCCC), held in Paris in 2015. As we will see, numerous initiatives at the summit targeted CM, which also figured in the formal outcomes of COP 21.

The presence of the future, the absence of the past

On the way to its current 'popularity', CM has been understood through a variety of competing framings (for a recent overview, see Ransan-Cooper et al. 2015), with agitated debates inside and outside the palaces of international climate diplomacy. Taken together, the shock waves originated by the recent 'refugees crisis' in Europe and the increasing likelihood of extremely severe climate impacts (IPCC 2013) confirm the pressing character of the phenomena CM points to. However, this chapter deliberately 'zooms out' of immediate questions on whether and how we should (or should not) understand and act upon CM. Instead, it interrogates the historical lineage of contemporary discourses. While the links between environmental change and human mobility have been researched within migration studies (cfr. Piguet 2012), demography (cfr. Hunter 2005; de Sherbinin et al. 2007), anthropology (Orlove 2005) and environmental history (Worster 1979), very seldom has there been a serious engagement with the question of where contemporary discourses on CM come from. This oblivion on the 'history' of CM arguably depends on the aura of novelty surrounding the issue. The link between mobility and climate change is discussed as something new and different (ontologically, epistemologically and politically) to what we have seen before—as symptomatized by the incessant calls for new research, new analytical tools, new policy designs[1]. For sure, the fact that human impacts have moved the whole planetary climate (and 'Earth System') into a new state configures climate change as an unprecedented phenomenon. Also unparalleled is the combination of intensity, spread and pace of the expected changes. But, of course, the fact that climate change and its impacts are in several ways unprecedented does not mean that the ways in which we make sense of and act upon them are detached from past and present politics. It goes without saying that the repression of these questions has political imports and effects. This chapter is motivated by the conviction that it is impossible to grasp the future implications of contemporary discourses without a substantial engagement with their past.

In the following, we will zoom out and explore the historical lineage of contemporary discourses on CM. When looking at their *longue durée*, the problematization of *population* in the 'global South' as a source of danger emerges as a thread linking future-oriented concerns over climate displaced to longstanding debates on economy, development, the environment. Focusing on population, this chapter will propose a heuristic periodization of the debate on CM into three phases – a prehistory, a history, and a contemporary period. Drawing on Harvey's work on the role of population in classic political economy (Harvey 1974), we will locate the deep roots of CM in the fear of population informing Malthus and his proto-definition of 'eco-scarcity'. The next stop on our journey through time will be in the 1960s, when

Northern environmental discourses erupted onto the scene, and out of which concerns over so called 'environmental refugees' emerged. In this phase, we will encounter Malthus' reincarnation in the fears for 'population bombs' and the swelling, unruly population in the 'global South' that ran through modern environmentalism. Moving towards the contemporary phases of the debate, we will still encounter the problematization of population as a source of danger, but this time articulated in new biopolitical discourses on climate change, development and resilience.

In the following sections, we will explore the three phases and trace signs of continuity and ruptures, concluding with some reflections on the political import of current debates on CM.

CM's prehistory, or the ecology of class hatred

When does our 'story' begin? The answer to this question cannot be innocent. In the literature, it is customary to point to the end of the 1970s (e.g. Laczko and Aghazarm 2009; Foresight 2011; Gemenne 2011; White 2011; Morrissey 2012), when the UN Environment Program (El-Hinnawi 1985) and the Worldwatch Institute (Jacobsen 1988) each published a seminal report, which effectively launched the concept of 'environmental refugees'. Although that was a crucial phase, if we zoom out and situate CM in relation to 'old' discussions on environment, population and mobility, a number of important political questions – which are kept out of sight in the contemporary future-oriented debates – come to the fore.

An obvious preliminary remark, which helps to de-naturalize CM and to see through its novelty aura, is that the links between ecological conditions and migration have been discussed in numerous contexts, disciplines, times (although not in relation to global warming). For instance, geographers, demographers, (environmental) historians and anthropologists for a long time have worked on the interaction between ecological conditions and mobility (on this, see Hunter 2005; de Sherbinin et al. 2007; Morrissey 2009; Adamo and Izazola 2010; Marino 2012). Ample discussions targeted both sides of the relation, i.e. both the impacts of migrants on ecosystems in the areas from and to which they move, and the ways in which ecological changes stimulate or inhibit movements. The wandering of Viking villagers under the push of advancing ices in northern Greenland is an archaic example dating back to AD 1000–1400 (for a brief summary, see Orlove 2005). The uprooting of peasants from the USA plains by a mixed ecological and economic crisis during the so-called Dust Bowl in the 1930s is a more recent case (for a critical introduction, see Worster 1979). Even the pioneers of migration studies – as early as in the 19th century – ranked environmental conditions among the principal factors of population movements (cfr. Piguet 2012).

Thus – obviously – it is not the first time the links between environmental change and human mobility are discussed. But the next and more important step is to interrogate the roots of contemporary concerns over CM. While it takes some effort to retune one's ears to discourses that sound archaic in comparisons with the current affairs of climate policy, the parallels with old debates on population and environment are staggering.

It could be argued that the not-so-friendly 'dialogue' on population between Karl Marx (1983 Notebook VI) and Thomas Malthus (1996) already contained the seeds for the problematization of population in contemporary discourses on CM. There is a striking assonance between the discussions on resource availability/scarcity and population that animated classic political economy, and the current concerns on climate change, displacement and conflict. In a nutshell, Malthus argued that, while populations grow geometrically, resources to feed them grow arithmetically, at a much slower pace. Thereby, in the graphs Malthusians love to draw, the lines representing population and food availability (or natural resources, or environmental quality; you choose) diverge. Such arguments build on three Malthusian assumptions – all controversial. First, the divergence of the two lines is assumed to be *natural*; second, this gap is said to *inevitably* cause the emergence of an (uprooted) *surplus population*; third, the dispossessed (because of their moral and material misery) are the cause of social unrest, turmoil and conflict. Thereby the scum (pardon, surplus population) becomes dangerous – in turn creating an imperative for 'society' to control it and restrain its reproduction. It is hard not to see the parallel with today's narratives that identify present and future 'victims' of climate change as the cause of armed conflict, where climate-induced stress assumes the same function of limited land productivity in Malthus' reasoning. According to neo-Malthusian perspectives on CM, climate change, by jeopardizing the resource base of vulnerable areas, will unavoidably create a sort of surplus population, displaced by global warming – the waves of climate refugees to be feared because of their destabilizing effects (for critique, see Hartmann 1998; White 2011; Bettini 2013). An illustrative example is the outrageous labeling of Syrian displaced as 'climate refugees', a rhetoric very popular in the run-up to the Paris COP. A few research papers provided evidence linking the drought that hit the Fertile Crescent from 2007 to 2010 to anthropogenic climate change, and suggested that the latter may have contributed to the events in Syria (Kelley et al. 2015; Cook et al. 2016). This shaky causal link (for a more articulated account, see e.g. Fröhlich 2016) was flagged up by many, including Prince Charles (Sky News 2015), as the anticipation of what a warmer planet would look like – with ecological stress said to directly cause armed conflict and originating 'hordes of climate refugees' menacing international security and stability. And all the politics is gone.

In opposition to Malthus' approach, Marx proposed a relational view on scarcity and what we nowadays call 'ecological stress', understood not as a product of an external *nature*, but as linked to specific modes of economic and social (re)production. In Marx' account, a 'surplus population' is functional to the reproduction of a class society, rather than a fact of nature. In the *Grundrisse*, Marx offers an observation that, in its simplicity, is *classic* and illuminating: while Malthusians measure and model overpopulation as the reason for the collapse of past civilizations (and here J. Diamond's work comes to mind), "we never hear that there were surplus slaves in the antiquity" (Marx 1983).

What these old, dusty political economic disputes unveil is that class matters – regardless of how globalized and evanescent class composition may appear today. This emerges as clearest in the climate-migration-security/conflict link. Such a link is not only analytically dubious (Buhaug et al. 2014; IPCC 2014). If we spell it out, it also enshrines a Malthusian class fear for the poor (or climate vulnerable). In the economy of the discourses that blame the poor for igniting climate-related conflicts and for future insecurity, there is a missing logical and causal link. Such discourses do not explain how a quarrel over a loaf of bread escalates into an armed conflict between states. It is a class fear (if not hatred) that makes up for that missing link and sustains the vulnerability–conflict causal inference. And this becomes embarrassingly clear against the backdrop of the old Malthus–Marx rivalry.

To be sure (and luckily!), a number of traditions (in academia and in political movements, both within and outside the Marxian field) have articulated the nexus between environment, population and development along progressive lines. Just to name a few, this has been the case for the tradition of political ecology (Blaikie 1985; Peet and Watts 2004), environmental justice movements and various forms of 'environmentalisms of the poor' (Martinez-Alier 2002; Bond 2012), theories of unequal exchange (Hornborg 2011), radical critiques to mainstream (sustainable) development (Shiva 1988; Escobar 1995). What we are stressing here is the fact that many of the narratives through which CM is narrated today (sometimes even by progressive forces) embed elements stemming from old conservative, neo-colonial takes on population in the global South. What we see is the continuity of narratives built (more or less ostensibly) on the fear of population (of certain classes) – which will emerge clearly even when moving into the green pastures of modern environmentalism, from which contemporary discourses on CM originated.

History – population and Northern environmentalism

In most studies, the story of CM begins with two reports, by the UN Environment Program (El-Hinnawi 1985) and by the Worldwatch Institute (Jacobsen 1988). These were key texts, although not only for the reasons most of literature focuses on. For sure, by re-launching the term 'environmental refugee' coined by environmentalist champion Lester Brown a few years earlier (1976), the two reports brought into the limelight the issue of environmentally induced displacement. But more importantly, the two landmark texts started 'spinning' an intelligible and evocative narrative on the nexus between ecological conditions and mobility (what we will call environmental migration, EM), firmly situating it in the landscape of the modern Northern environmental discourses. A closer look at the two texts (in terms of framing, authorship, contents and tones) reveals the imprint of the discourses arising in the 1970s on global environmental challenges such as biodiversity and desertification.

We can start by noting that EM was brought into the spotlight by key figures of environmental policy and advocacy of the time, such as the United Nations Environment Programme (UNEP, which commissioned El-Hinnawi's (1985) report), the Worldwatch Institute and its founder Lester Brown, and the vocal environmental scientist Norman Myers. It is revealing also that the first alarm bells over ecological displacement came from the 'desertification community,' which was concerned that land degradation would lead to large-scale uprooting of ecologically vulnerable populations, especially in sub-Saharan Africa (on this link, see El-Hinnawi 1985; Myers and Kent 1995; Black 2001; Leighton 2006 and 2011). From the environmental discourses of the time, the debates on EM inherited the quasi-messianic tone urging rescue of the planet from imminent catastrophe (and here it is hard not to think about the present alarmism on climate refugees), the imagined 'hero' (global environmental champions), as well as the belief that international institutions and legislation would 'solve the problem' (on these aspects, see Bettini and Andersson 2014). The emerging narratives on EM also contained the contradictions that carved environmental discourses; indeed, the critiques of the concept of environmental refugees (for some early examples, see Findley 1994; Suhrke 1994; Kibreab 1997) built on arguments similar to those put forward by early political ecology (Thompson and Warburton 1985; Blaikie and Brookfield 1987; Forsyth 1996; Leach and Mearns 1996) – including dominance of Northern science, the technocratic character, and a tendency to identify the poor, rather than the unequal resource distribution or economic growth, as the cause of environmental change (Adger et al. 2001). In sum, the nexus was understood in line with the epistemology and concerns of mainstream environment organizations and green advocacy – constructed as a 'problem to be solved' within their remit. This inscription strongly marked the nexus ecological conditions–migration as an 'environmental' one, something that probably explains the earlier reluctance to embrace the topic among development and migration specialists more than the often cited disciplinary boundaries between natural and social sciences (cfr. Morrissey 2012).

It is not a secret that environmental discourses beginning in the late 1960s – of which the UN Conference on the Human Environment (Stockholm 1972) and the Bruntlandt Report (World Commission on Environment and Development 1987) were key landmarks – problematized and pathologized *population* in the global South. The very title of one of the most influential, seminal books of the environmentalism of the time – Ehrlich's *Population Bomb* (1968) – speaks for itself. The fixation over the danger represented by a swelling population in the 'non-developed' world was (and arguably still is) one of the key ingredients of the discourses on environmental and climate change (Duffield 2001; Chaturvedi and Doyle 2015). Instructive, and showing a clear continuity with the 'prehistory' discussed above, is the analysis Harvey (1974, 270) proposes of another foundational work for 'green thought' and concerns over global environmental change, i.e. 'The Limits to Growth'(Meadows et al. 1972). The report, with its 'systems approach' and computer modeling of populations, applied a technically more refined but in principle analogous method to Malthus'. While already contested by perspectives such as political ecology and by non-Northern articulations of environmentalism (Martinez-Alier 2002 and 1995), a similar Malthusian logic informed the debates on the impacts of environmental and climatic changes on mobility and on CM, as the work of Norman Myers (Myers 1993; Myers and Kent 1995) most evidently shows (cfr. Hartmann 1998; Jakobeit and Methmann 2012).

The ascension of climate change

The proto-debates on environmental displacement discussed above took a decisive turn in the 1990s. At that point, climate change's ascension towards the highest spheres of international (environmental) politics entailed a semantic shift from the concerns over environmentally induced displacement, to narratives focussed specifically on global warming. A key step in this direction was IPCC's first assessment report in 1990. A passage from Working Group II's "Summary of findings" was to have a great impact: "[t]he gravest effects of climate change may be those on human migration as millions are displaced by shoreline erosion, coastal flooding and severe drought" (IPCC 1992, 103). That was a strong indictment, and its alarmed tones anticipated those echoing in the two following decades. Indeed, from that moment, a polarized debate started – opposing an 'alarmist' or 'maximalist' approach to a 'minimalist' or 'skeptical' school (on these classifications, see Morrissey (2009) and Gemenne (2011)). The former, with strong roots in environmental sciences, championed the view that climate change will cause large-scale displacement of vulnerable populations – a warning for the security implications of mounting waves of environmental or climate refugees (e.g. Myers 1997 and 2005). The latter, more closely related to social sciences, highlighted the analytical fallacies and potential normative risks of concepts such as climate and environmental refugees (e.g. Black 2001; Castles 2002).

This opposition lasted long, but did not hinder the debate from gaining growing attention. In the mid-2000s, a series of influential academic interventions stressed the pressing character of the issue of climate refugees (Byravan and Rajan 2006; McLeman and Smit 2006; Biermann and Boas 2008; Bronen 2009; Docherty and Giannini 2009). A number of influential actors (e.g. WBGU 2008; Stern 2007; Council of the European Union 2008) also framed CM as an emerging security issue, which also secured many headlines to the figure of 'climate refugees'. Nina Hall offers a thorough account of the growing engagement in CM debates by international organizations such as the UN High Commissioner for Refugees (UNHCR), the International Organization for Migration (IOM), and the UN Environment Program (Hall 2016). Various NGOs organized opinion campaigns and published reports on the need to protect climate refugees (Christian Aid 2007; Environmental Justice Foundation 2009), and various platforms were launched to spread the word on the issue. For instance, the Climate Change, Environment and Migration

Alliance (CCEMA) was initiated in 2008, as a multi-stakeholder partnership involving a cartel of influential organizations[2]. A few large-scale research initiatives were launched, such as the EU-funded EACH-FOR project, run between 2007 and 2009, with the substantial contribution of the UN University.

The contemporary phase – CM goes mainstream

Such important endorsements have led to CM's *mainstreaming*: while the polarization between skeptics and alarmist has been largely overcome, the tones have softened, and CM has firmly established itself as an important policy issue in the climate arena and beyond.

For instance, the Intergovernmental Panel on Climate Change (IPCC) devoted a large section of chapter 12 of the latest report by Working Group II (IPCC 2014) to CM. In the context of the UNFCCC, the Cancun Adaptation Framework (signed in December 2010) urged member countries to implement "[m]easures to enhance understanding, coordination and cooperation with regard to climate change induced displacement, migration and planned relocation" (UNFCCC 2010). This commitment was explicitly restated under the discussions on 'Loss and damage' at COP 18 in Doha in 2012. COP 21 in Paris hosted an unprecedented number of initiatives on various forms of CM, organized by a constellation of research and advocacy organizations. Both the IOM and UNHCR were very active, also being prominent members of the recently formed UN Advisory Group on Climate Change and Human Mobility. One of the outcomes of the Paris COP 21 was the decision, in line with the call to address climate migration made in Cancun, to "establish [...] a task force to develop recommendations for integrated approaches to avert, minimize and address displacement related to the adverse impacts of climate change" (UNFCCC 2016, par. 47).

What happened at COP 21 in Paris was the culmination of a period in which CM entered the agendas of an increasing number of mainstream organizations in the arenas of climate change and international development. For instance, while the World Bank has targeted the issue on various occasions and discussed it in its yearly flagship report in 2010 (World Bank 2010), the Asian Development Bank (ADB) went much further, promoting two high-profile initiatives. Namely, it funded "a regional project designed to generate policy options for addressing climate-induced migration in Asia and the Pacific", resulting in a series of case studies and a lengthy final policy report (ADB 2012). Furthermore, in collaboration with IOM, the ADB promoted the Asia–Pacific Migration and Environment Network (APMEN),[3] an online platform for sharing information and research results, as well as for 'spreading the word' on CM.

Another high-profile state-led project is the Nansen Initiative, which was launched by the Norwegian and the Swiss governments and inspired by UNHCR (Hall 2016, ch. 3). As a follow-up to the Nansen Conference on Climate Change and Displacement organized in 2011 by the Norwegian government, the initiative fostered a state-owned consultative process (which lasted 3 years) that created a vast consensus among countries on the need to formulate an agenda for tackling environmental-induced cross border displacement.

While it would be erroneous to understand the contemporary phase as a complete rupture with the past – for instance, the problematic figure of 'climate refugees' still has currency – it presents substantial elements of novelty. As detailed more extensively elsewhere, the mainstreaming of CM was made possible by the affirmation of a different discursive register (Bettini 2014), characterized by a different understanding and articulation of the links between migration, climate adaptation and development. The influential initiative on 'Migration and Global Environmental Change,' commissioned by the UK government to the Foresight Programme, was a watershed, crucial for the emersion of the contemporary discourses on CM and for the affirmation of sounder understandings of migration. It was a monumental project, involving more than 300 international experts and stakeholders, and producing about 70 background papers[4]. Its synthesis report, known as the Foresight Report, had a huge impact on academic and policy debates, and was widely echoed in the media[5]. Crucially, migration scholars such as Professor Richard Black – previously one of the fiercest critics of the maximalist position – had a key role in shaping the sounder and more accurate understanding of CM that informed the report. Indeed, today most interventions on CM are informed by a quite refined understanding of how ecological factors influence migration: the maximalist's determinism and simplistic model of migration have become marginal, supplanted by a conceptualization of CM as an array of mobility responses to climate change. While displacement is still a matter of concern (see the Nansen Initiative, a number of initiatives by UNHCR, and the wording of the Paris Agreement itself), the ways in which climate vulnerability might result in a *reduced* mobility are also considered (Black et al. 2013), as well as the ways in which planned relocation might be an option (de Sherbinin et al. 2011; UNHCR 2014; for some cautionary remarks, see Schade et al. 2015).

In particular, the idea that governed migration can represent a legitimate adaptation strategy has gained currency. Replicating the optimistic position in the decade-long debate on the so called migration–development nexus, labour migration is seen as source of remittances, which in turn are expected to play a key role in building up the resilience of vulnerable strata of the population (McLeman and Smit 2006; Barnett and Webber 2010; Black et al. 2011; Warner 2012).

A number of studies highlight the perils associated with the 'new' idea of migration as adaptation, in particular the ways in which it risks being symptomatic of the neoliberalization of climate policy (see Felli and Castree 2012; Felli 2013; Bettini 2014; Methmann and Oels 2015). For sure, the new register entails a different articulation of population, development and security centered on resilience and adaptive governance. As we have seen, modern Northern environmentalism has been characterized by a long tradition of fears for populations in the global South, of which the idea of climate refugees can be seen as an example. It would be wrong to state that this (post)colonial component has evaporated, but the contemporary register offers a re-articulation of (and to an extent, a rupture in relation to) the ways in which population is signified in discourses on environmental change. In the contemporary register we can see signs of a biopoliticization of adaptation and development. The narratives on migration as adaptation, behind a palatable facade, appear as a mechanism for disciplining populations through the imposition of neoliberal subjectivities – the figure at the centre stage is a docile temporary labour migrant, mobilizing her skills and human capital to become resilient (Bettini 2014). This was hardly a good prospect for progressive politics on climate and/or migration.

Back to the future

There is little doubt that the coming decade will entail decisive crossroads for the politics of both migration and climate change. Will the brunt of climate change fall on those in the peripheries of globalized capital, as the outcomes of international negotiations seem to indicate (Bond 2012; Ciplet et al. 2015; Morgan 2016)? Or will progressive movements manage to forge and force pathways of just climate action? If we look at mobility, the recent 'refugee crisis' around the Mediterranean – with the 'moral panic' it originated (Bauman 2015) and the cracks it highlighted in the very edifice of the European Union – once again confirmed the divisive, political character of migration, its function as symptom (in Lacanian terms) of globalized struggles around the production of space and distribution of resources (Mezzadra and Neilson 2013). Coming closer to this chapter's focus, the racialization of migrants and refugees is also a powerful reminder of how resilient postcolonial relations are, not least in the political field of climate change – with the resurfacing of the fear for some non-white being close to invading Europe.

Not in spite of, but because of the pressing character of these matters, this chapter has zoomed out of 'current affairs' to offer a lineage of contemporary concerns over CM. A worrying continuity has emerged, linking 'ancient' debates on populations and resources in classical political economy, the spectres of the unruly and swelling population in the 'global South' that has haunted Northern environmental discourses since the late 1960s (and from which discourses on CM originated), and contemporary concerns over 'climate barbarians' igniting conflicts and knocking on 'our' doors. The fact that such discursive elements are reproduced also by actors concerned about climate justice (Bettini et al. forthcoming) is a source of particular concern. Older and newer conservative narratives on population and environment share 'programmatic' implications (Robbins 2012, 17–18) – as they all identify the root cause of the problem in the poor – too many, too dangerous. Also, the emerging narratives on migration as adaptation appear less benign than they might seem at first glance: they represent an element of discontinuity, but rather than a rupture from the earlier problematization of population in the global South, they are a biopoliticized articulation of the same Northern takes on the migration-environment-development link.

These discourses share a depoliticizing potential, with the political kernel of climate justice and of migration foreclosed by the Malthusian invocation of environmental crisis or of the fantasy of labour migrants as docile, adaptive and resilient subject. Of course, the effect of these depoliticizing discourses is highly political – as they have to do with resource distribution (Robbins 2012, 18), and often the 'right to live'. Current discourses appear not only as a response to the new set of challenges posed by climate change, but as a (re)emergence of the fear of/fixation with populations in the global South (seen as a dangerous threat to socio-economic and/or ecological stability), even when rearticulated via neoliberal discourses that aim at ruling in the name of resilience, through the production of docile neoliberal subjects.

Notes

1 As acutely noted by Baldwin and colleagues, most interventions discuss the nexus in the 'future-conditional' tense (Baldwin et al. 2014). Climate refugees or migrants are discussed as figures of the future, outcomes of what will have happened (or not) after climate change and possibly 'our' responses to it have kicked in. To be sure, present and past do not disappear from these narrations of CM, but assume a peculiar role. As the plan of actuality (in the discourse) shifts into the future, current and past phenomena become anecdotal evidence of what will (finally?) happen *then*. This can be seen in the problematic way the recent Syrian tragedy has been mobilized as an anticipation of how a warmer world could look: the projection of the Syrian crisis into the future magically erases the political ecology of the conflict, displaced by a regression into an environmental deterministic reading of the events (more on this below).
2 See the homepage www.ccema-portal.org.
3 See the homepage available at www.apmen.iom.int/en/.
4 See www.bis.gov.uk/foresight/our-work/projects/published-projects/global-migration.
5 For instance, see the 'One-year review' available at www.bis.gov.uk/assets/foresight/docs/migration/12-1265-migration-one-year-review.pdf.

References

Adamo S.B. and Izazola H. 2010 Human migration and the environment, *Population and Environment* 32 105–108

ADB 2012 *Addressing Climate Change and Migration in Asia and the Pacific*, Asian Development Bank, Mandaluyong City, Philippines

Baldwin, A. and Gemenne F. 2013 The paradoxes of climate change and migration. *In: World Social Science Report 2013: Changing Global Environments*, UNESCO Publishing, Paris, 265–268

Baldwin A., Methmann C. and Rothe D. 2014 Securitizing 'climate refugees': the futurology of climate-induced migration, *Critical Studies on Security,* 2(2) 121–130

Barnett, J. & Webber, M. 2010 Migration as Adaptation: Opportunities and Limits. *In:* McAdam, J. (ed.) *Climate change and displacement: multidisciplinary perspectives*, Hart Publishing, Oxford, 37–55

Bauman, Z. 2015 The Migration Panic And Its (Mis)Uses. *Social Europe Blog.* [Online]. Available from: www.socialeurope.eu/2015/12/migration-panic-misuses/ [Accessed December 2015]

Bettini G. 2013 Climates barbarians at the gate? A critique of apocalyptic narratives on climate refugees, *Geoforum* 45 63–72

Bettini G. 2014 Climate migration as an adaption strategy: de-securitizing climate-induced migration or making the unruly governable? *Critical Studies on Security* 2 180–195

Bettini G. and Andersson E. 2014 Sand waves and human tides: exploring environmental myths on desertification and climate-induced migration, *The Journal of Environment and Development* 23 160–185

Bettini G., Nash S. and Gioli G. forthcoming. One step forward, two steps back? The changing contours of (in)justice in competing discourses on climate migration, *The Geographical Journal*, doi:10.1111/geoj.12192

Biermann F. and Boas I. 2008 Protecting climate refugees: the case for a global protocol, *Environment* 50 8–16

Black R. 2001 Environmental refugees: myth or reality? *New issues in Refugee Research – UNHCR Working Paper 70*

Black R., Arnell N.W., Adger W.N., Thomas D. and Geddes A. 2013 Migration, immobility and displacement outcomes following extreme events, *Environmental Science and Policy* 27 S32–S43

Black R., Bennett S.R.G., Thomas S.M. and Beddington J.R. 2011 Climate change: migration as adaptation, *Nature* 478, 447–449

Blaikie P. 1985 *The political economy of soil erosion in developing countries,* Longman, London and New York

Blaikie P. and Brookfield H. 1987 *Land degradation and society,* Methuen, London and New York

Bond P. 2012 *Politics of climate justice: paralysis above, movement below,* University of Kwazulu-Natal Press, Scottsville, South Africa

Bronen R. 2009 Forced migration of Alaskan indigenous communities due to climate change: creating a human rights response, *Amsterdam Conference on the Human Dimensions of Global Environmental Change,* Amsterdam

Brown L. 1976 *World population trends: signs of hope, signs of stress,* Worldwatch Paper 8, Worldwatch Institute, Washington, DC

Buhaug H., Nordkvelle J., Bernauer T., Böhmelt T., Brzoska M., Busby J.W., Ciccone A., Fjelde H., Gartzke E., Gleditsch N.P., Goldstone J.A., Hegre H., Holtermann H., Koubi V., Link J.S.A., Link P.M., Lujala P., O'Loughlin J, Raleigh C., Scheffran J., Schilling J., Smith T.G., Theisen O.M., Tol R.S.J., Urdal H. and von Uexkull N. 2014 One effect to rule them all? A comment on climate and conflict, *Climatic Change* 127 (3–4) 391–397

Byravan S. and Rajan S.C. 2006 Providing new homes for climate change exiles, *Climate Policy* 6 247–252

Castles S. 2002 Environmental change and forced migration: making sense of the debate, *New issues in Refugee Research – UNHCR working paper 70*

Chaturvedi S. and Doyle T. 2015 *Climate terror: a critical geopolitics of climate change,* Palgrave Macmillan, New York

Christian Aid 2007 *Human tide. The real migration crisis,* Christian Aid, London

Ciplet D., Roberts J.T. and Khan M.R. 2015 *Power in a warming world: the global politics of climate change and the remaking of environmental inequality,* MIT Press, Cambridge, Massachusetts

Cook B.I., Anchukaitis K.J., Touchan R., Meko D.M. and Cook E.R. 2016 Spatiotemporal drought variability in the Mediterranean over the last 900 years, *Journal of Geophysical Research: Atmospheres* 121(5) 2060–2074

Council of the European Union 2008 Climate change and international security – Report from the Commission and the Secretary-General/High Representative Brussels

De Sherbinin A., Carr D., Cassels S. and Jiang L. 2007 Population and Environment, *Annual review of environment and resources* 32 345–373

De Sherbinin A., Castro M., Gemenne, F., Cernea M.M., Adamo S., Fearnside P.M., Krieger G., Lahmani S., Oliver-Smith A., Pankhurst A., Scudder T., Singer B., Tan Y., Wannier G., Boncour P., Ehrhart C., Hugo G., Pandey B. and Shi G. 2011 Preparing for resettlement associated with climate change, *Science* 334 456–457

Docherty B. and Giannini T. 2009 Confronting a rising tide: a proposal for a convention on climate change refugees, *Harvard Environmental Law Review* 33 349–403

Duffield M.R. 2001 *Global governance and the new wars: the merging of development and security*, Zed Books, London

Ehrlich P.R. 1968 *The population bomb*, Ballantine Books, New York

El-Hinnawi E. 1985 *Environmental refugees*, UNEP, Nairobi

Environmental Justice Foundation 2009 *No place like home – Where next for climate refugees?* Environmental Justice Foundation, London

Escobar A. 1995 *Encountering development: the making and unmaking of the third world*, Princeton University Press, Princeton, New Jersey

Felli R. 2013 Managing climate insecurity by ensuring continuous capital accumulation: 'climate refugees'and 'climate migrants', *New Political Economy* 18 337–363

Felli R. and Castree N. 2012 Neoliberalising adaptation to environmental change: foresight or foreclosure? *Environment and Planning* A 44 1–4

Findley S.E. 1994 Does drought increase migration? a study of migration from rural Mali during the 1983–1985 drought, *International Migration Review* 28 539–553

Foresight 2011 *Final project report – Foresight: migration and global environmental change*, The Government Office for Science, London

Forsyth T. 1996 Science, myth and knowledge: testing Himalayan environmental degradation in Thailand, *Geoforum* 27 375–392

Fröhlich C.J. 2016 Climate migrants as protestors? Dispelling misconceptions about global environmental change in pre-revolutionary Syria, *Contemporary Levant* 1 38–50

Gemenne F. 2011 How they became the human face of climate change. Research and policy interactions in the birth of the 'environmental migration' concept. *In:* Piguet E., Pécoud A. & De Guchteneire P. (eds) *Migration and climate change*, Cambridge University Press, Cambridge

Hall N. 2016 *Displacement, development, and climate change: international organizations moving beyond their mandates*, Routledge, New York

Hartmann B. 1998 Population, environment and security: a new trinity, *Environment and Urbanization* 10 113–128

Harvey D. 1974 Population, resources, and ideology of science, *Economic Geography* 50 256–277

Hornborg A. 2011 *Global ecology and unequal exchange: fetishism in a zero-sum world*, Routledge, London

Hunter L. 2005 Migration and environmental hazards, *Population and Environment* 26 273–302

IPCC 1992 Climate Change: IPCC 1990 and 1992 Assessments. Available from: www. ipcc.ch/ipccreports/1992%20IPCC%20Supplement/IPCC_1990_and_1992_ Assessments/English/ipcc_90_92_assessments_far_full_report.pdf [Accessed January 2017]

IPCC 2013 Summary for Policymakers. *In:* Stocker T.F., Qin D., Plattner G.-K., Tignor M., Allen S.K., Boschung J., Nauels A., Xia Y., Bex V. and Midgley P.M. (eds) *Climate change 2013: The physical science basis. Contribution of Working Group I to the Fifth Assessment Report of the Intergovernmental Panel on Climate Change*, Cambridge University Press, Cambridge

IPCC 2014 *Climate Change 2014: impacts, adaptation, and vulnerability. Part A: Global and Sectoral Aspects. Contribution of Working Group II to the Fifth Assessment Report of the Intergovernmental Panel on Climate Change*, Cambridge University Press, Cambridge

Jacobsen J.L. 1988 *Environmental refugees: A yardstick of habitability*, Worldwatch Institute, Washington, DC

Jakobeit C. and Methmann C. 2012 'Climate Refugees' as dawning catastrophe? A critique of the dominant quest for numbers. *In:* Scheffran J., Brzoska M., Brauch H.G., Link P.M. and Schilling J. (eds) *Climate change, human security and violent conflict: challenges for societal stability*, Springer, New York

Kelley C.P., Mohtadi S., Cane M.A., Seager R. and Kushnir Y. 2015 Climate change in the Fertile Crescent and implications of the recent Syrian drought, *Proceedings of the National Academy of Sciences* 112, 3241–3246

Kibreab G. 1997 Environmental causes and impact of refugee movements: a critique of the current debate, *Disasters* 21 20–38

Laczko F. and Aghazarm C. (eds) 2009 *Migration, environment and climate change: assessing the evidence*, International Organization for Migration, Geneva

Leach M. and Mearns R. (eds) 1996 *The lie of the land: challenging received wisdom on the African* environment,The International African Institute in association with James Currey, Oxford

Leighton M. 2006 Desertification and migration. *In:* Johnson P.M., Mayrand K. and Paquin M. (eds) *Governing global desertification: linking environmental degradation, poverty and participation*, Ashgate, Aldershot

Leighton M. 2011 Drought, desertification and migration: past experiences, predicted impacts and human rights issues. *In:* Piguet E., Pécoud A. and De Guchteneire P. (eds) *Migration and Climate Change*, Cambridge University Press, Cambridge

Malthus T.R. 1996 *An essay on the principle of population*, London, Routledge

Marino E. 2012 The long history of environmental migration: Assessing vulnerability construction and obstacles to successful relocation in Shishmaref, Alaska, *Global Environmental Change* 22, 374–381

Martinez-Alier J. 1995 The environment as a luxury good or "too poor to be green"? *Ecological Economics* 13 1–10

Martinez-Alier J. 2002 *The environmentalism of the poor: a study of ecological conflicts and valuation*, Edward Elgar Publishing, Cheltenham

Marx K. 1983 *Grundrisse*, Penguin Books, London

McLeman R.A. and Smit B. 2006 Migration as an Adaptation to Climate Change, *Climatic Change* 76 31–53

Meadows D., Meadows D.L., Randers J. and Behrens W. 1972 *The limits to growth: a report for the Club of Rome's project on the predicament of mankind*, Earth Island, London

Methmann C. and Oels A. 2015 From 'fearing' to 'empowering' climate refugees: Governing climate-induced migration in the name of resilience, *Security Dialogue* 46 51–68

Mezzadra S. and Neilson B. 2013 *Border as method, or, the multiplication of labor*, Duke University Press, Durham

Morgan J. 2016 Paris COP 21: power that speaks the truth? *Globalizations* 13(6) 943–951

Morrissey J. 2009 *Environmental change and forced migration: a state of the art review*, University of Oxford, Oxford, Refugee Studies Centre, Oxford Department of International Development, Queen Elizabeth House

Morrissey J. 2012 Rethinking the 'debate on environmental refugees': from 'maximilists and minimalists' to 'proponents and critics', *Journal of Political Ecology* 19 37–49

Myers N. 1993 Environmental refugees in a globally warmed world, *BioScience* 43 752–761

Myers N. 1997 Environmental Refugees, *Population and Environment* 19 167–182

Myers N. 2005 Environmental refugees: an emergent security issue, Paper presented to the 13th Economic Forum, Prague, 23–27 May

Myers N. and Kent J. 1995 *Environmental exodus. An emergent crisis in the global arena*, Washington, Climate Institute

Orlove B. 2005 Human adaptation to climate change: a review of three historical cases and some general perspectives, *Environmental Science and Policy* 8 589–600

Peet R. and Watts M. eds 2004 *Liberation ecologies: environment, development, social movements*, Routledge, London

Piguet E. 2012 From 'primitive migration' to 'climate refugees': the curious fate of the natural environment in migration studies, *Annals of the Association of American Geographers* 103 148–162

Ransan-Cooper H., Farbotko C., Mcnamara K.E., Thornton F. and Chevalier E. 2015 Being(s) framed: The means and ends of framing environmental migrants, *Global Environmental Change* 35 106–115

Robbins, P. 2012 *Political ecology: a critical introduction*, J. Wiley & Sons, Chichester

Schade J., McDowell C., Ferris E., Schmidt K., Bettini G., Felgentreff C., Gemenne F., Patel A., Rovins J., Stojanov R. and Sultana Z. 2015 Climate change and climate policy induced relocation: A challenge for social justice. Recommendations of the Bielefeld Consultation 2014, *Migration, Environment and Climate Change: Policy Brief Series* 1, Geneva: IOM

Shiva V. 1988 *Staying alive: women, ecology, and development*, Zed Books, London

Sky News 2015 *Charles: Syria's war linked to climate change – 23 November* [Online]. SkyNews Online. Available from: http://news.sky.com/story/1592373/charles-syrias-war-linked-to-climate-change [Accessed 11 January 2017]

Stern N. 2007 *The economics of climate change: The Stern Review*, Cambridge University Press, Cambridge

Suhrke A. 1994 Environmental degradation and population flows, *Journal of International Affairs* 47 473–496

Thompson M. and Warburton M. 1985 Uncertainty on a Himalayan Scale, *Mountain Research and Development* 5 115–135

UNFCCC 2010 The Cancun Agreements: outcome of the work of the ad-hoc working group on long-term cooperative action under the convention. Available from: http://unfccc.int/resource/docs/2010/cop16/eng/07a01.pdf [Accessed 11 January 2017]

UNFCCC 2016 Report of the Conference of the Parties on its twenty-first session, held in Paris from 30 November to 13 December 2015. Addendum. Part two: Action taken by the Conference of the Parties at its twenty-first session. Available from: http://unfccc.int/resource/docs/2015/cop21/eng/10a01.pdf [Accessed 11 January 2017]

UNHCR 2014 Planned relocation, disasters and climate change: consolidating good practices and preparing for the future. Final report of the Expert consultation on Planned Relocation, Disasters and Climate Change: Consolidating Good Practices and Preparing for the Future, 2014 Sanremo, Italy, 12–14 March 2014. Available from: www.unhcr.org/54082cc69.pdf [Accessed 11 January 2017]

Warner K. 2012 Human migration and displacement in the context of adaptation to climate change: the Cancun Adaptation Framework and potential for future action, *Environment and Planning C: Government and Policy* 30 1061–1077

WBGU [German Advisory Council on Global Change] 2008 *Climate change as a security risk*, Earthscan, London

White G. 2011 *Climate change and migration: security and borders in a warming world*, Oxford University Press, Oxford

World Bank 2010 *World Development Report 2010: development and climate change*, World Bank, Washington, DC

World Commission on Environment and Development 1987 *Our common future*, Oxford University Press, Oxford

Worster D. 1979 *Dust Bowl: the southern plains in the 1930s*, Oxford University Press, Oxford

Index

nationalism 1, 54, 120, 124, 126, 139
nationality 112, 115, 121
Native Americans 152
nativism 12, 63, 109; anti-Filipino
    sentiment in California 112, 113,
    117, 118–119; Aspen 144, 147, 148,
    149–152; definition of 122n1;
    enviro-cultural context 120;
    environmental 111, 114–116;
    environmental privilege 143, 153;
    "Triumph of" 122n2; United States
    145–146
natural resources 5, 8, 9, 53, 54; Brazil 49,
    165; California 114; Chinese migrants
    in Australia 109, 124, 126, 133, 139;
    environmental nativism 111, 114, 115;
    environmental privilege 143–144;
    Hawai'i 27, 28; inter-ethnic conflicts
    55; population growth and 194; *see also*
    forests; mining; rivers
naturalization 114–115
nature 3, 5, 9, 17; drought in Brazil 160,
    165, 169, 174; German concept of 44;
    leisure and 55; personification of 99;
    responsibility for environmental crises
    175; taming of 8; workscape
    concept 54
neo-Malthusianism 194
neoliberalism 1, 147, 191, 199–200, 201
New Western History 7–8
New York 59, 61, 65–66
newspapers 94, 113, 130, 144, 186
Ngai, Mai M. 121
Ningxia 179
Nodari, Eunice Sueli 11, 41–52
Noiriel, Gérard. 90
Nordyke, Eleanor 38n1, 39n9
North American migrants 19, 20, 23–30,
    37–38

O'Connor, James 53
Okies 2–3
opium 83, 136–137
oppression 90, 104
orchards 56, 133
oriental despotism 177
Osborn, Henry Fairfield 145
Ossendowski, Ferdynand 72
Ōtani, Matsujiro 36
otherness: Chinese migrants in Australia
    126, 140; coal miners 89, 90, 97, 103,
    104; Italian backyards in the United
    States 59
overpopulation 12, 153, 157, 194–195

parentela 166, 168, 175n1
Park, Lisa Sun-Hee 12, 55, 109, 143–156
Parkes, Henry 137, 138
Patricinio, Jose do 161
Paulson, Terry 148, 149–150
peasants: China 179, 187; Russia 71, 72,
    74, 75–76, 78–79, 81; United States 193
Pedemonte, Thomas Arthur 59
Pellow, David Naguib 12, 55, 109,
    143–156
Perea, Juan F. 145
Pereira, Elenita Malta 9
personification of nature 99
pesticides 65, 122n5
Phelan, James D. 115, 122n4
pigs 24, 30, 44, 61, 76; *see also* hog farming
plantations: Brazil 50, 157, 161–162, 163,
    165, 171; capitalistic organization of
    17; Chinese migrants in Australia 133;
    Hawai'i 23, 25–26, 27–30, 31–34,
    36–37, 38; United States 58, 65; *see also*
    agriculture
plants 4, 5, 22, 45
policy: Aspen 147–148; Australia 125–126,
    134, 139; drought in Brazil 159, 167;
    environmental privilege 143; *see also*
    legislation
Polish migrants 58, 64
political ecology 65, 66, 90, 91, 195, 196,
    197, 201n1
political economy 191, 192, 194
politics: anti-immigration 12; Chinese
    party-state political system 189; climate
    change 192, 200; distributional 155;
    environmental 144, 154; Hawai'i
    24–25, 38
pollution 93, 143; Aspen 147, 152;
    environmental justice 155; immigrants
    blamed for 145; ski industry 150;
    Three Gorges Dam 183, 189; *see also*
    environmental degradation
Polynesians 19, 20–23
population: classical political economy
    192, 194; conservative narratives 200;
    demographic discourse 157; fear of 195,
    196, 199–200, 201; "population bombs"
    193, 196; *see also* overpopulation
population growth: Aspen 148, 149; Brazil
    47; Chinese migrants in Australia 134;
    gold rushes 130; Hawai'i 21–22, 37;
    "majority minority" populations 146;
    Malthus on 194; Ningxia 179; Three
    Gorges Dam resettlement 182
Portinari, Candido 170, 171

Wallonia 88–107
war 2
Warren, Louis 8–9, 55
water: Chinese migrants in Australia 109, 124, 126–131, 132, 139; drought relief in Brazil 166–167; environmental privilege 144; Hawai'i 38; *see also* dam construction; irrigation
Watsonville Riots (1930) 111, 112–113, 116, 118, 119, 120–121
Weber, Max 177–178
Weber, Regina 9
Whayne, Jeannie M. 62
White Australia Policy 125–126, 134, 139
White, Richard 84n2
whiteness 134, 147
Whyte, Martin 180
Wilder, Laura Ingalls 67n1
wilderness 4, 103–104; American 115; "coercive conservation" 152; Romantic image of 12
Wilson, Edward 135

Wittfogel, Karl 177–178
Wolf, Eric 31
Wolford, Wendy 167–168
women 7, 60, 146
Wood, James 119
workscape concept 54
World Bank 198
World Heritage Sites 94, 105, 106n18
Worldwatch Institute 193, 195–196
Worster, Donald 2–3, 7, 8, 42
Wright, Angus 12, 157, 159–176

xenophobia 1, 54, 55, 90; anti-Filipino riots in California 111; California 63; environmentalist discourses 9; protectionism 115; US immigration legislation 122n2; xenophobic spatialization 11, 96, 101, 103
Xing, Ying 12–13, 157, 177–190

yields 79–80
Young, William 133